Flood Hazards and Health

Flood Hazards and Health

Responding to Present and Future Risks

Edited by
Roger Few
and
Franziska Matthies

Tyndall°Centre
for Climate Change Research

EARTHSCAN
London • Sterling, VA

First published by Earthscan in the UK and USA in 2006
Reprinted 2007

ISBN-13: 978-1-84407-215-6 hardback
ISBN-13: 978-1-84407-216-3 paperback

Typesetting by JS Typesetting Ltd, Porthcawl, Mid Glamorgan
Printed and bound in the UK by Cromwell Press, Trowbridge
Cover design by Danny Gillespie

For a full list of publications please contact:

Earthscan
8–12 Camden High Street
London, NW1 0JH, UK
Tel: +44 (0)20 7387 8558
Fax: +44 (0)20 7387 8998
Email: earthinfo@earthscan.co.uk
Web: **www.earthscan.co.uk**

22883 Quicksilver Drive, Sterling, VA 20166-2012, USA

Earthscan is an imprint of James and James (Science Publishers) Ltd and publishes in
association with the International Institute for Environment and Development

A catalogue record for this book is available from the British Library

Library of Congress Cataloging-in-Publication Data

Few, Roger.
    Flood hazards and health : responding to present and future risks / Roger Few
and Franziska Matthies.
        p. cm.
    Includes bibliographical references and index.
    ISBN-13: 978-1-84407-215-6
    ISBN-10: 1-84407-215-0
  1. Floods–Health aspects. 2. Floods–Psychological aspects. 3. Global warming–
Health aspects. 4. Global warming–Environmental aspects. 5. Emergency medical
services. 6. Disaster relief. I. Matthies, Franziska. II. Title.
    RA645.9.F49 2005
    363.34'93–dc22

                                                                    2005027705

Mixed Sources
Product group from well-managed
forests and other controlled sources
www.fsc.org Cert no. TT-COC-2082
© 1996 Forest Stewardship Council

Contents

List of Figures, Tables and Boxes

Figures

Tables

Boxes

About the Authors

Mike Ahern is a research fellow in the Public and Environmental Health Research Unit, London School of Hygiene and Tropical Medicine (LSHTM), UK, and is a member of the school's Centre on Global Change and Health. He has a background in geography (School of Oriental and African Studies) and infectious disease control (LSHTM). The current focus of his research is on the health effects of global environmental change and, in particular, the effects of such change on communities in low-income countries.

Manuel Alvarinho is a civil engineer and has been working for the Mozambique government for more than 25 years in the water supply and sanitation sector. He is a senior adviser to the government on policy and strategy formulation and has been president of the Water Regulatory Council since December 1999. He is also a member of the World Bank's Water and Sanitation Programme council and serves on the board of the international network Building Partnerships for Development in Water and Sanitation.

Sandy Cairncross, a public health engineer by training and an epidemiologist by vocation, worked in Mozambique as a public health engineer from 1977 to 1984. He is now professor of environmental health at LSHTM, UK, and a member of Working Group II of the Intergovernmental Panel on Climate Change. He is also the technical director of WELL, a resource centre on water and environmental health for the UK Department for International Development (DFID).

Roger Few is senior research fellow in the School of Development Studies, University of East Anglia, UK, and is an affiliated researcher of the Tyndall Centre for Climate Change Research. His recent work examines the linkages between global environmental change, natural hazards and human health, with a focus especially on the social and political dimensions of vulnerability, resilience and adaptation. He currently holds an Economic and Social Research Council (UK) Research Fellowship on climatic hazards, health risk and response in developing countries.

Pham Gia Tran is a lecturer in the Department of Geography, University of Social Sciences and Humanities, Viet Nam National University, Viet Nam. He is also a member of the university's Centre for Research on Social Development and Poverty Reduction. He has worked on several recent research projects on flood risk policy and response within the Mekong Delta. Within this field he has a special interest in vulnerability and coping mechanisms at the local scale and in environmental and sanitation education.

Sari Kovats is a lecturer in environmental epidemiology at LSHTM, UK. Her research focuses on assessing the current and potential impacts of climate on human population health. Recent work has focused on the epidemiology of heatwaves and the public health impacts of weather extremes. She has been an expert adviser on climate variability, climate change and health to the World Health Organization (WHO), and is currently a lead author in the Fourth Assessment Report of the Intergovernmental Panel on Climate Change (IPCC).

Franziska Matthies is visiting fellow at the Tyndall Centre for Climate Change Research, UK, and research analyst for the German Advisory Council on Global Change to the Federal Government. Her recent work looks at the linkages between environmental change, human health and sustainable development, and is situated at the interface between research and policy. An assistant professor at the Department of International Health, University of Copenhagen, Denmark, she is also involved in the design and coordination of postgraduate courses in international health.

Christopher A. Ohl is an associate professor of medicine with the Section of Infectious Diseases, Wake Forest University School of Medicine, US. He is certified in internal medicine and infectious diseases by the American Board of Internal Medicine. His academic interests include the development and implementation of public health responses to emerging infections, antimicrobial resistance, bioterrorism and natural disasters, including flooding. He is the medical director for North Carolina's Public Health Response and Surveillance Team 5.

Sue Tapsell is a principal lecturer based at the Flood Hazard Research Centre, School of Health and Social Sciences, at Middlesex University, UK. Her recent focus has been on the 'intangible' impacts of flooding in the UK, in particular the health and social effects on individuals, households and communities. Other interests include public perception of flood risk, the social benefits of river restoration, public participation in flood risk management and the effectiveness of flood warning dissemination.

Sylvia Tunstall is an associate research manager and senior lecturer based at the Flood Hazard Research Centre, School of Health and Social Sciences, at Middlesex University, UK. She is a specialist in survey research methods whose research has focused on public perceptions of river environments, including river restoration schemes, children and rivers, flooding, flood warning systems, flood defence and public consultation processes. Recent interests include the 'intangible' impacts of flooding and the effectiveness of flood warning dissemination.

Acknowledgements

This book arose from the research project Health and Flood Risk: A Strategic Assessment of Adaptation Processes and Policies, funded by the Tyndall Centre for Climate Change Research. The editors and several of the contributing authors worked together on the project, and further chapters were drawn from participants in an international workshop held by the Tyndall Centre in 2004.

The book has also benefited from reviews, comments and assistance from a number of colleagues and workshop participants. We would therefore like to express our thanks to Neil Adger, Mozaharul Alam, Marie-Caroline Badjeck, Peter Baxter, Graham Bentham, Nick Brooks, Terry Cannon, Ngo Cong Chinh, Declan Conway, Suraje Dessai, Divya Donti, Torsten Grothmann, Trudy Harpham, Masahiro Hashizume, Madeleen Helmer, Philippe Hoyois, Mike Hulme, Paul Hunter, Bas Jonkman, Phillip Judge, Ilan Kelman, Tom Kosatsky, Iain Lake, Rony Maza, Laurence McKenna, Bettina Menne, Oliver Morgan, Robert Nicholls, Gordon Nichols, Tim O'Riordan, Mark Pelling, Sabina Rashid, Emma Tompkins, John Schellnhuber, Philip White, Paul Wilkinson, Alexandra Winkels and Ben Wisner. During the preparation of the book, continuing support to the editors has been provided by the UK Economic and Social Research Council, the Overseas Development Group of the University of East Anglia and the Tyndall Centre for Climate Change Research.

List of Acronyms and Abbreviations

AIDS	acquired immune deficiency syndrome
BRAC	Bangladesh Rural Advancement Commission
°C	degrees Celsius
CDC	Centers for Disease Control and Prevention
CFSC	Committee for Flood and Storm Control (Viet Nam)
cm	centimetre
CRED	Centre for Research on the Epidemiology of Disasters
CRPRSD	Centre for Research on Poverty Reduction and Social Development (Viet Nam)
CVM	Cruz Vermelha de Moçambique (national Red Cross in Mozambique)
DEC	Disasters Emergency Committee
Defra	UK Department for the Environment, Food and Rural Affairs
DHS	Department of Homeland Security (US)
EA	UK Environment Agency
ENSO	El Niño–Southern Oscillation
FEMA	Federal Emergency Management Agency (US)
GCM	global climate model
GDP	gross domestic product
GHQ	General Health Questionnaire
ha	hectare
HAV	hepatitis A virus
HEV	hepatitis B virus
HPS	hantavirus pulmonary syndrome
IFRC	International Federation of Red Cross and Red Crescent Societies
INTRAC	International NGO Training and Research Centre (UK)
IPCC	Intergovernmental Panel on Climate Change
ISDR	International Strategy for Disaster Reduction
JCAHO	Joint Commission for Accreditation of Healthcare Organizations
KAP	knowledge, attitude and practice
km	kilometre
m	metre
mm	millimetre

MSF	Médecins Sans Frontières
MVE	Murray Valley encephalitis
n	total sample population size
NGO	non-governmental organization
NOAA	National Oceanographic and Atmospheric Agency (US)
NWS	National Weather Service (US)
OFDA	Office of US Foreign Disaster Assistance
PADRU	Pan-American Disaster Response Unit
PAHO	Pan American Health Organization
PTSD	post-traumatic stress disorder
PTSS	Post-Traumatic Stress Scale
SLE	St Louis encephalitis
SPC	Storm Prediction Center (US)
TAR	Third Assessment Report
UK	United Kingdom
UNDP	United Nations Development Programme
UNICEF	United Nations Children's Fund
US	United States
VNRC	Viet Nam Red Cross Society
WHO	World Health Organization
WNV	West Nile virus

Introduction

In July 2004, as a group of experts on various aspects of flooding and health assembled for an international workshop in Norwich, UK, waters from several rivers swollen by heavy monsoon rains were spilling across the floodplains of Bangladesh. The excess rainfall had already brought catastrophic flooding to neighbouring parts of India, and now proceeded to bring an unprecedented depth of floodwater across much of central and north-east Bangladesh. During the course of the next three months, an estimated 36 million people were displaced from their homes, lost possessions and livestock, struggled to maintain a livelihood while their dwellings and communities were inundated, or were otherwise affected by this enormous flood event.

Floods continued to make the international headline news throughout the process of preparing this book, with catastrophic events reported, for example, from Haiti, India, China and the US, together with the devastating tsunami that overwhelmed coastlines around the Indian Ocean in December 2004, killing at least 227,000 people. Indeed, such is the frequency of extreme floods that many more will have occurred by the time this book goes to press. The reality is that flood hazards of various kinds and scales are ever present. Moreover, major floods are only part of the story. Yet more numerous are the 'minor' floods that take place more or less continually in one location or another across the globe. Seldom classified as 'disasters' (although their impact on individual households may be devastating) and seldom reported outside the local area, they, too, constitute flood events with potentially large cumulative effects. Floods do not have to be huge in scale to affect homes and livelihoods, and they do not have to be physically destructive to pose risks to human health. Indeed, vulnerability to certain disease risks may be highest in circumstances where people continue to live, work and play in the presence of floodwaters.

This book arose from a strategic assessment project that aimed to gauge how future society may respond to human health risks from floods in the context of climate change – a project that culminated in the international workshop noted above. In collating the current state of knowledge of health aspects of floods globally, it became clear to us that there was a pressing need not just for a book discussing future response, but also for a detailed analysis of how affected people and health systems cope with problems caused by flooding now. There was also a need to discuss how action to protect health during floods dovetails with broader aspects of hazard management and disaster risk reduction.

We see this book both as a means of synthesizing current knowledge and as a call for improving that global knowledge base. Indeed, as the following chapters show, to date there has been relatively little top-quality scientific research characterizing the health outcomes of flood hazards. This is the case in all countries, rich and poor. In discussions of health risk from floods in Europe, for example, Hajat et al (2003) and WHO (2002) emphasize the need for a stronger epidemiological information base and a better understanding of vulnerability factors. Similarly, there has been little research analysing health protection behaviour and the functioning of health care systems during floods. As well as improved understanding of the impacts of flood hazards on health, there is a need to focus on how people and institutions respond to health risks (McCluskey, 2001; Few, 2003). How, for example, do households in flood-prone contexts perceive and react to infectious disease risk? How does a health system cope with the simultaneous pressures from flood-related morbidity and flood-related disruption of the system itself?

The extent of future human vulnerability to flooding is yet more difficult to assess. There are many potential drivers of change. Populations may become more or less susceptible to flood impacts depending upon factors such as the distribution and growth of settlements, changes in the economy and levels of poverty, and investment in flood control engineering and other aspects of risk reduction. The nature of flood hazards themselves may alter as a result of environmental change at different scales, including alterations in global climate and sea level. The Intergovernmental Panel on Climate Change (IPCC) predicts that climate change is likely to cause an increase in flood hazards in many areas of the world (McCarthy et al, 2001). If climate change does act as a major driver of change in flooding, then the future health burden from floods may significantly alter. It is therefore important that existing information is assessed now so that global knowledge gaps can be strategically addressed.

The health implications of flooding

Floods pose risks to health, and emerging evidence from around the world suggests that their health impact penetrates far deeper than the immediate physical threat to life from floodwaters. Floods, for example, can carry water contaminated with wastes and toxic chemicals into living spaces, increase people's contact with disease vectors, and damage infrastructure, buildings and possessions. They can thereby increase human exposure to toxins and pathogens, may have implications for mental health, and can disrupt the capacity of health care systems to respond to health crises (McMichael et al, 2001; WHO, 2002; Hales et al, 2003). They can also impact on health in a more tangential sense by displacing people from their homes, disrupting livelihoods and access to food, and damaging infrastructure. Figure 0.1 indicates some of these pathways through which flood hazards can influence health outcomes.

The threats to health posed by floods generate a range of responses, both from the people who are at risk and from the agencies and institutions charged

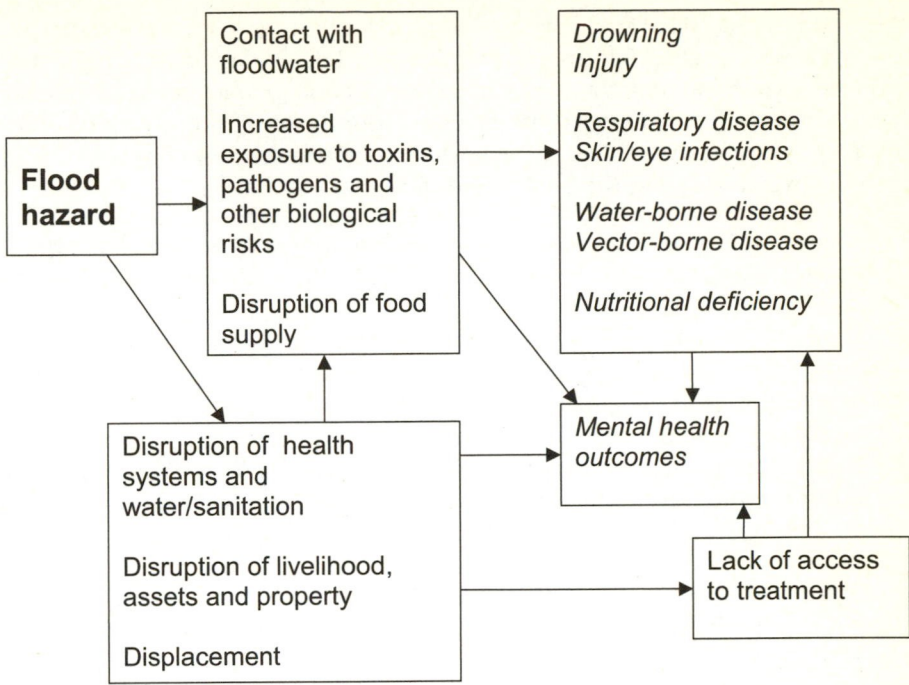

Figure 0.1 *How flooding may impact upon health*

with providing their health care and other life-supporting services, such as water supply and sanitation. Broadly, these include efforts to prevent impacts from occurring and to manage those that arise. As this book will show, they draw on many themes and approaches common in public health practice, including aspects of health promotion, environmental health, curative medicine and the upgrading of health facilities. As authors such as VanRooyen and Leaning (2005) and Waring and Brown (2005) point out, they also link closely with themes of mitigation, preparedness, emergency response and recovery that are prominent in the fields of disaster management and risk reduction.

Approach and scope of the book

The aim of this book is to bring together findings from epidemiological, envir-onmental, social and institutional studies to take stock of existing knowledge and discuss intervention needs in the critical field of flood risk and health. In doing so, the book frames health not merely as a medical or technical matter, but, crucially, as a social, cultural, economic and political issue. One of the most important advances in the analysis of natural hazards is the recognition that human vulnerability is a product of social processes such as impoverishment, marginalization and weak policy-making, and not just the physical presence of the hazard itself (see, for example, Cannon, 2000; Adger et al, 2003; Pelling, 2003; Bankoff et al, 2004; Wisner et al, 2004). This recognition of the social dimensions of vulnerability and related notions of coping capacity and adaptation has a close parallel with concepts of population health (Lindsay, 2003) and informs our discussions here of the health implications of flooding.

The overall scope of the book is as follows:

- It is concerned with flood events, in general, covering a variety of scales, intensities, speeds of onset and types (including riverine floods, flash floods and coastal floods).
- It examines a range of health risks connected with flooding, including drowning, injury, stress, communicable disease, the effects of exposure to pollution, and the effects of damage to health infrastructure and water/ sanitation facilities.
- It discusses responses to health risks at different levels (from household actions to international intervention) and at different stages in the hazard cycle (before, during and after the hazard event).

In order to maximize the *added value* of the book, we have concentrated thematically on health impacts and responses specific to flooding, rather than on health implications common to disaster events, in general. We are mainly interested here in documenting response to the specific health problems that arise for populations living within or near a flooded environment. Because of this focus there are several generic topics relating to health during disasters that we do not examine in depth in the book, including the effects of economic losses, disruption in food supply and concentration of displaced people in refugee camps. Their critical importance, however, is acknowledged in most of the chapters that follow.

Outline of the book

The book has three main elements. The early chapters (Chapters 1–3) introduce key concepts and provide global overviews of flood hazard, health impacts and responses to health risks. The middle chapters (Chapters 4–7) provide case studies presenting new research evidence from different regions on specific health aspects of floods. The final chapter (Chapter 8) synthesizes insights from the previous chapters and discusses priorities for policy, practice and research.

Chapter 1 by Roger Few sets the context for the book, introducing the geography, political ecology and management of global flood risk. It discusses the physical characteristics of floods, flood disasters, historical trends in flooding and the prospect of changes in flood patterns as a result of climate change. In this chapter the conceptual approach of the book is set out, drawing from existing work in the human geography and political ecology of hazards to discuss the social dimensions of flood risk, including concepts of vulnerability, coping capacity and adaptation and their inherently dynamic nature. It then introduces key principles of disaster management, including the roles of preparedness, risk reduction and community participation.

Chapters 2 and 3 are based on an extensive review of existing literature from around the world that relates to flooding health risks and responses. Health impacts are addressed primarily through an epidemiological review, assessing the quality of the existing evidence base for the health outcomes of flooding and analysing trends in the findings worldwide. In Chapter 2, Mike Ahern and Sari Kovats explore the evidence for a range of health outcomes, including drowning, injuries, infectious disease (water borne and vector borne) and mental health. To maximize added value, their survey focuses particularly on aspects of health that are specifically associated with the presence of floodwaters, rather than aspects that may be generic to disaster situations. The chapter makes clear the disparity in potential health outcomes between floods in high-income and low-income countries. It emphasizes the need for further evidence before firm conclusions can be made about specific disease risks and how these relate both to different flood types and differential human vulnerability.

Mechanisms of response to health risks from floods are addressed in Chapter 3 via a more discursive review of literature, in which the intention is not to provide an 'inventory' of specific health-related responses, but to highlight key practical and policy issues that arise in processes of response and adaptation. Roger Few and Franziska Matthies describe actions geared to preventing injury and illness resulting from flooding and to promoting treatment, including the continued functioning of health services. The chapter discusses six main categories of response, starting with health protection undertaken by vulnerable populations themselves, and moving through aspects of health education, disease surveillance and control, health care provision, protection of health infrastructure, and the protection and provision of water and sanitation systems. As well as reflecting different hazard management stages and scales of action, the chapter highlights key differences in response capacity between global regions. The authors identify a set of principles for enhancing coping capacity that apply across different aspects of response.

Chapters 4–7 present four thematic case studies based on recent research findings that describe and analyse specific health consequences and responses to flooding in different regions of the world. Examples from low-income as well as high-income settings have been chosen to illustrate issues in a range of settings. In Chapter 4, Sue Tapsell and Sylvia Tunstall present the findings of recent research in England and Wales, examining the effects of flood events on people's psychological health and the factors that appear to contribute to these impacts. Their chapter focuses attention on emerging concerns in academia and in health care provision on the potential for flooding to increase stress, psychological trauma and mental health disorders in affected populations. The authors examine how different social groups are affected, including groups that might be expected to show heightened vulnerability, such as the elderly. They discuss the quality of responses to mental health impacts and the implications for future policy and research.

The case study in Chapter 5 describes the health impacts of the catastrophic floods of 2000 in Mozambique, especially focusing on communicable diseases and the disruption of water and sanitation systems. One of the key effects of floods tends to be an increased risk of diarrhoeal disease linked with disruption and contamination of water supplies and sanitation – a source of infection that can have severe consequences in developing countries such as Mozambique. Sandy Cairncross and Manuel Alvarinho also examine the flood's long-term implications for physical and mental health. The authors discuss the challenges faced by government organizations and external agencies in responding to the immediate crises, before setting out the progress and costs to date of rehabilitation and the extent to which lessons can be implemented for future mitigation and preparedness.

Local-level responses to extreme floods in Viet Nam form the thematic focus of Chapter 6. Pham Gia Tran and Roger Few discuss health issues in the Mekong Delta, a setting in which annual floods are the norm, but where abnormally high seasonal peaks have occurred repeatedly in recent years. In Viet Nam, non-structural state responses to flooding are re-emphasizing the traditional 'living with floods' culture that is longstanding in the region. This policy context is linked with the results of a case study of response to health risks from flooding in two urban areas of the delta, where low-income communities, in particular, are often exposed to high water levels. The authors describe how local state agencies, health clinics and community-scale organizations perceive, prepare for and react to these risks. The chapter also refers to the vulnerability of children in the region, discussing research work on the high proportion of child deaths from drowning during floods and associated safety initiatives.

A detailed description and analysis of how individuals, health systems and other governmental agencies respond to flood events in the US is given by Christopher A. Ohl. Chapter 7 describes a complex layering and interweaving of responsibilities between different organizations and scales in a setting where levels of health care provision are generally high and the emergency services are relatively well resourced. Nevertheless, response to health issues associated with floods in the US presents many challenges, including the provision of medical care not only to those with acute injury or illness, but also to persons with chronic infirmity or disease who are unable to access their usual health care facilities. Shortcomings in the management of public health were dramatically exposed by Hurricane Katrina in 2005. The chapter discusses how this and other flood events in recent years have provided many important lessons in response, and how wider security issues since 2001 have altered funding and resources for disaster preparedness in the health sector.

In the concluding chapter, Roger Few, Franziska Matthies, Mike Ahern and Sari Kovats extend the analysis from the foregoing chapters, drawing out implications for present and future response to floods, set within a broader understanding of vulnerability and risk reduction. Chapter 8 discusses a series of insights on dimensions of vulnerability, coping capacity and adaptation to health risks from flooding, and places them in the context of potential changes in future flood hazards. The authors identify key opportunities and challenges for policy and intervention, emphasizing the importance of themes such as preparedness planning, integration, capacity-building, coordination, and dissemination of good practice for reducing health risk from flooding. They also point to inter-linkages with the wider context of public health and raise a number of critical areas for further research.

1

Flood Hazards, Vulnerability and Risk Reduction

Roger Few

Introduction

Flooding is one of the most frequent and widespread of all weather-related hazards. Floods of various types and magnitudes occur in most regions of the globe, causing huge annual losses in terms of damage and disruption to economic livelihoods, businesses, infrastructure, services and public health. Long-term data on disasters suggest that floods and wind storms (which frequently lead to flooding) are by far the most common causes of natural disaster worldwide. The International Federation of Red Cross and Red Crescent Societies reports that, in the ten years from 1993 to 2002, flood disasters 'affected more people across the globe (140 million per year on average) than all the other natural or technological disasters put together' (IFRC, 2003, p179). Further EM-DAT data collated by the Centre for Research on the Epidemiology of Disasters (CRED) indicate that this numerical dominance continued through 2003 and 2004.

In order to set the book's detailed discussions on health and flooding in context, this chapter provides a summary of the nature of floods and flood hazard now and in the future, a conceptual background to the analysis of flood risk, and an overview of some generic issues relating to flood risk reduction and hazard response. The chapter first describes the causes, types and variability of flood events, discussing recent trends in the incidence of flood hazard and disaster, and current understanding of the potential increased threat of flooding that may arise as a result of climate change. It then outlines theoretical insights from broader analysis of hazard and risk, discussing the concepts of vulnerability, coping capacity and adaptation. The final section provides generic information on overall response to flood hazards, including the balance between structural and non-structural mitigation, the importance of flood preparedness and the role of internal and external agents in flood risk reduction and emergency relief.

Floods and flood hazard

As Parker (2000) discusses in detail, floods can take many forms and it is not easy to pin down a precise definition for the term. Broadly speaking, however, and in the context of this book, a flood refers to an *excess* accumulation of water across a land surface: an event whereby water rises or flows over land not normally submerged (Ward, 1978). Floods can originate from a variety of sources, and Table 1.1 provides a simplified typology of the principal causes and associated flood types.

The leading cause of floods is heavy rainfall of long duration or of high intensity, creating high runoff in rivers or a build-up of surface water in areas of low relief. Rainfall over long periods may produce a gradual but persistent rise in river levels that causes rivers to inundate surrounding land for days or weeks at a time. In August 2002, for example, intense rainfall of long duration induced extreme flooding spanning five countries of Central and Eastern Europe (Caspary, 2004). Intense rain from storms and cyclones, on the other hand, may produce rapid runoff and sudden but severe flash floods across river valleys. The flooding from these events is typically more confined geographically and persists for shorter periods; but the violence of the event can be highly damaging and dangerous. Intense rain can also cause standing water to develop in urban areas when the capacity of storm drain systems is exceeded.

Table 1.1 *Causes of floods*

Cause	Examples of flood types
High rainfall	Slow-onset riverine flood Flash flood (rapid onset) Sewer/urban drain flood
Tidal and wave extremes	Storm surge Tsunami
Thawing of ice	Jökulhlaup Snowmelt
Structural failure	Dam-break flood Breaching of sea defences

Source: adapted from Parker (2000)

Coastal areas may face an added threat from the proximity of the sea. Tidal and wave extremes are another major cause of floods, bringing seawater across land above the normal high tide level. Cyclonic storms may create a dangerous storm surge in which low atmospheric pressure causes the sea to rise and strong winds force water and waves up against the shore. Tsunami waves originate from the displacement of water during undersea earthquakes and other massive disturbances such as landslides. They may have tremendous destructive power, as witnessed by coastal communities in 11 countries that were struck by the devastating Indian Ocean Tsunami of December 2004.

Other causes of severe flooding include rapid releases of water from snowfields and glaciers – a phenomenon known as jökulhlaup in Iceland where volcanic action beneath glaciers has produced highly destructive floods. Structural failure or overtopping of artificial river dams and sea defences may also result in damaging flood events. It is important to note further that flood causes may combine (Parker, 2000). For example, winter storms in North-West Europe may produce simultaneous inland flooding and storm surges that doubly afflict coastal areas adjacent to river mouths.

Flood events vary greatly in magnitude, timing and impact. Handmer et al (1999, p126) note that the term flooding can cover 'a continuum of events from the barely noticeable through to catastrophes of diluvian proportions'. There are a number of measurable characteristics through which events can be differentiated, including flood *depth, velocity* of flow, spatial *extent, content, speed of onset, duration* and *seasonality* (Parker 2000; Few, 2003). Floods may vary in depth from a few centimetres to several metres. They may be stationary or flow at high velocity. They may be confined to narrow valleys or spread across broad plains. They may contain sewage and pollutants, debris or such quantities of sediment that they are better termed mudflows. They may be slow to build up or rapid in onset as in flash floods. They may last from less than an hour to several months.

Floods may also be associated with regular climatic seasons such as monsoon rains and other annual heavy rainfall periods. In some locations, such as the major floodplains of Bangladesh, extensive flooding from seasonal rains is an expected annual occurrence to which human lifestyles and livelihoods are largely (pre) adapted (though such predictable flooding may still have health implications). However, seasonal flood levels vary from year to year, and such areas tend to be subject to occasional flood events that exceed the normal range of expectation. In 1998, Bangladesh experienced flooding of an unprecedented magnitude (depth and duration), surpassing the previous record flood that occurred in 1988 (Nishat et al, 2000). In 2004, the country was hit once again by floods of an equivalent scale (Alam et al, 2005).

Figure 1.1 indicates the distribution of extreme flood events during the period 1990 to 2004, drawing mainly on flood mapping data provided by the Dartmouth Flood Observatory. Severe floods from high rainfall (of long or short duration) have occurred in almost all the humid regions of the world, with flash floods also affecting many drier zones. Extreme flooding from wind storms and other causes tends to be more concentrated in distribution.

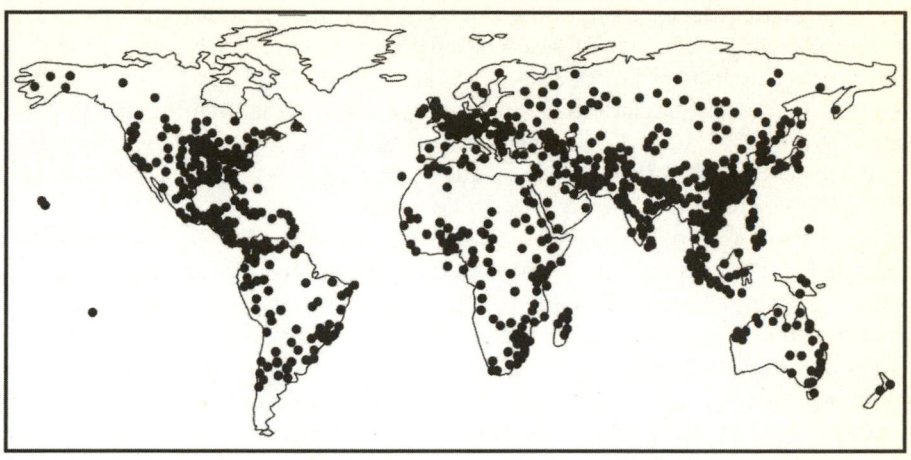

Figure 1.1 *Locations of extreme flood events 1990–2004*

Note: This map should be regarded as indicative only since there is no standard definition of what constitutes an extreme event. A depiction of all flood events of different magnitudes during this period would show an even wider distribution.

Source: developed from maps and data produced by Dartmouth Flood Observatory, Hanover, US, www.dartmouth.edu/~floods, and by EM-DAT: Office of US Foreign Disaster Assistance (OFDA)/CRED International Disaster Database, Université Catholique de Louvain, Brussels, Belgium

Hotspots for tropical storms (known as cyclones, typhoons or hurricanes) lie around the Bay of Bengal, the western Pacific coasts, the Caribbean and south-eastern US. Tsunamis historically have been associated mostly with the Pacific Ocean, although by far the most destructive event of recent years took place in the Indian Ocean in 2004. Floods associated with thawing of ice and snow occur predominantly in northern latitudes or in mountainous regions (note that there is likely to be an under-reporting of extreme flood events in sparsely populated regions, including the far north of Canada and Russia).

River and coastal defence engineers distinguish flood events using a statistical flood frequency measure, which uses historic data to define the probability of occurrence of a flood event of a given magnitude (Parker, 2000). Hence a 100-year flood refers to an event of a size likely to occur once in every 100 years, while a one-year flood might be expected annually. However, the physical parameters of a flood are not always effectively measured and are not necessarily reliable indicators of its impacts. Differing perceptions of and terminology for flood severity make it difficult to develop a standardized categorization of floods, and no such detailed categorization is attempted here. In any case, categorizing by flood magnitude can be misleading when considering severity of impacts since the same flood may differ in its effect at even an inter-household scale (Wisner et al, 2004).

The consequences of flooding are by no means solely negative. Seasonal river floods, in particular, play a crucial role in supporting ecosystems, renewing soil fertility in cultivated floodplains (Wisner et al, 2004). In regions such as the floodplains of Bangladesh, a 'normal' level of seasonal flooding is therefore generally regarded as positive: it is only when a flood reaches an abnormal or extreme level that it is perceived negatively as a damaging event (Parker, 2000).

It is this latter sense in which we use the term *flood hazard* in this book, meaning a flood event with the potential to cause harm to humans or human systems. In this conception, a flood event is a physical phenomenon, but a flood hazard is inherently 'social'. A flood event only constitutes a flood hazard when it threatens to have a negative impact on people and society (hence a river flood in an uninhabited area does not, for the purposes of this book, constitute a hazard). Flood hazards may, of course, have varying degrees of impact, from minor or small-scale damage to damage of catastrophic proportions. This book is concerned with all scales of impact because all forms of flooding can pose health risks. However, in public perception at least, it is flood *disasters* that tend to be of special concern.

Flood disasters

The definition of what constitutes a disaster is another contentious issue; but in its most basic sense it is used to describe an event that brings widespread losses and disruption to a community. Some definitions include the notion that it exceeds the ability of that community to cope using its own resources (ISDR, 2002; White et al, 2004). A number of studies and reports discussed in this book refer to flood disasters of different scales, and statistics on flood disasters provide a useful indicator for global flood risk.

We have already referred to the Centre for Research on the Epidemiology of Disasters (CRED), which manages a global database on disaster impacts known as EM-DAT. CRED classifies an event as a disaster if at least one of the following has occurred: 10 or more people killed; 100 or more people reported affected; a call for international assistance; and/or a declaration of a state of emergency. According to their disaster data, floods come second only to drought/famine during recent years in causing direct mortality (as defined) and account for more than half of all people affected by natural disasters. Since 'people affected are those requiring immediate assistance during a period of emergency, i.e. requiring basic survival needs such as food, water, shelter, sanitation and medical assistance' (IFRC, 2003, p180), this measure provides an indication of the scale of health impacts associated with flooding.

Though they have a number of limitations regarding the quality of information (see Chapter 2), disaster statistics also provide some indication of the geography of flood risk to human populations. Tables 1.2 and 1.3 compile flood and wind storm disaster statistics for different continents using the EM-DAT data from CRED (many of the deaths and other impacts attributed to wind storms are flood related). From the tables, it is clear that flood disasters and their mortality impacts are heavily skewed towards Asia, where there are high population concentrations in the floodplains of major rivers, such as the Ganges-Brahmaputra, Mekong and Yangtze basins, and in cyclone-prone coastal regions, such as around the Bay of Bengal and the South China Sea, Japan and the Philippines. Asia accounts for 98 per cent of all people affected by flood disasters and 90 per cent of all people affected by wind storms during the period 1990 to 2004.

Table 1.2 *Flood disasters by continent, 1990–2004*

Continent	Reported disasters[a]	People reported killed	People reported affected
Africa	319	11,223	23,058,000
North America and the Caribbean	130	4171	2,623,000
Central and South America	239	35,459	9,822,000
Asia	558	63,661	2,047,739,000
Europe and Russian Federation	272	3542	9,204,000
Oceania	44	46	264,000
Total	1562	118,102	2,092,710,000

Note: [a] There may be some double counting in this column since the regional statistics are aggregated from data on flood incidence per country (and some large-scale events may affect more than one country at a time).

Source: EM-DAT: OFDA/CRED International Disaster Database, Université Catholique de Louvain, Brussels, Belgium

Deaths from floods and wind storms are also notably high in Central and South America, where the impacts of two major events – Hurricane Mitch in Central America in 1998 and floods in Venezuela in 1999 – dominate the figures. It is important to note that specific events can have a major effect on regional disaster statistics. Other catastrophic events that strongly skewed regional figures upward were two major flood events in Haiti in 2004 and an enormously destructive cyclone disaster in Bangladesh in 1991. Extreme wave and surge events are not indicated in Tables 1.2 and 1.3, but the equivalent EM-DAT data in this category are dominated by the single tsunami event of 2004.

Table 1.3 *Wind storm disasters by continent, 1990–2004*

Continent	Reported disasters[a]	People killed	People reported affected
Africa	85	1939	7,217,000
North America and the Caribbean	328	7132	16,636,000
Central and South America	93	20,215	5,790,000
Asia	497	190,940	358,965,000
Europe and Russian Federation	137	1293	7,646,000
Oceania	103	376	4,746,000
Total	1243	221,895	401,000,000

Note: [a] There may be some double counting in this column since the regional statistics are aggregated from data on flood incidence per country (and some large-scale events may affect more than one country at a time).

Source: EM-DAT: OFDA/CRED International Disaster Database, Université Catholique de Louvain, Brussels, Belgium

Closer analysis of the statistics suggests that developing countries, in general, bear a disproportionate toll compared with industrialized countries. The Human Development Index compiled by the United Nations Development Programme (UNDP) lists countries according to a composite measure of mean income, educational attainment and life expectancy. The 55 nations listed as high human development countries, with index scores of 0.800 or above, represent 19 per cent of the global population (UNDP, 2004a). Yet, they account for only 3.3 per cent and 2.7 per cent, respectively, of all people killed by floods and wind storms from 1990 to 2004. The proportion of all people affected by floods who live in those countries is just 0.35 per cent. A recent UNDP report on disasters (UNDP, 2004b) provides a pilot Disaster Risk Index based on mortality from large- and medium-scale disasters during the period 1980–2000. This calculates the risk of death from selected hazards country by country, and is proposed as a measure of relative vulnerability because it takes the number of people exposed into account. For floods and cyclones, the risk index is found to have a broadly inverse relationship with measures of national economic development (UNDP, 2004b). This measure arguably reflects more realistically the high level of risk for individuals exposed to floods in many African countries. We return to issues of differential human vulnerability later in this chapter.

Recent trends in flood frequency

Flooding and its impacts not only vary across space, but also across time. One component of this variation is simply year-to-year short-term change in the incidence of floods caused by variability of climate. A major periodic influence on this variability is the cyclical climatic phenomenon known as El Niño–Southern Oscillation (ENSO), which may produce large-scale shifts in storm tracks and dramatic changes in rainfall patterns and flood risk (Glantz, 2001; Kovats et al, 2003). The second component – of key interest to this book – is longer-term change associated with significant shifts in flood trends over multiple decades. We now consider the evidence for recent global flood trends and, in particular, the notion that the incidence of flooding may already be increasing as a result of alteration of greenhouse gas levels in the atmosphere, leading to climate change.

To date, the evidence for a recent upward trend in global flooding remains inconclusive, with no strong consensus emerging from the different global and regional studies. Robson (2002) argues that no clear long-term evidence has emerged of an increased global flood trend during the last century. Milly et al (2002) report that the frequency of great floods – floods at 1/100-year levels – increased during the 20th century for large rivers in high-latitude regions of the Northern Hemisphere. However, they find no evidence for an upward trend in floods of lesser magnitude.

Europe has been the focus of much detailed analysis of flood trends. Mudelsee et al (2003) examined river flood patterns in Central Europe and found no increased trend in extreme flood frequency over recent decades, despite the occurrence of two events exceeding the 100-year flood level in 1997 and 2002. Frei (2003) contends that, although there may appear to have been an accumulation of high-magnitude flood events over the last decade in Europe, it is difficult to confirm statistically whether this constitutes a genuine trend because of the small number of actual events being considered. Rather, it is preferable to analyse lower-order 'intense' events that are more common and therefore make it easier to detect a trend signal out of the background noise of random variation. In this case, for Europe, there does appear to have been a significant trend towards increased intense winter rainfall events over much of the continent in the last five decades. However, it remains unclear whether this change is related to climate change (Frei, 2003).

One of the problems of attributing a causal link between flood trends and climate change is that flood dynamics may have multiple drivers. The incidence of flooding is strongly affected by a range of environmental changes (Bronstert, 2003; Woodworth et al, 2005). Alterations in land cover and urbanization influence the water absorption characteristics of land surfaces, in many cases increasing runoff rates and thereby exacerbating flooding from high rainfall. Loss of wetlands that can act as a buffer against tidal floods may heighten coastal flood risk. Though changes such as these take place at a local scale, they can combine to form cumulative trends in land-use change that might be associated with trends in flood events at a regional or global scale. Human vulnerability to floods is additionally affected by other drivers of change, including population growth, economic development and changes in settlement pattern such as urbanization in coastal zones (see later in this chapter and the discussions in Chapter 8). A final complicating matter to add to the uncertainty over present flood trends is the possibility that changes in the reporting and categorization of flood events may influence the pattern of statistics. As Jonkman (2005) discusses, these include cumulative improvements in data collection on disasters over recent decades.

Future climate change and flooding

Although information on recent flood trends is inconclusive, global trends in sea level and temperature now provide strong evidence of a climate change signature. The weight of international scientific opinion has swung decisively towards the perspective that a process of global climate change is now under way, over and above normal background climatic variability. Though climate change is only one of many potential drivers of future global flood risk, its direct link with the physical sources of flooding makes it of special interest.

The Third Assessment Report (TAR) of the Intergovernmental Panel on Climate Change (IPCC) draws on a series of modelling approaches to estimate how climatic parameters might change (in future) and to set out a range of potential impacts resulting from these changes. The magnitude of change depends partly upon whether society succeeds in reducing greenhouse gas emissions. Yet, even with strenuous efforts in climate change mitigation, the TAR concludes that some climate impacts would be inevitable. Over the next 100 years, yearly average near-surface temperatures across the globe are therefore predicted to rise by between 1.4°C and 5.8°C, causing an increase in flood hazard in some areas because of sea level rise, changes in seasonal precipitation or the pattern of wind storms (Houghton et al, 2001; McCarthy et al, 2001).

Because of uncertainties over future greenhouse gas emissions and the complexity of hydrometeorological processes, however, confident prediction of the scale of flooding changes in specific geographical regions remains an elusive goal. Increasing attention is even being given to the possibility of *rapid* or *catastrophic* climate change (Hulme, 2003), which, though of low probability, could render climate systems highly unstable. The predictive picture also becomes greatly obscured by the potential effect of other environmental changes that may exacerbate or counteract climate-induced changes, such as land-use alterations, deforestation and mangrove clearance, construction of coastal defences and river channel engineering (Bronstert, 2003; Woodworth et al, 2005). For extreme events of low probability but high consequence, the challenges for quantification and prediction are especially great.

Inland flooding

As Milly et al (2002) state, the intensification of the global water cycle expected under climate change is likely to lead to an increased threat of riverine flooding from high rainfall over catchments. This may result in changes to several aspects of a river basin's flood regime, including changes in timing, magnitude, frequency, spatial extent and temporal duration of floods (Mirza, 2002). There may also be alterations in the timing of peak flows and the synchronicity of peaks from different tributaries of large river basins. Moving from such generalized statements to predictions for specific rivers presents a major challenge, partly because of the coarse spatial scale on which most global climate models (GCMs) tend to run (Hunt, 2002; Bronstert, 2003). GCMs have typically had grid sizes of hundreds of kilometres, although advances are being made in downscaling models to a finer resolution for individual regions. Predicting extreme flood events is yet more difficult because of their inherent rarity (Palmer and Rälsänen, 2002). The high uncertainty surrounding future storm patterns and extreme weather events means that future flooding can be considered a potential threat for virtually any region.

As already noted, despite recent upward trends in high river flows in some locations, it is not yet clear whether a climate change signature can be detected in present-day global flooding statistics. However, warming of the climate in the next 50 to 100 years is widely expected to lead to changes in rainfall and flood risk in all continents. The major problem is pinpointing exactly where levels of rainfall will increase or decrease. Results from a series of different climate models analysed by Arnell (2004, p36) point toward reduced annual runoff from precipitation in 'much of Europe, the Middle East, Southern Africa, North America and most of South America' and increased annual runoff in 'high latitude North America and Siberia, Eastern Africa, parts of arid Saharan Africa and Australia, and South and East Asia'. Rising trends may be especially apparent in areas of maritime climate, monsoon regions and zones where precipitation is strongly associated with tropical cyclones (Hunt, 2002). Seasonality of rainfall can, however, be masked by annual totals. Predictions by Palmer and Rälsänen (2002) for Northern Europe, for example, suggest that high rainfall winters (with precipitation two standard deviations above normal) will become three to five times more frequent than at present.

Making the link between increased rainfall and flooding is not necessarily straightforward, because the flood outcome will also depend upon other river basin and flow regime characteristics. However, some authors have explicitly addressed future flood risk. Interestingly, Christensen and Christensen (2003) predict a greater frequency of flooding in summer within Europe resulting from intense rainfall events, despite an expected reduction in overall summer precipitation. A major recent report for the UK produced by the Foresight Future Flooding project envisages a twofold to fourfold increase in inland flood risk across the country by the 2080s (Evans et al, 2004). If the connection between rainfall and flooding is strong, the predictions from GCMs are particularly worrying for South Asia, already the world's leading flood-prone region. The work by Palmer and Rälsänen (2002) predicts an increase of three to seven times in the probability of high monsoon precipitation in the next 100 years, producing increases in peak discharges of the region's major rivers. The highest rainfall increases are in the upper basin of the Brahmaputra. The study by Mirza (2002) also suggests that the predicted discharge from the

Brahmaputra River is sensitive to mean temperature rise, with major implications for future flooding in Bangladesh.

Coastal floods

Rising sea level is likely to lead to an increase in flood events experienced by coastal populations (Kabat and van Schaik, 2003). This is especially likely to be the case in low-lying coastal sites as a prelude to their eventual permanent inundation and abandonment (Nicholls, 2002). But it is not only rise in mean sea level that may heighten the risk of sea floods: the more complex effects of climate change may also bring changes in storm conditions (increasing storm surges), tide patterns and wave heights (Woodworth et al, 2005). Moreover, sea level rise may not only exacerbate the effect of increased storm surges, but also pond back the outflow from rivers during peak discharges – it has been estimated that a sea level rise of 90 centimetres (cm) would raise flood heights in the Mekong River, Viet Nam, up to 400 kilometres (km) inland (Nicholls et al, 1995).

Sea level rise has already been observed during the past century, and GCMs robustly predict that global mean sea level will continue to rise over the next 100 years. The TAR estimates a rise of 9–88cm, depending upon the level of future greenhouse gas emissions (Church et al, 2001). In addition to this, different regions may experience further relative sea level rise owing to land subsidence and regional oceanic changes (Woodworth et al, 2005). Any increase in the frequency and magnitude of offshore wind storms will further increase the risk of floods, although, as noted, predicting the future geography of storm events is extremely problematic.

Nicholls (2004) reports on modelling work that combines sea level rise predictions with different sets of assumptions about the implications of future global political, economic, social and technical developments. The model calculates that in 1990 approximately 10 million people per year worldwide experienced coastal flooding arising from storm surges. By the 2080s, depending upon the socio-economic scenario adopted, the model predicts that between 2 million and 50 million additional people per year will experience flooding. The model generally assumes that coastal flood defence measures would be improved during this period. In an earlier paper, the same author suggests that if no measures are taken to adapt to sea level rise, the worst case scenario could see nearly 40 times more people per year affected by sea floods by 2100 (Nicholls, 2002).

Regionally, the global pattern of coastal flooding impact on human populations will relate not just to coastal topography, but also to the number of people potentially exposed to storm surges. Nicholls et al (1999) argue that the greatest increase in vulnerability to sea level changes lies in the coastal strips of South and South-East Asia, and the urbanized coastal lowlands around the African continent. All have high concentrations of relatively unprotected people living in low-lying (and sometimes cyclone-prone) coastal locations. In addition, though they hold relatively small populations, many of the small island states of the Caribbean, Indian Ocean and Pacific Ocean are under especially severe threat from sea level rise and tropical cyclones (Woodworth et al, 2005). A recent report by the World Bank draws attention to the potential vulnerability of major urban agglomerations concentrated in coastal areas of both the North and South (Kreimer et al, 2003).

What can we conclude about future flood risk resulting from climate change?

All in all, though major limitations remain in our ability to make robust projections of future rates of climate change and its effects, increasing predictive evidence of heightened global risk of inland and coastal flooding is emerging. It is perhaps premature and misleading to attempt to produce a future flood risk map; but it is apparent that some areas, at least, are highly likely to experience more intense or frequent flood events over the next 100 years – many of these are humid areas that already experience high rainfall/flood events or low-lying coastal sites that are now prone to tidal inundation.

It is also prudent to assume that the changes may not only mean just 'more of the same'. There might not be evidence from the GCMs of coarse regional changes in flood distribution; but we cannot take that assumption too far. It does not preclude the possibility of there being significant geographical changes in flood distribution at a smaller scale – areas not previously affected by flooding that may become newly afflicted as a result of climate change. Lack of experience could then become a contributory factor towards greater vulnerability in the populations exposed.

Social dimensions of flood risk

Galvanized, in part, by questions of societal adaptation to climate change impacts, there has been much recent theoretical work on hazard risk and related concepts of vulnerability and resilience (for a recent review, see Wisner et al, 2004). Contributions from literature on disaster management, the political ecology of hazards and climate change adaptation, for example, have highlighted the social construction of risk, root causes of vulnerability and the differential vulnerability and coping capacity of social groups – themes we return to below.

Navigating through a series of competing terminologies from different academic disciplines is a complex undertaking, but Box 1.1 provides a list of working definitions for some of these concepts to indicate how they are being applied in this book. It reflects, in part, the conceptual definitions provided by the International Strategy for Disaster Reduction (ISDR, 2002).

Flood *risk* is defined here in terms of risk to humans and human society, and is seen as a product of the severity and probability of occurrence of flood hazard and the vulnerability of the population/system. The concept of *vulnerability*, in turn, encompasses both the likelihood of physical exposure

> **Box 1.1** *The terminology of 'risk': Working definitions*
>
> The following working definitions of the concepts of risk, hazard, vulnerability, coping capacity and adaptation have been adopted in the book:
>
> - *Risk* = the probability of harmful consequences to a human population resulting from flooding (a function of flood hazard and vulnerability).
> - *Flood hazard* = a flood event that has the potential to cause harm to humans or human systems.
> - *Vulnerability* = a set of conditions and processes that determine the likelihood of exposure and the resulting susceptibility of humans or human systems to the adverse effects of a flood hazard.
> - *Coping capacity* = the ability of people/systems to avoid exposure to flood hazard and to avoid, tolerate or recover from adverse effects (the converse of vulnerability).
> - *Adaptation* = change in behaviour, resources, infrastructure or the functioning of a system that reduces vulnerability.

to the hazard and the likelihood of coming to harm as a result of exposure. An alternative means of expressing vulnerability is to refer to *coping capacity*, which emphasizes the ability to respond to risk. Response to flood risk that involves a demonstrable change in action or policy is referred to as *adaptation*, and the ability of people and systems to bring about such changes is referred to as adaptive capacity.

Vulnerability and social differentiation

Human vulnerability to floods is shaped by a combination of physical, social, economic and environmental factors – the attributes of the person/system that condition the impacts resulting from flooding. In the past, physical aspects of vulnerability – the spatial distribution of populations and infrastructure in relation to flood hazard – tended to receive more attention in hazards research (Hilhorst and Bankoff, 2004). But there is now increasing recognition given to the social aspects of vulnerability. For individuals, susceptibility to hazards depends largely upon behaviour, well-being and the resources people have to enable them to avoid and recover from harm. These, in turn, are largely determined by wider social, economic and political patterns and processes that differentiate how flooding affects people and human systems (Cannon, 2000; Wisner et al, 2004). Analyses of vulnerability have therefore increasingly highlighted its socially constructed nature (Cutter, 1996), underlining the importance of understanding how socio-political processes can create vulnerability and thereby create disaster (Pelling, 2003; Hilhorst and Bankoff, 2004).

Wisner et al (2004) develop an analytical model that shows how under-lying causes rooted in inequality generate a progression of vulnerability that creates the unsafe conditions in which hazard events turn to disasters. This process of vulnerability creation operates at different scales. That the impact of flood disaster is so heavily skewed to developing countries is undoubtedly linked to disparities at the global level in resources available for risk reduction by governments and citizens. Equally, at the intra-community level, poverty and marginalization can create differential vulnerability, with the poor being both more susceptible and more exposed (UNDP, 2004b; White et al, 2004). Flood-prone marginal land in cities of low-income countries, for example, often becomes the site of squatter settlements for the urban poor (Bernstein, 1992; McCluskey, 2001).

But poverty and vulnerability are not one and the same: floods can reach the wealthy, too (Few, 2003). Indeed, inappropriate floodplain and coastal development can generate vulnerability in all countries (see, e.g. Baxter et al, 2001), affecting both rich and poor. It is also important to recognize that vulnerability is differentiated by social dimensions other than wealth. In both developing and industrialized nations, health and other impacts may fall dis-proportionately on women, children, people with disabilities and the elderly (Guha-Sapir, 1993; Tapsell and Tunstall, 2001; Twigg, 2004). Jabry (2002) especially highlights the vulnerability of children during the onset and after-math of natural disasters.

Coping capacity and adaptation

Because the term has negative connotations, a focus on vulnerability may run the risk of labelling, alienating and disempowering those it describes (Bankoff, 2001; Handmer, 2003). The concept of coping capacity, although in essence the converse of vulnerability, emphasizes instead the positive potential and actions of people and societies to combat the adverse effects of flooding. As such, it too depends upon policies and actions at the systems level and upon a range of assets at the local level, including the knowledge and capability to utilize coping mechanisms and strategies. At the local level, for example, people accustomed to living in flood-prone environments may follow a range of actions designed to help them avoid and manage harm from floods, including creation of dykes, raised house construction, community food stores, livelihood diversification and reliance on social networks (Buckland and Rahman, 1999; Few, 2003).

Adaptation, in the terminology employed here, refers to a process of change in coping mechanisms and strategies. It can refer to changes in human behaviour, technology, organization or policy that serve to increase capacity to cope with floods and other hazards. Ideas relating to adaptation and adaptive capacity have come to particular prominence in the global literature on the future impacts of climate change. Drawing on concepts from broader hazards theorization emphasizing the positive aspects of human resilience, the IPCC argues that planned adaptation to climate change impacts has to be considered by society in tandem with actions to reduce greenhouse gas emissions (climate change mitigation). In this sense:

> *Adaptation is adjustment in ecological, social or economic systems in response to actual or expected climatic stimuli and their effects or impacts. This term refers to changes in processes, practices or structures to moderate or offset potential damages or to take advantage of opportunities associated with changes in climate.* (Smit et al, 2001, p881)

In this conception, adaptation may be anticipatory as well as reactive. It can also be either purposeful or incidental in relation to the risk in question. It is the more purposeful adaptations designed to reduce or avoid future risk to health from floods that are of key interest in this book, although the role of broader changes such as poverty reduction and general improvement in health systems are also of crucial relevance (see Chapter 8). As with coping capacity, adaptive capacity – the capability to adapt – is shaped not only by the attributes of individuals and organizations, but also by social, economic and political contexts (Adger et al, 2003; Grambsch and Menne, 2003).

Cycles and spirals

Processes of long-term adaptation underline the dynamic rather than static nature of societal response to flooding. Before moving on to discuss general trends in flood management and risk reduction, it is also important to note other aspects of change in response to floods over time.

On the shortest time scale lies the progression of the flood event itself. Flood events, by definition, are inherently dynamic in that they represent a process of short-term change in environmental conditions. Single events can therefore be divided into pre-onset, onset and post-onset phases. In parallel, Wisner et al (2004) describe how hazard coping strategies may comprise preventive, impact-minimizing or post-event recovery strategies. These strategy options map on to the concept of a hazard cycle – a descriptive device that is influential in disaster management approaches (Wisner and Adams, 2002). Figure 1.2 depicts a simplified disaster management cycle, with stages before and after flood events relating to mitigation, preparedness, emergency response and recovery. The terms mitigation and preparedness are, to some extent, overlapping; but the former generally refers to actions in advance to limit the impact of hazards, while the latter denotes actions in advance to ensure effective response when impacts occur (ISDR, 2002). Emergency response includes coping actions by affected populations, as well as relief interventions from external agencies. The recovery stage may include efforts in rehabilitation and reconstruction of services and infrastructure (note that the term mitigation in relation to hazard has a distinct meaning from its use in relation to climate change policy, where mitigation refers to the reduction of net greenhouse gas emissions).

The disaster management cycle has been applied in many contexts, including public health response to disaster (VanRooyen and Leaning, 2005), and reference is made to the different stages in the following chapters. It has

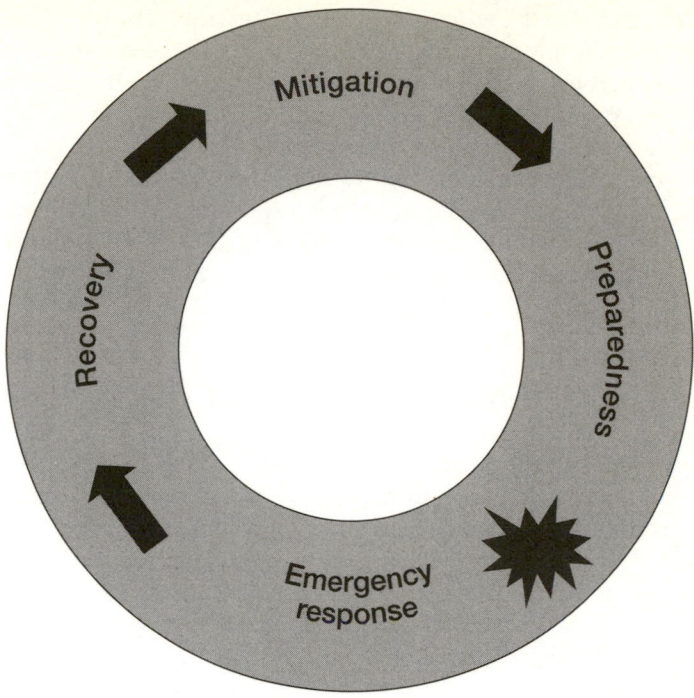

Figure 1.2 *Disaster management cycle*

also played a key role in highlighting the inadequacies of a focus purely on emergency relief (see below). However, the concept has also attracted criticism for the very fact that it portrays hazard response in a circular fashion. It has been suggested that the cycle reinforces the perception of disasters as exogenous, implying that the hazard event is a physical aberration from normal conditions and that circumstances will return to normal once the event has passed (White et al, 2004). This downplays the notion that social vulnerability to hazards may be pre-existing in normal circumstances and that flood disasters are, in part, endogenous. Arguably, it also fails to acknowledge that hazard impacts may have long-lasting effects on coping capacity at individual, community and national scales. In particular, under conditions of poverty, livelihood losses sustained during floods may lead to an exacerbation of vulnerability, so that households become yet more susceptible to the next major flood (Bankoff et al, 2004; Wisner et al, 2004). The result is a negative spiral, rather than a closed circle.

On the other hand, the notion of a spiral can have positive connotations if allied with effective progress in risk reduction. Just as vulnerability is seldom static, so coping capacity at all levels may be transformed by the influx of new ideas, technologies and practices and by the lessons learned from previous flood experiences. White et al (2004, p18) therefore promote the concept of 'virtuous spirals' of risk reduction in which 'learning from a disaster event can stimulate adaptation and modification in development planning rather than a simple reconstruction of pre-existing social and physical conditions'. Processes of learning and adaptation are just as much part of the social fabric of flood risk as changes in human vulnerability.

Present coping mechanisms and future adaptive strategies that relate to health risk from floods form the prime interest of this book and are explored in detail in the chapters that follow. The remainder of this chapter introduces broader generic aspects of the practice of flood hazard management and risk reduction.

Flood hazard management and risk reduction

Reflecting the ideas expressed in the previous section, the last two decades have witnessed considerable re-thinking on how society should approach the management of hazards. This process has, in part, been shaped by a series of international initiatives that have stressed the inter-linkage between environmental and social dimensions of vulnerability, including, during recent years, the establishment of the United Nations International Strategy for Disaster Reduction, the staging of the World Summit on Sustainable Development and the declaration of the Millennium Development Goals for poverty reduction (Wisner et al, 2004). Their influence fed into the World Conference on Disaster Reduction held early in 2005, which affirmed the need to take a holistic approach to tackling hazards that emphasizes long-term sustainable risk reduction.

Broadening the scope

In the past, flood response by governments and other agencies focused largely on emergency relief efforts for affected populations and on structural mitigation – attempts to prevent hazards through flood control engineering. Although structural mitigation measures, such as embankments and tidal barriers, will continue to play a major role in flood management, there is also a strong trend now towards advocating broader aspects of flooding preparedness and a less ready reliance on structural responses (Smith, 2000; Wisner et al, 2004). Non-structural flood mitigation and preparedness options include appropriate land-use planning, enforcement of building codes to avoid construction in flood-prone sites, insurance schemes, and effective flood forecasting, warning and evacuation procedures (Parker, 1999). According to the International Federation of Red Cross and Red Crescent Societies (IFRC, 2002, p3), priority disaster preparedness activities include 'risk and vulnerability mapping, disaster awareness and education, early-warning and evacuation systems, stockpiling relief materials, training in response skills, and planning at all levels to ensure coordination of disaster response'. All of these activities can play their part in reducing risks to health.

Although the organization of warning and evacuation is not addressed in detail in this book, it plays a critical role in risk reduction and public safety. In Mozambique, for example, given the threat of future increases in flood intensity/frequency and the generally prohibitive cost of local-scale structural defences, Christie and Hanlon (2001, pp151–152) stress the need for clearly marked evacuation routes and better and clearer public warning systems. Box 1.2 stresses the role that preparedness planning can play in forging an integrated and effective warning and evacuation system.

Box 1.2 *Integrated approaches to warning and evacuation*

Flood warnings and measures to ensure appropriate response by citizens can play a crucial role in saving lives and reducing injury during the onset of floods (Menne, 1999). Evidence provided by studies and reports from many sources emphasize the importance of setting up well-planned, integrated emergency systems. In Australia, the concept of a 'total flood warning system' combines planning for flood prediction, impact assessment, warning dissemination, agency response and community response, and emphasizes processes of community involvement, institutional cooperation and continuous review and improvement of procedures (Handmer, 2000).

According to the International Federation of Red Cross and Red Crescent Societies, all links in the chain from high-tech meteorological forecasting to local evacuation announcements and plans must be in place (IFRC, 2002). Too often, however, there has been an overemphasis in investment in scientific and technical aspects of forecasting and a relative neglect of effective systems for warning dissemination (Parker, 1999). Palakudiyil and Todd (2003) report that in Orissa, India, the lack of a truly integrated warning system meant that communication of the approach of the 1999 super-cyclone was not effective. Warnings were scientific rather than user friendly – they did not enable people to assess the risk to themselves and take appropriate evacuative action. Wisner and Adams (2002) stress the use of simple language, clear statements of the threat and implications, and identification of the potential victims.

Coordination of warning with evacuation is then often dependent upon relations of trust between the public and those issuing warnings. An integrated system may require a presence on the ground: leaders and volunteers to help persuade people to take warnings seriously, take avoidance action and, if necessary, evacuate their dwellings (Wisner and Adams, 2002; Palakudiyil and Todd, 2003). If evacuation is advised, it is vital that appropriate shelter is available – adequate in size and accessible. The 1991 cyclone in Bangladesh revealed early problems with large purpose-built cyclone shelters constructed in the flood-prone coastal lands on the Bay of Bengal (UNICEF Cyclone Evaluation Team, 1993). The population interviewed complained of an inadequate number of shelters, separated by long distances, and that some were hard to reach because the access roads to them were themselves flooded. Instead of these large shelters, the evaluation report suggested a better alternative might be the reinforcement of a series of small (multipurpose) buildings within communities that people could reach more quickly.

Integration of warning and evacuation activities can benefit greatly from community involvement in their design and execution. For example, during Hurricane Mitch in 1998, there was no loss of life along the Coyolate River in Guatemala, although 300 people perished in floods along other rivers in the region. There, communities had jointly worked to map flood hazard, establish a high-rainfall alarm system, monitor river levels and build evacuation shelters (IFRC, 2002). In northern Cambodia, the aid organization Action Against Hunger has helped to establish safe areas for flood evacuation in rural areas (British Red Cross, 2001a). The agency consulted villagers to identify traditional safe areas both within the village (higher-placed houses) and external to the village (other villages on higher ground).

Good practice in flood preparedness is widely seen to involve cross-sectoral coordination by public authorities, non-governmental organizations (NGOs) and external agencies in developing response plans at different scales that are in place before disaster strikes (Biswas et al, 1999a; ISDR, 2002; Hajat et al, 2003). For example, the Red Cross in Latin America has set up the Pan-American Disaster Response Unit (PADRU), based in Panama, to coordinate and strengthen regional and local capacity in disaster preparedness and response capability. It views the optimum scale of organization for disaster preparedness as dependent upon the type of activity, with strategic relief stockpiles and international relief coordination best managed centrally, but search-and-rescue operations and evacuation procedures best organized at a local level (IFRC, 2002).

Participation and long-term risk reduction

Linked with the idea of local management is the role of community participation in response to flood risks. Interventions that fail to recognize the knowledge, capabilities and resilience of affected communities are likely to miss vital opportunities for sustainable risk reduction (Anderson and Woodrow, 1998; IFRC, 2004). If imposed from outside without effective public involvement, these interventions raise questions over equity and legitimacy. They may even do more harm than good. Bankoff (2001) warns against creating a discourse of vulnerability that casts populations as disaster prone, and thereby undermines their own actions and potentials. Lambert et al (2003) advance ethical principles of open discourse on environmental health risks, arguing that communities have a right to be involved in understanding risks and in developing preventive measures. Contributions to a publication marking the close of the United Nations International Decade for Disaster Reduction of 1990–1999 strongly emphasize greater community involvement in strengthening local coping capacities (Davis and Hall, 1999; Maskrey, 1999). As Lichterman (2000) and others demonstrate (see Chapter 3), these arguments apply equally in high- and low-income countries. However, the principles of community involvement have perhaps been elaborated upon most strongly in developing country contexts.

Victoria (2002), for example, reports on community-based disaster pre-paredness and mitigation initiatives established in Orissa, India, after the floods and super-cyclone of 1999. These included organization of disaster management committees and community volunteer teams; identification of response gaps observed in 1999 and development of community contingency plans; and promotion of alternative housing technologies and local radio alert networks. The project was deemed successful in building capacity in disaster preparedness, raising the profile of risk reduction, and putting local disaster management systems in place that enabled more effective response to further floods in 2001 and a cyclone threat in 2002.

Response to flood risk that is rooted in public inclusion and local-scale capacity building is a key element of long-term risk reduction. Together with a movement towards greater preparedness for flood events, there is a growing drive to ensure that flood response activities provide greater security and positive benefits for communities over sustained periods rather than simply addressing immediate crises. In particular, it is argued that measures introduced during the recovery phase of disasters should be designed so as to reduce, rather than replicate, vulnerability of lives, livelihoods and infrastructure in the future (IFRC, 2003; White et al, 2004). Hence, wherever possible, rehabilitation and reconstruction projects should incorporate future risk assessment and measures to increase resilience against future floods.

Issues of human health are intimately tied with these arguments and trends in flood hazard management. As subsequent chapters show, the themes of preparedness, planning, coordination, participation, capacity-building and long-term risk reduction all have a key role to play in reducing human vulner-ability to the health impacts of flooding and in promoting effective responses to health risks.

2

The Health Impacts of Floods

Mike Ahern and Sari Kovats

Introduction

Floods have the potential to exact a major impact on the health of human populations, and for a given flood event the range of possible health outcomes is broad (see Table 2.1). These outcomes can result directly from health risks associated with the presence of floodwaters (e.g. drownings, injuries and water-related diseases) or indirectly via the impact of floods on shelter, livelihoods, infrastructure and health systems. The degree to which a particular flood will affect human health depends upon a host of factors, including the:

*   nature of the flood event (i.e. regularity, speed of onset, velocity and depth of water, spatial and temporal scale of flood);
*   degree to which human populations and systems are vulnerable (e.g. socio-economic status, construction of houses, current status of population health, status of health care infrastructure); and
*   capacity of human populations and systems to adapt to (i.e. coping strategies) and mitigate against the flood (e.g. early warning, evacuation and disaster preparedness).

The mechanisms by which human health is affected by flooding are often complex but are generally well understood. In Table 2.2 the main health outcomes are considered in terms of whether or not they require human contact with floodwaters, either in the home or the local environment. Health outcomes may also occur during different time periods. For example, in the period immediately before the flood (pre-onset), injuries may occur as individuals remove themselves and their possessions from the rising floodwater. Injuries may also occur during (onset phase) and after the flood (post-onset). Elevated levels of infectious disease may continue to occur some time after the flood, and

Table 2.1 *Potential health effects of flooding*

Direct	• Drowning
	• Injuries (e.g. cuts, sprains, fractures, punctures, electric shock)
	• Diarrhoeal disease
	• Vector- and rodent-borne diseases (e.g. malaria, leptospirosis)
	• Chemical contamination (e.g. of water, food)
	• Respiratory infections
	• Skin/eye infections
	• Mental health
Indirect	• Damage to health care infrastructure and loss of essential drugs
	• Damage to water and sanitation infrastructure
	• Damage to crops and/or disruption of food supplies
	• Damage/destruction of property (e.g. lack of shelter may lead to increased exposure to disease vectors)
	• Disruption of livelihood and income
	• Population displacement

Table 2.2 *Mechanisms through which humans may be affected by flooding*

Health outcome	Flooding of house	Walking in or contact with floodwaters	Existence of flood nearby (but no direct contact with flood)
Death from drowning and trauma	Yes	Yes	No
Injuries	Yes	Yes	No
Diarrhoea	Yes	Yes	Possible (e.g. flooding of water treatment works)
Malaria	Generally unlikely	Generally unlikely	Yes
Leptospirosis	Rarely	Yes	Possible
Mental health (e.g. depression and anxiety)	Yes	Possible	Possible (e.g. if evacuated but not flooded)

adverse effects on mental health may only become apparent several months after the floodwaters have subsided.

In the following sections, we review the epidemiological evidence for the health impacts of floods and focus on deaths and injuries, diarrhoeal disease, vector- and rodent-borne disease, mental health impacts, and risks from chemical hazards and respiratory disease. We consider health in the broadest sense, covering all aspects of physical and mental well-being. Our review does not address in detail the health impacts associated with population displacement, economic losses and disruption of food supplies following major flood events, although we provide a brief overview of these issues towards the end of the chapter.

Our review describes the impact of floods as they are reported in the literature (note that not all of the flood events discussed would be classified as 'disasters'). We also address the evidence for impacts by flood type and regional location. To date, published reviews on the health impacts of floods have focused on health effects in high-income countries (Western, 1982; Seaman, 1984; Malilay, 1997; Hajat et al, 2003). While the focus of the chapter is on epidemiological studies (see Box 2.1), we recognize that the reporting of health effects in the academic literature is heavily biased towards effects in high-income countries (including effects on rare diseases). This is unfortunate as the health effects are likely to be greatest in other regions. There are also insightful sociological studies on the health effects of flooding. However, we do not provide a detailed analysis of this qualitative work here.

Deaths due to flooding

Flood-related mortality is commonly understood to mean drownings or fatal injuries received during the onset of the flood. Compared with many other health outcomes associated with floods, statistics on such deaths are relatively easy to access, at least for events classed as disasters. But it is important to note that deaths from other causes can also be attributed to flood events, such as those from infectious diseases – a theme we return to at the end of this section.

Currently, there are three global databases that record the impacts of a range of events that have been classified as disasters (see Box 2.2). Although these datasets have some limitations, they do provide the best indication of the global impact of flood disasters in terms of numbers of deaths. They also highlight important differences between countries and regions. Globally, it is difficult to obtain information on non-disaster flood events, although these are generally reported in high-income countries. National statistics are available, but there has been no serious attempt to produce a comprehensive picture of flood mortality. We focus on the EM-DAT database produced by the Centre for Research on the Epidemiology of Disasters (CRED) since this is the only one that provides public access.

Box 2.1 *Epidemiology of flood hazard*

Epidemiology is 'the study of the distribution and determinants of health-related states or events in specified populations, and the application of this study to control of health problems' (Last, 2001, p62). Epidemiological data are essential for setting priorities within health, and for designing and evaluating public health interventions, and are also an important tool for advocacy. In the context of flood disasters, epidemiological data are important to enable public health officials and various disaster relief organizations to gain a better understanding of the different health outcomes that may arise from these kinds of events, the various population groups that may be affected, and how best to minimize the health impacts of future events. Broadly, the most rigorous epidemiological studies on flooding are those which provide details of the following:

- a clearly stated hypothesis;
- individuals included in the study and how they were selected (i.e. using some form of randomization or probability sampling procedure);
- a sample that includes those who were affected by the flood event and those who were not – the latter are often referred to as the control or comparison group;
- data collection in both the pre- and post-flood period – prospective data collection is given higher weighting than retrospective data collection as the latter is particularly susceptible to recall bias;
- results that should include *p*-values or confidence intervals; limitations of the study should also be highlighted; and
- clinical (e.g. mental health outcomes) or laboratory (e.g. leptospirosis) diagnosis that is given greater credence than self-reported diagnosis.

These criteria represent an ideal, and it will not always be possible for them to be met. By their very nature floods present a number of methodological challenges to the epidemiologist, and these challenges vary depending upon the location and nature of the flood event. For instance, one of the key challenges facing epidemiologists is being able to compare human health before the flood (baseline data) with that afterwards (post-flood data). It is reasonable to assume that the health impacts of a *non-seasonal catastrophic flood* will be significantly greater than those which might result from a *seasonal non-catastrophic flood*. One could also reasonably assume that the health impacts of the latter will be much more difficult to detect since the seasonal nature of the flood is likely to have led individuals and communities to develop adaptive/coping strategies.

Epidemiological studies are likely to be more feasible in settings where routine surveillance data are available. For example, in most European and North American countries, routine surveillance data are collected on many of the health outcomes that are associated with flooding. Hospital admissions data and general practice consultation data are readily available, and these facilitate research on the health effects of floods. In lower-income countries, these data are not always readily available, thus making epidemiological research more difficult.

> ## Box 2.2 *Global datasets on disaster deaths*
>
> There are three global datasets on disasters. Two are operated by the re-insurance industry (by the companies Munich Re and Swiss Re) and are not publicly accessible, although selected outputs from the datasets are published. The third (EM-DAT) is operated by the University of Louvain and is freely available on the internet (www.em-dat.net/who.htm). The EM-DAT Disaster Events Database includes reports of the number of deaths per event and is generally considered to be the most comprehensive of the disaster databases currently available. In EM-DAT, a disaster is defined as an event where:
>
> - 10 or more people are reported killed; or
> - 100 people are reported affected; or
> - there is a call for international assistance or declaration of a state of emergency (CRED, 2005).
>
> EM-DAT relies on a variety of sources for information, including United Nations agencies, non-governmental organizations (NGOs), insurance companies, research institutes and press agencies. This information is cross-checked for consistency and in order to avoid double counting. One of the major limitations of EM-DAT is that the database does not provide details on the cause of death, or report death by age or sex. Little information is provided on vulnerability, other than by location.

As Chapter 1 has shown, the average annual death toll from floods and wind storms runs into tens of thousands; but there are huge disparities between countries in terms of the number of flood deaths (and the number of deaths per event). Table 2.3 describes annual rates of flood deaths for different groups of countries, based on EM-DAT data from 1980–1999. The greatest incidence (mortality per 10 million per year) due to river flooding and landslides are in countries in Central and South America. The greatest incidence of death due to coastal flooding is seen in the Caribbean and Central America, and South Asia (Bangladesh and India).

It should be noted that population growth and other factors have increased the population at risk of flooding; therefore, it is extremely difficult to interpret observed trends over time and to attribute the causes of increased or decreased vulnerability. Nevertheless, the risk of drowning is certainly greatest in low-income countries where flood defences and flood preparedness measures tend to be less robust than in high-income settings. Major disasters in recent years have included a cyclone in Bangladesh in 1991, in which nearly 140,000 people died, and severe floods in Venezuela in 1999 that killed 30,000. Total deaths from the Indian Ocean Tsunami of December 2004 amounted to at least 227,000.

Table 2.3 *Annual incidence of deaths per 10,000,000 population, for the period 1980–1999 (reported data from EM-DAT database)*

World Health Organization (WHO) region	Sub-region (mortality stratum)	Countries	Inland floods and landslides	Coastal floods
Africa	Afr D	Algeria, Angola, Benin, Burkina Faso, Cameroon, Cape Verde, Chad, Comoros, Equatorial Guinea, Gabon, Gambia, Ghana, Guinea, Guinea-Bissau, Liberia, Madagascar, Mali, Mauritania, Mauritius, Niger, Nigeria, São Tome and Principe, Senegal, Seychelles, Sierra Leone, Togo	2.7	0.0
	Afr E	Botswana, Burundi, Central African Republic, Congo, Côte d'Ivoire, Democratic Republic of the Congo, Eritrea, Ethiopia, Kenya, Lesotho, Malawi, Mozambique, Namibia, Rwanda, South Africa, Swaziland, Uganda, United Republic of Tanzania, Zambia, Zimbabwe	6.5	0.0
Americas	Amr A	Canada, Cuba, US	2.2	0.0
	Amr B	Antigua and Barbuda, Argentina, Bahamas, Barbados, Belize, Brazil, Chile, Colombia, Costa Rica, Dominica, Dominican Republic, El Salvador, Grenada, Guyana, Honduras, Jamaica, Mexico, Panama, Paraguay, Saint Kitts and Nevis, Saint Lucia, Saint Vincent and the Grenadines, Suriname, Trinidad and Tobago, Uruguay, Venezuela	52.2	2.00
	Amr D	Bolivia, Ecuador, Guatemala, Haiti, Nicaragua, Peru	52.1	0.40
Eastern Mediterannean	Emr B	Bahrain, Cyprus, Iran (Islamic Republic of), Jordan, Kuwait, Lebanon, Libyan Arab Jamahiriya, Oman, Qatar, Saudi Arabia, Syrian Arab Republic, Tunisia, United Arab Emirates	14.9	0.0
	Emr D	Afghanistan, Djibouti, Egypt, Iraq, Morocco, Pakistan, Somalia, Sudan, Yemen	32.2	0.0

Table 2.3 *Annual incidence of deaths per 10,000,000 population, for the period 1980–1999 (reported data from EM-DAT database) (continued)*

World Health Organization (WHO) region	Sub-region (mortality stratum)	Countries	Inland floods and landslides	Coastal floods
Europe	Eur A	Andorra, Austria, Belgium, Croatia, Czech Republic, Denmark, Finland, France, Germany, Greece, Iceland, Ireland, Israel, Italy, Luxembourg, Malta, Monaco, The Netherlands, Norway, Portugal, San Marino, Slovenia, Spain, Sweden, Switzerland, UK	1.3	0.0
	Eur B	Albania, Armenia, Azerbaijan, Bosnia and Herzegovina, Bulgaria, Georgia, Kyrgyzstan, Poland, Romania, Slovakia, Tajikistan, Macedonia, Turkey, Turkmenistan, Uzbekistan, Yugoslavia	8.9	0.0
	Eur C	Belarus, Estonia, Hungary, Kazakhstan, Latvia, Lithuania, Republic of Moldova, Russian Federation, Ukraine	1.2	0.10
South-East Asia	Sear B	Indonesia, Sri Lanka, Thailand	9.9	0.10
	Sear D	Bangladesh, Bhutan, Democratic People's Republic of Korea, India, Maldives, Myanmar, Nepal	20.3	1.20
Western Pacific	Wpr A	Australia, Brunei Darussalam, Japan, New Zealand, Singapore	3.7	0.10
	Wpr B	Cambodia, China, Cook Islands, Fiji, Kiribati, Lao People's Democratic Republic, Malaysia, Marshall Islands, Micronesia (Federated States of), Mongolia, Nauru, Niue, Palau, Papua New Guinea, Philippines, Republic of Korea, Samoa, Solomon Islands, Tonga, Tuvalu, Vanuatu, Viet Nam	13.8	0.90

Note: sub-regions within WHO regions are based on mortality 'strata', ranging from A (very low mortality) to E (high/very high mortality).

Source: adapted from McMichael et al (2004)

It is also widely acknowledged that vulnerability to disasters is socially differentiated (see Chapter 1). For example, women may be more at risk of drowning in floods due to a range of cultural factors, including being more responsible for the children, having restricted mobility, receiving less education and access to information, and undertaking occupations that put them at more risk (Briceño, 2001; Cannon, 2002). It was reported that women were much more likely to be killed in the 2004 Indian Ocean Tsunami than men. Oxfam surveyed villages in Indonesia and found that in some locations male survivors outnumbered female survivors by a ratio of three to one (Oxfam, 2005).

Overall, the speed of flood onset is generally considered to be the main factor determining the number of flood-related deaths. Rapid-onset floods are particularly hazardous as there is little opportunity to warn individuals of the impending danger. The average rate of mortality, in terms of numbers killed as a proportion of numbers affected, are highest for flash floods (Jonkman and Kelman, 2005). Speed of onset also helped to account for the huge number of deaths in the Indian Ocean Tsunami.

Few scientific papers have reviewed the available information on flood deaths, and those that do exist have focused on floods in high-income countries. Jonkman and Kelman (2005) analysed 247 flood fatalities from Europe and the US, and found that two-thirds were due to drowning. A review of flash flood reports in the US for the period 1969–1981 found that 177 (93 per cent of all flood deaths) were due to drownings, with 46 per cent of these being car related (Table 2.4). Other papers from the US have highlighted the importance of motor vehicle occupancy as a risk factor for flood-related drownings (Donnell and Hamm, 1993; Duke et al, 1994; Kremer et al, 2000), and this was also found to be a significant risk factor for flood-related mortality in Puerto Rico (Staes et al, 1994). Rescuers are also at risk of drowning during flash floods (Duclos et al, 1991).

As noted earlier, mortality may result from other flood-related causes, as well as drowning and fatal injury. A few studies have investigated the impact

Table 2.4 *Circumstances of 190 deaths in 16 survey reports of flash floods, US, 1969–1981*

Circumstances of death	Number	Percentage
Drownings	177	93
Car related	80	46
Swept into water (in home, at campsite or when crossing bridge)	81	46
Rafting or sailing	4	2
Storm water	2	1
During evacuation (not involving car)	4	2
Performing rescue	6	3
Trauma	2	1
Heart attack	7	4
Electrocution	2	1
Buried in mud	2	1
Total	190	100

Source: French et al (1983)

of flooding on mortality using routine data sources. An increase in diarrhoea mortality was seen after the 1988 floods in Khartoum, Sudan (Woodruff et al, 1990), and in Bangladesh a cross-sectional survey of households flooded in 1998 found that seven people (0.23 per cent of 3109) died during the flood, two of whom died of apparent diarrhoea and two were suspected of dying of a heart attack (Kunii et al, 2002). The rather weak evidence for disease-related mortality from floods in developing countries may, in part, stem from data limitations. It is not possible to conduct a household survey where populations are displaced, although surveillance is undertaken in camps or other centres where people have gathered. It should also be remembered that in many low-income countries the health care infrastructure is weak, and routine reporting of infections is a low priority.

In contrast, some studies on individuals in flooded households in high-income countries found an excess in mortality several months after the flood event (Lorraine, 1954). In the UK, a retrospective study of the 1968 Bristol floods reported a 50 per cent increase in the number of deaths among those whose homes had been flooded, with the most pronounced rise in the 45- to 64-year age group (Bennet, 1970). Similar studies in Australia, however, found no such effect (Abrahams et al, 1976; Handmer and Smith, 1983). The suggested mechanism for these deaths was increased stress or anxiety caused by the flood. We discuss the impact of flooding on mental health in more detail below.

Injuries

Flooding can be associated with trauma from being hit by objects in fast-flowing waters. Injuries can be relatively minor and self-treated, such as cuts and abrasions, or may be more serious (e.g. fractures, crush injuries and punctures). There is also potential for injuries after the flood, when people return to their homes and businesses and begin the clean-up operation. Anecdotal evidence indicates risks from unstable buildings and from electrical power cables. Surprisingly little information on the burden of injuries due to flood events is available, and injuries caused by floods are not routinely reported in most countries. There is some evidence that the burden of injuries due to floods is low in high-income countries, and in those surveys that have reported injuries, the injuries were all relatively minor.

After the 1993 Midwest floods in the US, injuries were reported through the routine surveillance system (Schmidt et al, 1993). Approximately 500 flood-related conditions were reported, and of these 250 (48 per cent) were injuries. The most common injuries reported were sprains/strains (34 per cent), lacerations (24 per cent) and abrasions/contusions (11 per cent). Similar data were reported from Iowa (Atchison et al, 1993). Following the 1988 floods in Nîmes (France), 6 per cent of households reported mild injuries (contusions, cuts and sprains) related to the flood (Duclos et al, 1991). In addition to the flooded community, rescue workers and other emergency teams are also at risk of injury.

Diarrhoeal diseases

Diarrhoeal disease is a major cause of childhood mortality and morbidity in low-income countries (Kosek et al, 2003). The transmission of many diarrhoeal diseases shows seasonal variation that may be associated with seasonal rains and flooding, although the evidence for this is not well established. Diarrhoeal disease can be caused by both viral and bacterial pathogens. Due to improvements in the treatment of diarrhoea (such as oral re-hydration therapy), diarrhoeal mortality has decreased in many countries, but morbidity remains high. Table 2.5 summarizes the main water- and excreta-related infections.

Diarrhoeal diseases are generally transmitted through the faecal-oral route, and flooding is thought to lead to increased transmission of diarrhoea via increased contact of individuals with faecal matter. Flooding will also lead to decreases in basic hygiene if toilets or latrines become inaccessible and clean water is not available for washing (see Chapter 3). These conditions could persist for a long time, depending upon the severity of the flood.

Diarrhoeal disease is endemic in low-income countries such as Bangladesh that are also subject to frequent flooding. There is some evidence that diarrhoeal mortality and morbidity increased following major floods in Bangladesh (Siddique et al, 1991; Kunii et al, 2002). In a study of the 1998 flood, diarrhoea was reported as the major cause of illness in children, and accounted for 27 per cent of the 154 flood-related deaths reported. Flood-related increases in diarrhoeal disease have also been reported in India (Mondal et al, 2001) and Brazil (Heller et al, 2003).

Rotavirus is a common cause of diarrhoea in children and infants, and two further studies from Bangladesh (Ahmed et al, 1991; Fun et al, 1991) focus on the floods of 1988. Although the findings of both studies could not conclusively state that there was a causal association between the floods and increased cases of rotavirus infection, Ahmed et al (1991, p2275) did find that 'an increase in the proportion of rotavirus diarrhoea also seemed to correspond to the spread of the flood after August'.

In high-income countries, where health surveillance is much better and is often enhanced following floods, the available evidence suggests that there is not an increase in diarrhoeal disease following floods (Cervenka, 1976; Atchison et al, 1993; Schmidt et al, 1993; Aavitsland et al, 1996) However, surveys where people report their own symptoms have indicated an increase in diarrhoeal episodes following flooding (e.g. Waring et al, 2002; Reacher et al, 2004; Wade et al, 2004).

Since the 1990s, there have been several reports of cholera following flood events. These include reports from Djibouti (Morillon et al, 1998), the Horn of Africa (WHO, 1998), India (Sur et al, 2000), Indonesia (Korthuis et al, 1998) and Mozambique (Naidoo and Patric, 2002). Cholera is an acute and severe form of diarrhoeal disease, caused by the infectious agent *Vibrio cholerae* 01 (a more recent strain, *V. cholerae* 0139, has also been identified). Humans are the main reservoir, although in recent years environmental reservoirs have been

Table 2.5 *Environmental classification system for water- and excreta-related infections*

Category	Infection	Pathogenic agent
1 Faecal-oral (water borne or water washed)	• Diarrhoeas and dysenteries:	
	– Amoebic dysentery	P
	– Balantidiasis	P
	– *Campylobacter* enteritis	B
	– Cholera	B
	– Cryptosporidiosis	P
	– *E. coli* diarrhoea	B
	– Giardiasis	P
	– Rotavirus diarrhoea	V
	– Salmonellosis	B
	– Shigellosis (bacillary dysentery)	B
	– Yersiniosis	B
	• Enteric fevers:	
	– Typhoid	B
	– Paratyphoid	B
	• Poliomyelitis	V
	• Hepatitis A	V
2 Water washed:		
• Skin and eye infections	• Infectious skin diseases	M
	• Infectious eye diseases	M
• Other	• Louse-borne typhus	R
	• Louse-borne relapsing fever	S
3 Water based:		
• Penetrating skin	• Schistosomiasis	H
• Ingested	• Guinea worm	H
	• Clonorchiasis	H
	• Diphyllobothriasis	H
	• Fasciolopsiasis	H
	• Paragonimiasis	H
	• Others	H
4 Soil-transmitted helminths	• Ascariasis (roundworm)	H
	• Trichuriasis (whipworm)	H
	• Hookworm	H
	• Strongyloidasis	H
5 Water-related insect vector:		
• Biting near water	• Sleeping sickness	P
• Breeding in water	• Filariasis	H
	• Malaria	P
	• River blindness	H
	• Mosquito-borne viruses:	
	– Yellow fever	V
	– Dengue	V
	– Others	V

Note: B = bacterium; H = helminth; P = protozoan; M = miscellaneous; R = rickettsia; S = spirochaete; V = virus.

Source: adapted from Cairncross and Feachem (1993, Tables 1.2, 1.3)

shown to exist, apparently in association with copepods or other zooplankton in brackish water or estuaries (Chin, 2000; Naidoo and Patric, 2002).

After the 1998 floods in West Bengal there was a severe outbreak of diarrhoeal disease with 16,590 reported cases and 276 deaths. A quarter of the cases and most of the deaths were in children under five. The main pathogen was identified as *V. cholerae* 01, biotype El Tor (Sur et al, 2000, p181). The epidemic however, may have been caused by the inappropriate siting of emergency tube wells in low-lying areas.

In Indonesia, Katsumata et al (1998) conducted a hospital- and community-based study to understand the prevalence and mode of transmission of *Cryptosporidium parvum* infection. Although exposure to flooding was found to be a risk factor for *C. parvum* infection, it was not clear how exposure to flooding was measured, or whether this association referred to both the hospital- and community-based studies. Another Indonesian study (Vollaard et al, 2004) found an increased risk of contracting paratyphoid infections when homes were flooded. These studies refer to frequent monsoon flooding, rather than catastrophic flooding.

The hepatitis A and E viruses (HAV and HEV) are transmitted primarily through the faecal-oral route (Chin, 2000). Common source outbreaks for HEV include contaminated water, and for HAV both contaminated food and water. A recent review suggested that many of the large outbreaks of HEV have occurred after heavy rains and flooding (Piper-Jenks et al, 2000). There have also been reports of flood-related outbreaks of HAV and HEV from Sudan (McCarthy et al, 1994), the US (Mackowiak et al, 1976), and Viet Nam (Corwin et al, 1999; Hau et al, 1999).

In their cross-sectional study of the prevalence of hepatitis A and E in Viet Nam, Hau et al (1999) suggested that 'periodic flooding of the Mekong River and tributaries probably contributes to the contamination of water sources with human and/or animal waste material, adding to the risk of exposure [and this] regular flooding favours the epidemic potential of HEV spread' (Hau et al, 1999, p279). However, such an association cannot be confirmed by this study. In contrast, an outbreak investigation in Indonesia (Sedyaningsih-Mamahit et al, 2002) found no climatic influences (flood or drought) which favoured epidemic HEV transmission.

Infection from helminths

Infection by helminths (parasitic worms) can be either water based or soil based (see Table 2.5). Water-based infection (e.g. schistosomiasis) results from infection by helminths that depend upon an aquatic intermediate host such as a snail to complete their life cycle. Soil-transmitted helminths are not immediately infective, but first require a period of development in favourable conditions, usually in moist soil (Cairncross and Feachem, 1993). Both water-based and soil-based infections are associated with conditions of poor sanitation and hygiene, as infective eggs are passed in either human urine or (usually) faeces.

Humans become infected with schistosomiasis when the parasite released by the snail intermediate host penetrates human skin. The parasite is subsequently transported to the veins around the bladder or to those which deliver blood to the liver. The transmission cycle is completed when infected humans urinate or defecate in waters in which the intermediate snail host is found. The disease is particularly associated with large-scale irrigation projects, where relatively stagnant waters provide an ideal environment for the intermediate snail host, and tends to occur in communities with inadequate sanitation infrastructure. There is increased risk of transmission when floods inundate the irrigation project and enable the intermediate snail host to be more widely dispersed. Several papers from China focus on the changes in snail intermediate host distribution and on the prevalence of human infection in relation to various flood events during the 1990s (Huang YiXin et al, 1998; Chen MingGang, 1999; Lin DanDan et al, 1999; Chen Wei et al, 2000; Li Tao et al, 2000; Chen Jiran et al, 2001; Yang MeiXia et al, 2002; Zhang YuQi et al, 2002). None, however, provide strong epidemiological evidence of a causal relationship between flooding and increased disease transmission.

Hookworm – a chronic parasitic infection – is widely endemic in tropical and subtropical countries where sanitary disposal of human faeces is not practised, and soil, moisture and temperature conditions favour development of infective larvae (Chin, 2000). In a longitudinal study of risk factors for Bancroftian filariasis in Haitian children (Lilley et al, 1997), the prevalence of *Ascaris* (a roundworm) and *Trichuris* (a whipworm) remained relatively stable, while over the six-year follow-up period of the study the prevalence of hookworm increased from 0 per cent to 12–15 per cent. Lilley et al (1997, p392) report that this increase 'may be an indirect consequence of deforestation, which led to silt accumulation in the local river, subsequent flooding, altered water drainage patterns and saturation of soil near homes', and that sandy loam soil deposited after flooding events 'may also have been more conducive to hookworm development and survival, thus heightening the effects of the increased soil moisture'.

Mosquito-borne diseases

Infections transmitted by water-related insect vectors represent an important category of disease that can be affected by flooding (see Table 2.5). Mosquitoes breed in, or close to, stagnant or slow-moving water (such as puddles and ponds) and are responsible for transmitting many important infectious diseases. Heavy rainfall and flooding can trigger epidemics of mosquito-borne disease in areas where the climate is usually too dry to maintain a sufficiently abundant mosquito population. Floodwaters and heavy rain can also be beneficial, however, in the sense that they can wash away breeding sites, and in areas where mosquito-borne disease is endemic, this can lead to reduced transmission (Lindsay et al, 2000; Sidley, 2000), at least during the period when water levels are high.

The collection of stagnant water due to the blocking of drains in urban settings is also associated with increases in risk of transmission. Here, we cite only those papers where a flood event is also reported. However, there is a large and separate literature on the role of weather, particularly rainfall, in triggering mosquito-borne disease outbreaks that cannot be adequately addressed in this chapter. Overall, there is little rigorous epidemiological evidence to support the suggestion that outbreaks of malaria or other mosquito-borne disease are a common consequence of a flood event. The studies that relate to particular diseases are discussed in more detail below.

Malaria

Malaria is a parasitic disease that occurs in humans when one of four infectious agents – *Plasmodium vivax*, *P. malariae*, *P. falciparum* and *P. ovale* – is transmitted into the blood stream through the bite of a female mosquito (Chin, 2000). Flood-related malaria outbreaks have been reported from Africa, Asia and Latin America. For example, the 1982 El Niño event caused extensive flooding in several countries in Latin America, and a number of papers (Moreira Cedeno, 1986; Russac, 1986; Hederra, 1987) reported sharp increases in the number of cases of malaria following these floods.

Likewise, the 1988 floods in Khartoum, Sudan, were also reported to have led to an increase in the transmission of malaria, which was over and above the annual rainy season increase that one would normally expect (MMWR, 1989; Woodruff et al, 1990; McCarthy et al, 1996; El-Sayed et al, 2000). However, due to a lack of baseline population data, morbidity and mortality rates could not be calculated, and while the increase in the number of cases reported in August 1988 was greater than that of August 1987, it is not clear if this was statistically significant (MMWR, 1989; Woodruff et al, 1990). Other flood-related outbreaks of malaria have been reported from Costa Rica (Saenz et al, 1995) and India (Mathur et al, 1992; Sharma et al, 1997; Nandi and Sharma, 2000); but none provide strong evidence of a flood-related increase in transmission.

Arboviruses

Mosquitoes are also responsible for the transmission of a number of arboviruses (arthropod-borne viruses), including dengue, and several forms of encephalitis. Dengue fever is an acute febrile viral disease and is transmitted to humans by the *Aedes aegypti* mosquito, which predominates in urban environments and whose preferred breeding habitat is in man-made containers, such as drinking-water storage containers. Dengue is unlikely to be a particular problem during the onset phase of a flood, as many breeding habitats of *A. aegypti* are likely to be overwhelmed by floodwaters. However, in the post-onset phase there is a possibility that receding floodwaters may provide ideal breeding habitats. Only one paper (Rigau-Perez et al, 2001) made reference to dengue in the context of flooding, and reported that 'widespread flooding in 1996 did not affect the shape and height of the dengue epidemic [in the inter-epidemic period]' (Rigau-Perez et al, 2001, p81).

West Nile virus (WNV) has caused outbreaks in Egypt, India, Israel and several countries in Central Europe, and is widespread in parts of Africa (Chin, 2000). Several papers refer to WNV in Europe (Tsai et al, 1998; Han et al, 1999; Hubalek and Halouzka, 1999; Hubalek et al, 1999; Hubalek, 2000) and report that environmental factors such as flooding can facilitate the re-emergence of WNV. There have also been reports of outbreaks of Murray Valley encephalitis (MVE) and St Louis encephalitis (SLE) following floods, and although these diseases are relatively rare they are important in high-income countries. MVE is found in parts of Australia and New Guinea (Chin, 2000), and in the period of 1990–1998, 14 cases of MVE were notified in Western Australia; 9 of these cases followed heavy rain and flooding during the 1993 wet season in Western Australia and the Northern Territory (Smith et al, 1993; Cordova et al, 2000). Heavy rainfall and flooding were seen as possible contributory factors to transmission.

SLE is found in North America, parts of the Caribbean and Latin America. One study (Hopkins et al, 1975) reports on an epidemic of SLE in the US during 1966. In late April 1966, unusually heavy rains caused flooding in many areas of Dallas, Texas, and 'overloaded the drainage and sewage management system, causing back-up of water in the drains and creating pools of standing water enriched with organic waste favourable for mosquito breeding throughout the low-lying parts of the city' (Hopkins et al, 1975, p2) More recent outbreaks linked to flooding of the lower Colorado River have also been reported (Lauerman et al, 1984).

Rodent-borne diseases

Hantavirus pulmonary syndrome

Hantavirus pulmonary syndrome (HPS) is an acute zoonotic viral disease, and multiple hantaviruses have been identified in the Americas; the disease was first recognized in 1993 in New Mexico and Arizona, US (Chin, 2000). The natural reservoir for the disease includes various species of rodent, such as the deer mouse, and infection in humans occurs after inhalation of aerosolized virus or direct contact with infected rodents or their excreta (Bayard et al, 2000).

Flooding can affect the ecology of certain species and change local disease transmission by upsetting the balance between hosts, vectors and prey. These interactions are complex and difficult to study. The role of weather in the emergence of HPS in the US during the 1990s has been well investigated (Engelthaler et al, 1999). In Panama in 1999, an increase in cases occurred around the same time as an increase in peri-domestic rodents, which was associated with increased rainfall and flooding in surrounding areas (Bayard et al, 2000). Bayard et al (2000) have also suggested that an increased incidence of HPS was linked with periods of above average rainfall in parts of the south-western US.

Leptospirosis

Leptospirosis is a zoonotic disease caused by the bacterial pathogen *Leptospira interrogans* and is transmitted in urine from animals to humans, either directly, when urine from an infected animal (including dogs, cats, cattle, rodents and wild animals) enters the body through a break in the skin, or indirectly, in contaminated water and soil (Ingraham and Ingraham, 1995; Bharti et al, 2003). The pathogen enters the bloodstream and after reaching the kidneys multiplies and is excreted in the urine. The disease occurs worldwide in urban and rural areas, and in both the North and South (Chin, 2000); but there is a higher incidence of human infection in tropical regions (Bharti et al, 2003). There is often a lack of awareness of the disease, and with diagnosis difficult (even in the laboratory) there is likely to be a general underestimation of incidence rates (Bharti et al, 2003, p759).

Leptospirosis infection is more common in men (Park et al, 1989; Morshed, et al, 1994), and the disease is generally seen as an occupational infection in sewer workers and agricultural labourers; the first apparent outbreak in sewer workers was in 1883 (Fuortes and Nettleman, 1994). However, there have also been outbreaks among water sports enthusiasts who were infected when using flooded rivers (Reisberg et al, 1997). In general, 'flooding after heavy rain is particularly favourable to leptospires; it prevents animal urine from being absorbed into the soil or evaporating so leptospires may pass directly into the surface waters or persist in mud' (Sanders et al, 1999, p401).

While leptospirosis is not solely associated with heavy rainfall and flooding, there have been reports of flood-associated outbreaks from a wide range of countries, including Argentina (Vanasco et al, 2000), Brazil (Corrêa, 1975; Marotto et al, 1997; Ko et al, 1999; Barcellos and Sabroza, 2000; Kupek, et al, 2000; Barcellos and Sabroza, 2001; Sarkar et al, 2002), Cuba (Suárez Hernández et al, 1999), India (WHO, 2000; Karande et al, 2002; Sehgal et al, 2002; Karande et al, 2003), Korea (Park et al, 1989), Mexico (Leal-Castellanos et al, 2003), Nicaragua (Muñoz et al, 1995; Trevejo et al, 1998; Ashford et al, 2000), the Philippines (Easton, 1999) and Portugal (Simões et al, 1969).

In November 1967, Lisbon, Portugal, experienced heavy precipitation (109mm in 24 hours), which resulted in homes being flooded. There were 32 cases of leptospirosis (all males aged 14 to 59 years), and according to Simões et al (1969), similar heavy precipitation occurred in the past, but cases were not reported. The authors suggest that this may be due to the lower density of the human population. In Korea, Park et al (1989) claim that the 1987 outbreak 'seemed to be due to the wash-out of leptospira-laden rodent urine into fields where workers were tying up fallen rice stalks after severe flooding. The outbreaks of leptospirosis in 1975, 1984 and 1985 also occurred after severe floods before harvesting season' (Park et al, 1989, p348).

There is good evidence that flooding can lead to outbreaks of leptospirosis. After a series of tropical storms in 1995, two health centres in western Nicaragua reported increased numbers of patients with a fever-like illness, and some deaths from haemorrhagic manifestations and shock (Trevejo et al, 1998).

Dengue and dengue haemorrhagic fever were initially suspected (Muñoz et al, 1995). A case-control study was conducted to identify and characterize aetiology, to describe the epidemic and to identify possible risk factors. Case patients were found to be 'significantly more likely than controls to have reported walking through creeks or swimming in rivers' (Trevejo et al, 1998, p1459). The authors report 'the most likely explanation for this epidemic was increased exposure to floodwaters that had become contaminated by urine from animals infected with leptospira species' (Trevejo et al, 1998, p1461). Although several articles (Muñoz et al, 1995; Trevejo et al, 1998; Ashford et al, 2000) indicate that contact with floodwaters was the likely cause of the outbreak, none of these papers have provided details of the flood.

After the floods of 2000 and 2001 in Mumbai, India, Karande et al (2003, p1071) conducted two hospital-based observational studies among children and found that 'contact with contaminated floodwater was significantly associated with the diagnosis of leptospirosis, [and children] had either played in the floodwater or waded through it while going to school, and in some cases the floodwater had even entered their homes'. However, neither of the studies in Mumbai used a control group, making it difficult to establish whether there was an association between contact with floodwaters and both outbreaks. As already noted, there have been several papers on leptospirosis in Brazil, and the findings of two of these are discussed in more detail in Box 2.3.

Box 2.3 *Leptospirosis in Brazil*

The City of Salvador is located along the north-east coast of Brazil and has a population of over 2 million. During the rainy season of 1996, the city experienced a large epidemic of an acute illness associated with jaundice and acute renal failure. As a result, an active surveillance system for leptospirosis was established at a state-run infectious disease hospital, which also serves as the reference centre for leptospirosis in the metropolitan region.

Between 10 March and 2 November 1996, patients meeting the case criteria for severe manifestations of leptospirosis were recruited into a study (Ko et al, 1999). The surveillance system identified 326 clinically defined cases, of which 193 (59 per cent) were confirmed by laboratory diagnosis or were classed as 'probable' cases. Ko et al (1999) found that rainfall had exceeded 75mm per week in the one to four weeks before each peak in the number of cases, and that severe flooding occurred during the heaviest period of rainfall between 21 and 27 April. The largest number of cases per week (39) was reported two weeks after this event. The majority of the cases were adults in employment and 80 per cent were male. Of those who were employed, 40 per cent had an occupation that brought them into contact with flood or sewage water. In interviews with patients, 69 per cent of respondents stated they had been in contact with flood or sewage water within the four weeks before identification of leptospirosis, and 77 per cent reported seeing rodents in their home or place of work.

Sarkar et al (2002) investigated another outbreak that occurred in the same city in 2000. Using a case-control study design, they found that residence in proximity to an open sewer, peri-domiciliary sighting of rats and workplace exposure to contaminated environmental sources were independent risk factors for acquiring leptospirosis. They also found that those with the disease reported flooding in front of their residence more frequently than those who did not have the disease

The effects of flooding on mental health

In their 2001 *World Health Report* (WHO, 2001), the World Health Organization (WHO) stated:

> ...*mental health has been defined variously by scholars from different cultures. Concepts of mental health include subjective well-being, perceived self-efficacy, autonomy, competence, intergenerational dependence, and self-actualization of one's intellectual and emotional potential, among others. From a cross-cultural perspective, it is nearly impossible to define mental health comprehensively. It is, however, generally agreed that mental health is broader than a lack of mental disorders.* (WHO, 2001, p5)

Box 2.4 sets out typical symptoms and forms of mental illness. It should be noted that there are complex interactions between physical and mental health. In general, major life stressors such as natural disasters can influence the constitutional status of the body and increase susceptibility not only to physical illness but also to effects on mental health (Phifer et al, 1988). As shown in previous sections of this chapter, flooding can lead to a range of adverse outcomes on physical health, and many of these can, in turn, lead to impacts on mental health status. Mental health impacts may also result from personal losses and disruption caused by floods (see Chapter 4). Loss of a loved one can have a tremendous impact on the mental well-being of close family and friends. Stress and emotional trauma can also result from the loss of livelihood (e.g. loss of employment or loss of property), and this can be exacerbated in circumstances where social networks and social welfare systems are less than adequate. In most low-income countries, many families will not have insurance polices, and when property is damaged or destroyed there is likely to be increased stress and anxiety.

Furthermore, the mental health consequences of exposure to disasters 'have not been fully addressed by those in the field of disaster preparedness or service delivery' (Gerrity and Flynn, 1997, p101). This is especially the case in low-income countries. WHO (2001, p43) emphasizes that natural disasters, such as floods and hurricanes, 'take a heavy toll on the mental health of the people involved, most of whom live in developing countries, where capacity to take care of these problems is extremely limited'.

In this section we focus on three aspects of mental health:

- common mental health disorders;
- post-traumatic stress disorder (PTSD); and
- suicide.

Common mental health disorders (anxiety, depression, and stress)

There have been numerous studies of the effects of flooding on common mental health disorders, and most of these refer to flood events in high-income

---

Box 2.4 *Symptoms and categories of mental illness*

There are five major types of symptoms for the diagnosis of mental illness:

1 *Physical – 'somatic' symptoms.* These affect the body and physical functions, and include aches, tiredness and sleep disturbance. It is important to remember that mental illnesses often produce physical symptoms.
2 *Feeling – emotional symptoms.* Typical examples are feeling sad or scared.
3 *Thinking – 'cognitive' symptoms.* Typical examples are thinking of suicide, thinking that someone is going to harm you, difficulty in thinking clearly and forgetfulness.
4 *Behaving – behavioural symptoms.* These symptoms are related to what a person is doing. Examples include behaving in an aggressive manner and attempting suicide.
5 *Imaging – perceptual symptoms.* These arise from one of the sensory organs and include hearing voices or seeing things that others cannot (hallucinations).

In reality, these different types of symptoms are closely associated with one another. There are six broad categories of mental illness:

1 common mental disorders (depression and anxiety);
2 'bad habits', such as alcohol dependence and drug misuse;
3 severe mental disorders (the psychoses);
4 mental retardation;
5 mental health problems in the elderly; and
6 mental health problems in children.

Source: adapted from Patel (2003)

countries, including the US, Australia and a number of European countries such as Poland, The Netherlands and the UK. In addition to those cited below, they include studies by Price (1978); Logue and Hansen (1980); Ollendick and Hoffman (1982); Powell and Penick (1983); Melick and Logue (1985); Tobin and Ollenburger (1996); Neuberg et al (1999); Hegstad (2000); Neuberg et al (2001); and Ferraro (2003). As far as we are aware, there has only been one epidemiological study (Durkin et al, 1993) of the mental health impacts of flooding in a low-income country.

After the 1968 floods in Bristol, UK, Bennet (1970) found a significant increase in the number of new psychiatric symptoms (considered to comprise anxiety, depression, irritability and sleeplessness) reported by flooded female respondents compared with the non-flooded group. However, there was no significant difference in the psychiatric symptoms reported by males. These results concur with a study of the 1974 Brisbane floods (Abrahams et al, 1976), except that in this case flooded males were more affected than non-flooded males.

In the US, two studies (Melick, 1978; Logue et al, 1981) were conducted after Tropical Storm Agnes caused extensive flooding in Pennsylvania in 1972. Respondents who were flooded demonstrated more mental health symptoms than non-flooded respondents, but this difference was not statistically significant. The second study was carried out five years post-flood; but again no statistically significant effect of increased anxiety was found in the flooded persons (Logue et al, 1981, p239).

A major difficulty with these types of studies is that they cannot take into account the fact that some people were depressed before the flood, and therefore their depression after the flood cannot be solely attributed to the flood. A well-conducted study in the US had information on mental health before the flood, and the authors found that flood exposure was associated with significant increases in depression and anxiety in older persons (Phifer et al, 1988; Phifer, 1990). Those with high levels of pre-flood depressive symptoms experienced greater increases in symptoms post-flood. Flood exposure was also associated with reports of increased physical symptoms. The study also found that anxiety effects were increased in low socio-economic groups (Phifer, 1990). These findings have since been confirmed by another study that was able to follow up people who were flooded and control for their pre-flood symptoms (Ginexi et al, 2000).

The majority of the papers reviewed here focused on the mental health of adults. Flooding has also been shown to affect the mental health of children. In Bangladesh, Durkin et al (1993) found post-flood changes in behaviour and bedwetting in children aged two to nine years. In The Netherlands, Becht et al (1998) interviewed children and their parents six months post-flood, and found 15–20 per cent of children having moderate to severe stress symptoms. After the 1997 floods in Opole, Poland, children were found to have long-term negative effects, including post-traumatic stress disorder, depression and dissatisfaction with ongoing life (Bokszczanin, 2000; Bokszczanin, 2002).

Post-traumatic stress disorder

Post-traumatic stress disorder (PTSD) 'arises after a stressful event of an exceptionally threatening or catastrophic nature and is characterized by intrusive memories, avoidance of circumstances associated with the stressor, sleep disturbances, irritability and anger, lack of concentration and excessive vigilance'(WHO, 2001, p43). The specific diagnosis of PTSD, however, 'has been questioned as being culture specific and also as being made too often' (WHO, 2001, p43), and has been called 'a diagnostic category that has been invented based on socio-political needs' (Summerfield, 2001, cited in WHO, 2001, p440).

There have been studies of flood-related PTSD undertaken in Canada (Auger et al, 2000; Maltais et al, 2000), France (Verger et al, 2003), Poland (Norris et al, 2002), Puerto Rico (Canino et al, 1990) and the US (Moinzadeh, 1999; Waelde et al, 2001; McMillen et al, 2002). Verger et al (2003) conducted a retrospective cross-sectional study in adults over 18 years of age, five years after the 1992 floods in Vaucluse, France, to study the association between the severity of psychological exposure to the flood and symptoms of PTSD. A significantly higher PTSD score was observed for females and for subjects older than 35 years. However, the authors state 'the subjects' reports of their disaster-related experiences are by nature subjective and were collected, retrospectively, five years after the event [and are therefore] not entirely reliable' (Verger et al, 2003, p440).

McMillen et al (2002) interviewed those who were affected by the 1993 US Midwest floods in areas around St Louis, and found 60 subjects (38 per cent) who met criteria for post-flood psychiatric disorder. Thirty-five subjects (22 per cent) met criteria for flood-related PTSD. The authors recognized that there were several limitations with this study, and these included the retrospective collection of data, the fact that interviewees were self-selected, lack of clinical diagnosis, and the lack of a non-flooded comparison group. In Puerto Rico, Canino et al (1990) found that the higher the level of exposure to the disaster, the greater the number of new depression and PTSD symptoms.

Suicide

We identified only two studies that refer to suicides in the context of flooding. Reporting on natural disasters in the US, Krug et al (1998, 1999) found that the results for countries affected by a single natural disaster did not support the hypothesis that suicide rates increase afer such events. However, these results were subsequently retracted after the authors found a computational error in their original findings, and conceded that 'the new results for counties affected by a single natural disaster do not support the hypothesis that suicide rates increase after natural disasters' (Krug et al, 1999, p148). A paper from China (He, 1998) reports that suicide rates in the Yangtze Basin are 40 per cent higher than in the rest of the country. This area resembles the rest of the country in terms of socio-demographic variables, and the author reports that 'the major difference in this region is the periodic flooding' (He, 1998, p287). However, the paper provides no epidemiological evidence to support any link between these suicide rates and flooding.

Chemical contamination and respiratory disease

Floods and chemical contamination

Chemical contamination may result when floodwaters inundate industrial plants and waste storage facilities, damage pipelines, or facilitate the release of chemicals from land that may be already contaminated. Floodwaters can also cause structural damage to housing and heating systems, releasing fuel oil into floodwater, and these oils can seep into walls and stairwells, later releasing toxic hydrocarbons into indoor air (Potera, 2003). These accidental releases of chemicals may result in adverse effects on human health through various biological pathways, including inhalation of contaminated air and ingestion of contaminated water or foodstuffs.

Euripidou and Murray (2004) reviewed the public health impacts of chemical contamination following flood events and describe a number of flood events in the UK. Although these events led to increased self-reporting of earache, gastrointestinal upsets, nausea, skin rashes, sore throat, stinging faces and impacts on psychological health, the epidemiological evidence linking such contamination with mortality and morbidity is not strong.

In Honduras, Balluz and colleagues (2001) evaluated chemical contamination of potable water, and the extent of human exposure to chemicals, after the floods associated with Hurricane Mitch in October 1998. Using an environmental exposure assessment and cross-sectional survey of households with adolescents aged 15 to 18 years, the study showed that the floods had produced little contamination of water supplies, with only one sample containing a higher than expected level of detectable contaminants. 'This suggested that chemicals from agricultural land and chemical manufacturing and storage facilities, which were released into the water during the hurricane and subsequent flooding, were diluted or washed away with the floodwater' (Balluz et al, 2001, p291). However, in contrast, all of the soil samples contained detectable levels of pesticides, and as exposure through inhalation and ingestion of food were not studied, 'these may represent significant exposure pathways' (Balluz et al, 2001, p292).

Respiratory disease

Respiratory disease is commonly reported as a possible health outcome of exposure to flooding (see, e.g. Ahmed et al, 1999; Menne, 1999; Franklin et al, 2000). It has been suggested, for instance, that damp caused by flooding leads to accumulation of mould in dwellings with consequences for respiratory health (Patterson et al, 1981; Jarvis et al, 1998; Elidemir et al, 1999). However, the epidemiological evidence linking flood-related moulds and respiratory infections is not particularly strong, and a study in the US by Curtis et al (1997) found allergen levels to be significantly higher in those homes that had not been flooded.

For low-income countries, there is also little evidence in relation to respiratory infections. In their study of the 1993 West Bengal floods, Biswas et al (1999b) compared rates for respiratory infections between the pre- and post-flood period, and found that rates increased from 2.8 per cent to 9.6 per cent. More recently, Kunii et al (2002) report that respiratory infections accounted for 14 per cent of the health problems reported by those surveyed after the 1998 floods in Bangladesh. However, it is again difficult to draw any firm conclusions from this study design.

Floods can often lead to a temporary loss of electrical power supply, and this shortage is often met by using petroleum-fuelled equipment. This equipment may be used in clean-up operations, and there is potential for adverse health effects. For example, after the April 1997 Red River flood, a surveillance system was established in North Dakota, and this system detected an outbreak of carbon monoxide poisoning, which was related to the use of such equipment (Daley et al, 2001).

Flood disasters and social disruption

Major flood disasters can be associated with disruption of infrastructure, economic losses and population displacement, with further implications for health. Although we do not focus on these impacts in this chapter, we recognize that each of these has the potential to exact a burden of disease on human populations.

Floods can bring severe disruption to key sectors, such as roads and transport systems, agriculture, industry, commerce and utilities, as well as health services (see Chapter 3 for detailed discussion of damage to health infrastructure and water supply and sanitation systems). Floods may result in short- and long-term economic losses, which affect households, businesses and the wider community. In higher-income countries, insurance facilitates the economic recovery of those affected by floods, whereas in many low-income countries such insurance is not readily available, and this makes recovery much more difficult (Wisner et al, 2004). Floods, and particularly catastrophic floods, are liable to result in population displacement, when individuals may lose their homes, possessions and livelihoods. Displacement may occur locally, within national borders or can be cross-border, and can result in emergency accommodation within refugee camps.

These impacts can influence health status in a number of ways, including access to medical treatment, water, sanitation and food. Access to medical services, for example, can be affected by impacts on household income and the wider economy, as well as by direct physical damage to health systems (Parker and Thompson, 2000; Wisner et al, 2004). Severe floods can weaken the health care infrastructure through damage to buildings and equipment, materials and supplies. The Pan American Health Organization (PAHO, 1998a), for example, describes a series of major impacts to the health care infrastructure in Ecuador and Peru during the 1997/1998 El Niño. Disruption of transport can also create problems of travel to health care facilities, especially in rural areas.

Displaced populations may be especially at risk of ill health (Wisner and Adams, 2002; The Sphere Project, 2004). Their access to essential medicines and health care may be acutely affected, and they may lack an adequate alternative source of water and shelter. In the crowded conditions that often exist in refugee camps, infectious disease outbreaks are a serious risk. Moreover, large-scale population movements will place an additional major burden on the local and national health care infrastructure.

As with other aspects of flooding, however, securing conclusive data linking the wider effects of flood events with health impacts is difficult. To date, very few studies have attempted to document the health impacts of reduced access to normal primary and secondary care caused by flooding. An outbreak of Poliomyelitis (polio) in KwaZulu-Natal, South Africa, was attributed to major floods that led to a temporary breakdown in vaccination services and possibly contamination of surface water with the polio pathogen (van Middelkoop et al, 1992).

Nutritional status can also be affected by flooding. Access to foodstuffs may prove difficult, if not impossible, when food distribution networks are unable to operate (Parker and Thompson, 2000). If one assumes that most households are unlikely to have food reserves to last more than a few days, and that access is not restored within a relatively short period, increased morbidity may result. While the impact of disruptions to the food supply system will generally be confined to the area of the flood, the impacts of inundation of agricultural land are likely to be much wider in scale. The latter is likely to affect not just the local community, but also those who live further away and are reliant on this agricultural land for their food consumption. Disruption of economic livelihood may also affect household incomes and capacity to purchase food, especially in low-income countries (Parker, 2000).

Two surveillance reports from the Khartoum floods of 1988 have highlighted the difficulties in measuring the impacts of flooding on nutritional status (CDC, 1989; Woodruff et al, 1990). Woodruff et al (1990) established that of the 17,639 children (aged one to five years) assessed during the period of 19–30 August 1988, 13.6 per cent were moderately malnourished and 9.5 per cent were severely malnourished. The Centers for Disease Control and Prevention (CDC) report emphasizes that 'the direct impact of the flood disaster on the nutritional status of the assessed children is difficult to evaluate without prior survey information [which in this case was not available]; however, the extent of their current under-nutrition is associated with an increased risk of mortality' (CDC, 1989, p787).

Conclusion

The health impacts of floods are wide ranging and depend upon a host of factors, including the characteristics of the flood hazard, patterns of exposure and underlying vulnerability of the population. Clearly, the impacts of a particular flood event are context specific, and are also substantially different between rich and poor countries. Overall, however, there is a surprisingly weak scientific evidence base to assess the health impacts of flooding. Few rigorous epidemiological studies have been undertaken, and it is extremely difficult to assess the duration of symptoms and disease, and the attribution of cause without longitudinal data. In general, the incompleteness of the information entailed that:

• Our review of the available evidence is not limited to high-quality epidemiological studies.
• There was insufficient information to evaluate specific public health interventions (see also Chapters 3 and 8).
• There was insufficient information to address more detailed questions about differential social vulnerability to the health impacts of flooding.

In low-income countries, outbreaks of infectious diseases have been reported following major flood events, and these outbreaks vary in magnitude and mortality. There is some evidence from India and Bangladesh that diarrhoeal disease increases after flooding, but this is based on only a few studies. There is, at present, only weak epidemiological evidence that flooding leads to outbreaks of other infectious diseases (e.g. cholera, hepatitis and vector-borne diseases). Since the early 1990s, there have been numerous studies, particularly in the Americas, on leptospirosis, and these indicate flooding as an important cause.

The majority of flood-related mental health studies are from the US and Europe. In general, there is strong evidence that flooding has an adverse effect on common mental health disorders. Evidence from Bangladesh of increased behavioural problems in children derives from one of the few studies that have addressed mental health impacts of flooding in low-income countries. The dearth of mental health studies from low-income countries may be due to a lack of research expertise on mental health epidemiology and related services, as well as a focus of resources on other priorities (that are perceived as more acute) or a perception that the mental health burden from floods is relatively small.

In broad terms, we have limited knowledge of how different types of flood affect human health. The majority of the flood events covered in this chapter are of the slow-onset type, and these are less likely to result in deaths and injuries, at least in the onset phase. The range of health outcomes described in the chapter are likely to arise in the context of a flood of this type, although certain outcomes are more likely to arise in low-income countries than high-income countries. For example, the evidence cited here would suggest that flood-related outbreaks of infectious disease are less likely to occur in high-income regions such as Europe and the US. Such outbreaks are more likely to occur in low-income countries where infectious disease transmission is an existing public health problem; in many of these countries the public health infrastructure is also less well established and there are many more vulnerable individuals.

There is a general paucity of epidemiological studies in both the North and South, and we suggest that further studies need to be funded (though we recognize that there are ethical concerns about conducting research following major disasters – see Chapter 8). Due to the difficulties in obtaining relevant information on flood events (including flood surveys and reports), we also recommend that an information system be created to improve access to this literature. There is also a need to improve monitoring and surveillance of infectious diseases in order to improve public health responses, but also to improve the epidemiological evidence. For example, leptospirosis is difficult to diagnose and is often misdiagnosed as dengue. There are few specialist laboratories that can make the diagnosis. On the other hand, there is a need to develop and enhance surveillance following flood events. Surveys and research should be conducted following flood events in order to determine mortality, morbidity and the associated risk factors (such as age, sex, housing types, socio-economic status and access to warning information).

3

Responses to the Health Risks from Flooding

Roger Few and Franziska Matthies

Introduction

Drawing on the conceptualizations of risk outlined in earlier chapters, the health outcomes of floods can be seen as the result of a series of events whereby a flood generates a flood hazard that brings physical risk effects, leading to mortality and morbidity. Just as social processes can intervene at all stages in this chain to heighten vulnerability, so interventions can be made at various points to reduce vulnerability and strengthen coping capacity. Such actions include efforts to avoid the incursion of floodwaters into the local environment and living spaces, such as flood control engineering and raised house construction. However, these general flood avoidance actions are not the focus of this chapter.

Our purpose here is to provide an overview of specifically health-related coping mechanisms and strategies – both private actions and external interventions that reduce vulnerability to health impacts and strengthen coping capacity in the face of health risks. By that we mean responses geared to preventing injury and disease resulting from flooding and to promoting treatment, including the continued functioning of health services and provision of safe water and sanitation. These actions can take a variety of forms. Hence, exposure to infection can be avoided – for example, by the flood-proofing of latrines or the use of bed nets; development of disease can be prevented by vaccination, provision of first aid or stress counselling; and recovery can be promoted by stockpiling medicines or ensuring that health care services continue to function effectively.

Organization of the chapter

This chapter draws on a major review of processes and policies of adaptation to the health risks from floods reported in Few et al (2004a). It brings together material from a wide range of studies and reports to discuss the scope and characteristics of societal responses to the health impacts of flooding. These responses are grouped under six main categories, starting with health protection undertaken by vulnerable populations themselves, and moving through aspects of health education and public safety; disease surveillance and control; health care provision; protection of health infrastructure; and the protection and provision of water and sanitation systems.

In each section we set out in broad terms the types of coping mechanisms and strategies described in the literature. It should be noted from the outset that relatively few independent studies of flood hazards and disasters directly focus on health issues. One result of this is that there is a paucity of existing analytical material by which to gauge the utility of many of the mechanisms and strategies described. Nevertheless, broad lessons can be drawn from many of the studies cited, and the concluding section of the chapter draws out some key generic issues that may shape the effectiveness of present and future responses.

The range of responses considered in this chapter loosely maps on to the *phases* of the hazard cycle introduced in Chapter 1. Coping strategies relating to health are particularly concentrated in preparedness and emergency response, with some linkage, too, with recovery for formal health systems. However, many of the actions cannot be too closely tied to one phase, either practically or conceptually – much preparedness, for example, is concerned with preparation to facilitate emergency response, and recovery activities can evolve into mitigation of future flood damage. Hence, it has not been feasible to organize this chapter in terms of phases of the hazard cycle.

Responses to health risks also take place at a variety of *scales*, a variation we try to convey in the substantive sections that follow. Responses may take place at individual, household, community, city/district, regional, national and international levels. Of these scale categories, 'community' is perhaps the most problematic to define, with only vaguely defined connotations of local-scale social linkages and shared place-based identity. In applying the term it is particularly important to avoid the simplistic idea that communities are necessarily consensual or socially homogenous entities (Leach et al, 1997). As with other scale categories, communities are characterized by internal differences and divisions that may become manifest in response to crises (Asthana, 1994; Wisner and Adams, 2002).

Actions by different *actors*, with different sets of assets and capabilities, loosely map on to these scale categories. The principal types of actor in this context include individual people and households (affected by floods, in proximity to floods or subject to flood risk); community-based organizations; local health care providers (dispensaries, surgeries, clinics, health centres, hospitals); local service providers in preventive health (health education, public safety and environmental health teams); local water and sanitation providers; regional and national government departments; non-governmental organizations (NGOs); and international agencies.

As well as reflecting different hazard management stages and scales of action, we also try to depict as far as possible actions in different global *regions*. One of the key dimensions of geographical variation is the disparity in health outcomes between richer and poorer countries that has been indicated in Chapter 2, and which is reflected further in this chapter. However, it is important to underline that the disparities are more complex and less bipolar than any North–South division might suggest. Differential coping capacity relates not just to the distribution of material resources, but also to context-specific aspects of culture, social organization and political institutions that may shape human vulnerability, risk perception and risk behaviour.

Actions in the home and the community

We focus first on actions undertaken in the home and within the community to prepare for and cope with the health risks of floods. Although they have received little attention to date from academic studies (Few, 2003), health-related coping mechanisms at the grassroots provide the front line of defence for people who are at risk from floods. In a recent report, the aid organization Tearfund stressed that 'the ability of local people to resist the impact of disasters should not be underestimated. In fact, local coping mechanisms must form the basis of international development support' (Tearfund, 2004, p15). The importance of local capacity-building to strengthen the skills and resources of at-risk communities in flood response has already been highlighted in Chapter 1.

As with all aspects of vulnerability, the coping options available to people are shaped by attributes both of the society in which they reside and of the individual, including material assets and access to social networks. Shahaduzzaman (1999, p47) notes: 'How people cope will be determined by their personal strengths, those of their families, friends and community and on the resources, which they have or receive.' Equally, there may be economic, political and cultural factors that serve to undermine personal health protection. Rashid and Michaud (2000) and Ahmed et al (1999), for example, note that during the extreme floods in Bangladesh in 1998, social conventions discouraged many women from visiting alternative public toilet sites when household latrines were flooded. They report that many women had little choice but to squat in water after dark, defecate in the home, or even 'drink less water and take less food so that they would have to urinate and defecate less frequently' (Ahmed et al, 1999, p12).

The nature of action at the grassroots to protect against floods also depends fundamentally upon how people perceive the risks. Stephens et al (1994) provide one of the few academic studies that look explicitly at perceptions of environmental health risk from flooding. They found that flood-prone urban communities in Indore, India, broadly understood the health effects that floods might bring and especially the relationship between sewage contamination and water-borne disease. However, they freely traded that risk off against the livelihood advantages of an inner city location, and were prepared to 'live with' flood hazard, making only simple modifications in housing and behaviour to try to avoid its worst effects.

Household actions

Analysis of household coping strategies against floods has seldom concentrated on health protection. Most studies that we have identified examine efforts to maintain income and economic livelihood – strategies that may themselves have negative, as well as positive, implications for health. Del Ninno et al (2001), for example, report on how borrowing, selling belongings and reducing food consumption became short-term economic coping mechanisms for poor families affected by the Bangladesh flood of 1998, and Skoufias (2003) points out that such actions can have adverse long-term health and nutritional impacts.

Although few coping actions relating explicitly to health have been discussed in the literature surveyed, the material that does exist suggests that this may reflect a lack of reporting. Parkinson (2002), for example, notes that people may make adjustments to their dwellings, both to resist the incursion of floodwater and also to prevent exposure and injury when floods enter. Placing electrical wiring high up on walls in flood-prone environments is one such example. Prior to flood seasons, households may make advance purchase of medicines to tackle common diseases that arise during floods, such as skin infections. Reporting from Viet Nam, Few et al (2004b) list a number of household coping actions, including avoidance of exposure to water within houses by creating raised walkways from planks and raising furniture on bricks, and removal of unused vessels where mosquitoes can breed after flooding has receded (see also Chapter 6).

In low-income countries, where flooding often poses severe threats to water supplies, evidence suggests that people make major efforts to obtain clean drinking water. An evaluation of relief efforts for the 1999 cyclone disaster in Orissa, India, suggests that mortality resulting from polluted water following the event was low and that this 'was caused as much by strong local coping mechanisms amongst the people themselves as it was by the initial relief efforts' (INTRAC, 2000, p24). People generally recognized the need to avoid sources of water polluted by nearby carcasses and made widespread use of fluid in coconuts for drinking (coconuts were abundant on the ground because of the destruction of palms). Ahmed et al (1999) report that after the 1998 Bangladesh floods, people switched to fetching water from distant non-contaminated tube wells and from alternative local sources, such as schools and mosques, that had not been inundated. We return to issues of water provision later in the chapter.

A number of studies of household-level coping responses relating to mental health come from the US, detailing psychological coping mechanisms and the role of emotional support within the household. Smith (1996), in a study of the 1993 Midwest flood, identified how a 'problem-focused' active coping mentality was positive for mental health: active coping efforts directed at clean-up and recovery were associated with lower levels of psychological distress. Russoniello et al (2002) examined coping strategies of children after the flooding events of Hurricane Floyd in 1999. They noted how ineffective coping patterns such as social withdrawal, self-criticism, problem solving (unresolved) and blaming of others were strongly related to post-traumatic stress disorder (PTSD). Effective coping strategies included 'wishful thinking (hope), distraction, social support, cognitive restructuring and resignation (accepting the reality of the event)' (Russoniello et al, 2002, p69). From work with flood victims, Deering (2000) stresses the strong role that parents and significant adults play in conditioning children's response. Providing emotional support for children is crucial, through activities such as comfort, reassurance, restoring routine and talking through events.

Community actions

As for the household level, there is little material analysing communal activities in health risk reduction in relation to flooding, although we again suspect that this may be a reflection of lack of critical attention to the subject. A survey of the material that does exist suggests that several types of response at the community level may be of key importance in influencing public health.

One crucial area in terms of public safety is warning and evacuation, for which community-based activities may provide the key to survival. Some such mechanisms are traditional, such as the practice reported from northern Pakistan of tying ropes with bells attached across rivers upstream from where fishermen work to provide last-minute warning of flash floods (Davis and Hall, 1999). Others have been fostered via external support. When Hurricane Mitch struck Central America in 1998, few communities were prepared for the impact of high winds, floods and landslides. In contrast with neighbouring sites, however, there were no deaths among the inhabitants of La Masica on the coast of Honduras, where external agencies had supported a local capacity-building programme for risk reduction featuring a community-based flood early warning system (Maskrey, 1999; Tearfund, 2004).

Further studies provide examples where communities have responded to the efforts of public and external agencies to foster general community preparedness for hazards, including their health aspects. Lichterman (2000) describes a number of successful community-based 'citizen disaster preparedness programmes' in different parts of California, US, which include training in reducing household hazards, preparing emergency kits, evacuation plans, first aid, and also advanced training in disaster medical aid and disaster mental health for volunteers to work alongside professional personnel. One scheme provides 'first-responder' training to make communities as self-sufficient as possible in the immediate aftermath of disasters. Luna (2001) discusses the work of NGOs in the Philippines in community-based flooding and disaster management, including the establishment of village committees and training in fields such as evacuation management and health and sanitation.

In terms of emergency response to floods, there are examples of both spontaneous relief efforts by community members and efforts coordinated by external bodies. Studies of the 1998 floods in Bangladesh, for example, yield various reports of spontaneous communal coping mechanisms relating to health. Karim et al (1999) note how a group of students opened a centre at a school in Dhaka for preparing oral re-hydration packets to a standard World Health Organization (WHO) formula and distributed them to affected households. A study by the Bangladesh Rural Advancement Commission (BRAC) during the same flood notes distribution of food and other materials by richer families to poor neighbours in rural areas, and people sharing boats with neighbours for essential travel. 'In one slum area, a group of ten women bought together a boat for Tk [Taka] 1800 to move about and go to private places for their personal hygiene and bathing' (Ahmed et al, 1999, p23). Nishat et al (2000) report that volunteers often organized themselves into groups to provide relief, including shelter, food, drinking water, treatment of the sick and distribution of water tablets.

Nishat et al (2000, p232) add that 'in future, this kind of cooperation from the general population may be of great help, and proper planning and coordination of these efforts are required'. They recommend that formal health systems should encourage participation from the community in medical teams during crises. The potential for coordinated volunteer action was demonstrated in Orissa, India, after the 1999 cyclone, when the government appealed for volunteers to help dispose of human bodies and animal carcasses, and thousands came forward (INTRAC, 2000). In Viet Nam, local voluntary effort in rescue and medical assistance during floods is coordinated on a large scale by a network of mass organizations, including the Viet Nam Red Cross (Few et al, 2004b). However Hoque et al (1993) caution against reliance on disaster volunteers who are inadequately trained or supervised. They note that during the 1991 cyclone in Bangladesh, many relief workers, who, for example, helped to repair tube wells, remove corpses and distribute water purifying tablets, admitted in interviews that they did not know enough about appropriate environmental health measures or that they failed to instruct people on how to store and use the water tablets they provided.

Research by Gillard and Paton (1999) in Fiji notes the role that local religious organizations can play in preparedness and response, particularly in providing spiritual and social support to help alleviate stress among victims. Clemens et al (1999) note that informal support networks within communities can also help to lessen negative emotional impact from the experience of flooding. Social and emotional support for flood victims by fellow community members is reported in both low- and high-income countries. Enarson (2001, p6) reports that in the 1997 flood of the Red River Valley, US, women drew on extended networks to share hazard information, make contingency plans and organize 'non-family or institutional care of the young, old, sick and disabled'.

Research on the social psychology of floods and other disasters has yielded insights into the processes through which community bonds tend to be disrupted and reorganized in the post-impact phases. Gordon (2004), for example, defines stages of initial 'de-bonding' and then temporary high levels of social 'fusion' in the immediate emergency phase, commonly leading to a disruptive stage of social 'cleavages' in the early recovery phase (when many of the psychosocial problems associated with flooding tend to develop). Efforts to foster community preparedness, facilitate social communication and establish appropriate local organizational structures to manage recovery can all serve to smooth the rehabilitation process and minimize social disruption.

Broad-based involvement of community members in flood response actions is seen as a keystone for improving local coping capacity by many agencies (see, for example, Action Aid, 2002; IFRC, 2003; Tearfund, 2004). Community participation, however, can prove more straightforward on paper than it is in practice, as experience from many fields of development amply shows. It raises major issues in terms of power relations between agencies and stakeholders, intra-community divisions, and motivation and capacity to participate (Cooke and Kothari, 2001; Few et al, 2003; Pugh and Potter, 2003). In an emergency setting it may prove even more problematic. To round off this section, Box 3.1 provides some perspectives on community involvement in relief and recovery from floods and other natural disasters.

Box 3.1 *Perspectives on community involvement in disaster relief/recovery*

An evaluation of the activities of UK-based agencies in Orissa in the aftermath of the 1999 cyclone strongly advocated greater inclusion of affected populations in decision-making:

> *Future emergency responses need to build on the innovative participatory work of some DEC [Disasters Emergency Committee] agencies and their local NGO partners in increasing the involvement of poorer people in the planning and monitoring of relief and rehabilitation activities.* (INTRAC, 2000, p58)

The 2003 *World Disasters Report* (IFRC, 2003) stresses that, in order to facilitate community-based decision-making, a crucial role for external agencies should be that of capacity-building. But there is a fine line between fostering action and directing action, and before any intervention crucial questions should be asked:

> *The issues can be distilled down to two very simple but fundamental questions: first, what do vulnerable people and disaster victims really want and need; second, do our actions contribute in meeting those needs in any real way?* (IFRC, 2003, p62)

A report on relief efforts after Hurricane Mitch in 1998, however, suggests that effective community involvement may not be feasible in the early stages after disaster: 'Many community members recall a state of shock and disbelief that would have precluded any serious effective participation in the humanitarian assistance programmes that served them' (Espacios Consultores, 2000, p17).

Health education

This section focuses on health education, including public safety and hygiene education, specific to flood situations. Like the preceding section, it examines aspects of health promotion for vulnerable populations; but the prime interest here is on 'exogenous' efforts by non-local agencies (governmental and non-governmental) to advise the public directly on practices that reduce health risk. Education efforts may be provided as part of preparedness efforts in flood-prone environments or deployed as part of emergency response activities during and in the aftermath of flood events. Whatever the timing of its delivery, however, education appears to work most effectively when it is well planned in advance – maximizing the chance that the information provided is accessible, appropriate and widely disseminated (Perez and Thompson, 1995; Menne, 1999; Caribbean Environmental Health Institute, 2003).

Content and delivery

Health education relating to floods spans many themes. Wisner and Adams (2002, p202) define it as 'the communication of information that enables people to make informed decisions about health-related activities at all stages of the disaster-management cycle'. It therefore includes information on the physical risk of flooding in specific sites; how to prepare the home in advance to prevent injury and disease; flood warnings and evacuation messages and prior information on how to react to them; how to avoid health risks once floods occur; and where to seek emergency health care. In the US, for example, the website of the Centers for Disease Control and Prevention (CDC) provides specific health advice for the US public in order to prepare and recover from floods. The guidance covers purification of drinking water; disinfection of wells; food safety; sanitation and personal hygiene; precautions during return to and cleaning up of flooded homes; mosquito control; and threats from animals, chemicals and swift-flowing water. Becker et al (1999) add to this that education materials should include information on safe evacuation routes and warnings to drivers not to drive in flash flood risk areas or across roads/bridges covered by rapid water. Draft guidelines designed to reduce health risks from flooding provided by the Public Health Laboratory Service in the UK cover general hygiene to prevent exposure to contaminated water and surfaces, cleaning and drying of surfaces and materials, food and drinking water safety, and avoidance of electrical hazards (PHLS, 2000).

It is beyond the scope of this chapter to discuss these guidelines for health, safety and hygiene measures in detail; but it is worth noting that the overall content (if not the detail) of guidance in flood situations is broadly similar across different regions. For example, general themes for hygiene practices during disaster situations described by Wisner and Adams (2002) apply across both high- and low-income countries: it is the key considerations that vary according to development context (see Table 3.1).

Table 3.1 *Household health and hygiene during disasters: Key themes*

Theme	Consideration
Water safety	Sources of water Collection and storage Use of water
Excreta disposal	Hygienic places for defecation Children's sanitation
Waste disposal	Solid waste Liquid waste
Vector control	Removal of breeding sites Personal protection
Personal hygiene	Water for washing Washing of hands
Shelter	Continued use of the home Return from shelter
Food safety	Food handling and preparation Feeding babies

Source: adapted from Wisner and Adams (2002, pp250–252)

During and immediately after flood emergencies there may be a case for focusing education messages on priority topics. The Sphere Project handbook on humanitarian assistance suggests that hygiene promotion in general disaster response should target the key risks in each context – these are likely to relate to excreta disposal, toilet use and maintenance, hand washing, water collection and storage, and food storage and preparation (The Sphere Project, 2004). One of the most important functions of such efforts should be addressing key misconceptions about effective hygiene. Malilay (1997) similarly underscores the importance of health education, addressing common gaps in public understanding such as the link between driving and drowning deaths during flash floods.

The delivery of education messages may be by various means, depending upon context and resources, including written materials, websites, radio and television broadcasts, public meetings and demonstrations, and household visits. In Viet Nam, much of this work is undertaken through conventional propaganda channels, such as broadcasts over the local government loudspeakers sited throughout communities (Few et al, 2004b). Following the 1999 cyclone in Orissa, India, the United Nations Children's Fund (UNICEF) assisted with the production of handbills and loudspeaker announcements, and supported a series of hygiene education programmes for 3900 teachers (Palakudiyil and Todd, 2003). In situations where literacy is low, it may be more culturally appropriate to communicate hygiene messages through participatory techniques rather than written instruction (The Sphere Project, 2004).

During floods the mass media may play a crucial role. Floods were a major hazard associated with Hurricane Michelle in Cuba in 2001; but, though the storm was extremely powerful and destroyed 8700 homes, only five people died (Palakudiyil and Todd, 2003; Thompson and Gavira, 2004). Effective dissemination of emergency information through state-run media helped to enable the evacuation of 700,000 people to shelters before the storm struck (IFRC, 2002). Private media organizations may also take on a vital public information role. A newspaper article on public safety during the 2004 floods in Bangladesh illustrates the role of the press in information provision, offering specific advice for householders on topics such as the use of salvaged food, the disconnection of electrical appliances and the threat from venomous snakes taking refuge in homes (*The Daily Star*, 2004).

One key lesson that emerges on health, safety and hygiene education is that it must be flexible enough to match the needs and capacities of different groups. Not only is there social differentiation in vulnerability to hazards, but there is variation in receptivity to messages because of differing sensitivities to risk, abilities to understand information and abilities to take action (Handmer, 2000; Glantz, 2004). Kircher et al (1987), for example, note that the likelihood of individuals taking emergency action or evacuating their home following flash flood warnings tends to be higher than the mean for those with recent disaster experience and significantly lower for the elderly or for people living alone. Messages may therefore need to be tailored to different audiences and perhaps targeted to particularly vulnerable groups, including children (Jabry, 2002). In many contexts, the design and delivery of the message will also need to take account of educational status, gender and cultural barriers (Pilon, 2004), and the process may work most effectively if community members are involved from the outset in its production (Wisner and Adams, 2002).

Disease surveillance and control

Disease surveillance refers to the systematic collection and analysis of data on communicable diseases. It is important for efficient resource allocation, planning of preventive strategies and public health interventions, and the identification of special needs (Dietz et al, 1990; CDC, 1993a). Two dimensions of disease surveillance are crucial in relation to response and adaptation to flooding. First, an ongoing public health surveillance system provides the baseline data against which changes in disease incidence can be detected after an extreme event such as a flood. Second, a specific disaster-related surveillance programme covering infectious diseases, injuries and vector populations can be established following a flood (Malilay, 1997). Such a post-flood surveillance system helps to identify detailed changes in disease patterns and outbreaks. Noji and Toole (1997) argue that timely data collection and analysis provides the foundation for effective disaster response, and Franklin et al (2000) suggest that academic medical institutions can play a key role in emergency response in this respect, providing specialist support and expertise to boost the surveillance capacity of the public health system. Both types of surveillance system need to be well defined with regard to the selection of diseases, case definitions, methods, documentation and duration. Data need to be collected, compiled, documented and analysed, and results should be shared with decision-makers on a regular basis (Malilay, 1997).

Utilizing surveillance information, control measures can be put in place that specifically tackle disease risk associated with floods. As well as preventive control measures, responsive control strategies (including treatment) need to be in place in order to react as soon as possible to irregularities or outbreaks of infectious diseases. Disease outbreak control can include actions to protect susceptible populations, such as immunization and hygiene education, as well as direct efforts to combat the disease organism and its vectors, such as water treatment and mosquito control (The Sphere Project, 2004). In many cases, routine practices such as vector control may become disrupted by flood events, and it is important to ensure that they are able to resume as rapidly as possible (Caribbean Environmental Health Institute, 2003). Piarroux (2002) suggests that volunteer help can play an important role in enabling disease control in emergency situations. Discussing cholera outbreaks, the author argues that teams of volunteers can provide an effective service if they are adequately supervised by professional staff able to translate general cholera-control techniques to the specific field conditions. Generic principles and guidelines for both surveillance and control are set out in detail in a WHO manual on disease control in emergencies (Connolly, 2005), including guidance on how to set monitoring and prevention priorities in different contexts.

Priority measures

As Chapter 2 has shown, literature on severe floods from high-income countries suggests that the risk of infectious disease outbreaks is relatively minor; hence, control measures tend to be of low priority. Nevertheless, surveillance relating to the range of health impacts from floods may take place. Following the floods in Iowa, US, in 1993, the CDC assisted in implementing a surveillance system to monitor flood-related injury and disease impacts (CDC, 1993b). A surveillance system was established by the North Carolina Department of Health and Human Services following floods in 1999, registering 150 reportable health effects (Booker, 2000). Data were compared with results from 1998, underscoring the value of reliable baseline data.

In developing countries, where the threat of infectious diseases poses more pressing concerns after floods, the potential value of surveillance and control systems is heightened. However, needs do not match capacities – it is precisely in low-income countries that both routine and emergency surveillance mechanisms tend to be weakest (Guha-Sapir, 1991; see also Chapter 2).

The need for epidemiological surveillance was emphasized in the aftermath of Hurricane Mitch in Central America (PAHO, 1998b). Due to physical damage to health services and water and sanitation facilities, overcrowding in shelters and movements of populations, the incidence of cholera and other water-borne diseases, leptospirosis, dengue and malaria increased in urban areas and especially in poor populations. In Puerto Rico, following tropical storm Isabel in October 1985, a shelter surveillance system was established monitoring 19 acute and chronic conditions (such as fever, diarrhoea, conjunctivitis, upper respiratory tract infections, pediculosis, injuries, stress, vomiting and asthma) in 28 shelters over a five-week period (Dietz et al, 1990). The authors emphasize that such a system needs to be standardized and representative for the entire hazard area (not just the most affected locations).

Biswas and colleagues (1999b), who report on increases in diarrhoeal diseases and acute respiratory tract infections as a consequence of severe flooding in West Bengal, India, also stress the need for improved disease surveillance and control. Reporting from their experience during the 1998 floods in Bangladesh, Hossain and Kolsteren (2003) assign top priority to the control and the treatment of diarrhoeal diseases in flood-affected areas. Following severe floods in Sri Lanka in 2003, the WHO especially recommended surveillance of diarrhoeal diseases and vector-borne diseases because of the increased risk from damage to water and sewage systems and the displacement of people to overcrowded camps (WHO, 2003a).

Surveillance and control of vector-borne disease is often a major concern following floods in poorer countries. Risk of increase in mosquito-borne diseases, for example, may be associated with increased formation of breeding sites for aquatic mosquito larvae. Control of breeding sites is commonly achieved through environmental modifications or control spraying to kill larvae, both prior to and following flood events (Wisner and Adams, 2002). However, such measures may not always be feasible during widespread flood conditions, and in such circumstances disease control may have to rest on preventive behaviour in the home, including use of topical repellents and impregnated bed nets. Durrheim and Govere (2002), for example, report on effective control of a post-flood malaria epidemic in a community in South Africa through the promotion of a twice-nightly application of insect repellent on ankles and feet. Guha-Sapir et al (1991) focus on control of leptospirosis epidemics in Brazil following severe flooding. Their main recommendations for strengthening existing surveillance and control include compulsory notification of disease cases and protection of susceptible groups (especially use of protective clothing by at-risk workers, such as those engaged in sewerage repair).

In selecting and designing disease control strategies, it is important that the utility of specific control measures is carefully assessed in relation to the threat. Chosen control measures and the manner in which they are implemented should be appropriate to the specific disease, its risk and its context, and flexibility of approach is often required in order to ensure that interventions by different agencies are coordinated and compatible (PAHO, 1999). In particular, the utility of a reactive approach of mass immunization against potential disease outbreaks during flood disasters is questioned by some authors. Parker and Thompson (2000) note that although there is often public demand for immunization, such measures can absorb critical resources and divert them from other priority relief activities. They may also give people a false sense of security in terms of hygiene behaviour and health protection. Menne (1999) points out that heightened disease risk during floods is usually limited to diseases that are already endemic to a flooded area: the chance of new infectious diseases being introduced is generally low.

Advance knowledge on existing environmental health risks can help assessment and control teams to identify priority measures (The Sphere Project, 2004). Guidelines provided by the Caribbean Environmental Health Institute (2003) particularly emphasize the development of vector profiles for flood-prone areas. Such profiles should include gathering knowledge on sites that are likely to develop pools of stagnant water where mosquitoes can breed, and the locations of commercial or domestic sites where food sources are likely to accumulate for rodents and other vectors.

Health care services

This section focuses on the provision of health care for populations affected by flood. Its principal concern is with the actions of formal health systems (from primary to tertiary level); but the discussion also brings in the actions of a range of other organizations engaged in health-sector response, including environmental and social support agencies, and NGOs and external aid organizations providing health-related services.

During hazard and disaster events, the demands on a health system tend to multiply. Authorities with responsibility for public health and social care provision have to be able to organize and coordinate response to the specific needs of injured and displaced people and to changing disease patterns. The demand for health services may change after a flooding event, and these changes have been observed to persist longer than the acute phase of the event. In the US, for example, changes in health care demand (e.g. from injuries, consumption of contaminated water and food, and the consequences of stress) were reported following the 1993 Midwest floods (Axelrod et al, 1994). At the same time, ongoing provision of 'normal' health care has to be maintained as far as possible, or at least quickly re-established (Rahman and Bennish, 1993; Poncelet and de Ville de Goyet, 1996). This is especially the case for essential services such as care for the chronically ill. All of this should be undertaken on an equitable basis for the client population, at a time when access to and from health facilities may be greatly disrupted (Menne, 1999). During flood disasters, health systems themselves may experience functional disruption, including staff shortages owing to deaths, injuries, disease, displacement and preoccupation with personal concerns – as highlighted in the aftermath of the Indian Ocean Tsunami of 2004 (WHO, 2005a). Floods may also cause direct physical damage and disruption to health infrastructure – a theme taken up later in the chapter.

The precise nature of health care provision and prioritization during floods, as with most aspects of response relating to health, varies greatly according to context. It is shaped by:

- the pre-existing health status of the affected population;
- the health risks posed by the hazard event; and
- the resources and capacity of the health system (The Sphere Project, 2004).

Differences in terms of health care needs, response capabilities and the need for external support arise from these factors.

The following discussion looks first at emergency planning and needs assessment activities, and then examines the problems and principles of general health care delivery and mental health care. Once again, it should be made clear that very few studies exist that attempt to evaluate the effect of the measures described on health outcomes.

Emergency planning and needs assessment

Well-planned emergency procedures for health systems, designed and put in place well in advance of hazard events, provide the foundation for effective health care during and after flooding. Preparedness of health services for natural disasters aims at minimizing mortality and reducing morbidity. In Mozambique, for example, health-sector preparedness for the February/March 2000 floods started in November 1999, when warnings of impending flood risk began to be issued (Christie and Hanlon, 2001). The Ministry of Health oversaw efforts to prepare cholera treatment plans at the provincial level and to ensure that health posts were adequately stocked with routine medicine supplies, and issued extra stocks of malaria medicines and re-hydration fluids. The Mozambique Red Cross also distributed medicine kits in late 1999. In this sense, effective emergency preparedness in the health sector depends upon reliable and effective hazard early warning information (Wisner and Adams, 2002).

Preparedness can, however, be taken still further in advance – well before the advent of flood crises – and can be more comprehensive in approach. Bradt et al (2003) argue that health care providers need the skills and support to generate guidelines for disaster preparedness. CDC (2005a, p61) highlights how 'written and rehearsed disaster plans' enabled rapid response to the health needs of coastal populations in Thailand affected by the Indian Ocean Tsunami of 2004. According to Quayle (1995), systematic disaster preparedness plans for health facilities form the best defence in any emergency. A well-crafted plan consists of information and guidelines on the availability of staff, decision-making structures, communication with the media, and supply and storage of medicines and equipment. The author also underlines the importance of undertaking practical drills. Menne (1999) adds the need to compile inventories of existing resources in order that they can be rapidly mobilized, and the need to undertake a public health vulnerability analysis.

Disaster preparedness plans for the health sector may apply at local, regional and national scales. Milsten (2000) provides a review of hospital-level disaster planning in the US, indicating commonplace shortfalls in quality and staff awareness of the plans that have been produced, and cases where plans have failed to be implemented when crises strike. The author argues that detailed preparation is needed for the disaster plan to be effective in providing structure to an organization in a chaotic situation. It needs to be specific for each facility, rather than simply generic in format, and should address three disaster phases: preparation following warnings; dealing with the event itself; and recuperation.

A case study by Xiaohong (1993) describes the role of health system planning for disaster preparedness in eight provinces of south-east China affected by floods in 1991. The author contends that adequate preparedness of the health sector played a key role in preventing infectious disease epidemics in the affected areas, and in reducing mortality rates from cases of infectious disease compared to earlier severe flood events in the same region. To enhance preparedness, the state medical sector established an organizational framework with a detailed plan for decision-making and to provide training in techniques of rescue and the treatment of victims. Intensive care units of hospitals (field hospitals, rural hospitals and city-level hospitals) needed to be prepared to treat large numbers of patients. Cooperation with different sectors such as military forces, fire-fighters, civil engineers, mechanics, the police force and others was another important aspect of planned response.

However, preparedness plans for the health care system can only go so far. Health care needs vary in each disaster situation, and it may not always be feasible to prepare for unanticipated or extreme-magnitude flood events. Peters (1996), for example, describes how the overall emergency response to the US Midwest floods in 1993 was built partly on disaster preparedness and partly on improvisation and flexibility. When a flood event occurs, an emergency needs assessment gives the necessary information to fine tune responses.

CDC (2002) underlines the usefulness of rapid needs assessment techniques (combining epidemiological, qualitative and statistical methods) for directing response measures and response planning following flood events. A rapid needs assessment is a streamlined, low-cost analysis designed to identify key health risks and impacts, and to minimize misinformation. Information gathered following floods typically includes population health status and medical needs, the condition of water, sanitation and electricity supply systems, and the state of health services (Menne, 1999).

Guha-Sapir (1991) reviewed concepts and methods of rapid assessment. The most immediate assessment following an acute disaster may be required within 24 to 48 hours of the event, particularly in the case of rapid-onset wind storm and flash flood disasters. Its purpose is to estimate the magnitude of the disaster, to measure present and potential health impact (mortality and expected morbidity patterns), to assess the resources needed, and to plan appropriate responses. Inevitably in such rapid analyses, there is a trade-off to be made between accuracy and timeliness: the need for scientific precision may have to be relaxed in order to permit the swift reporting of critical information (WHO, 1999a). Building on such principles, the WHO has developed standardized reporting templates for such assessments, providing guidance on how to select and summarize data.

Rapid assessments may not be limited to the immediate flood phase. Clinton et al (1995) stress the need for continuous reassessment of health and medical needs in changing conditions as an event unfolds into its post-onset phase. Assessments also should take account of the special needs of population groups such as pregnant women, children, people with disabilities and the elderly. The NGO Help Age International draws attention to the special needs of older people in disasters, including problems of access to health relief and treatment for chronic medical conditions (British Red Cross, 2001b). In some cases, targeting of health care towards especially vulnerable groups may be required, especially if resources are likely to become overstretched (Handmer, 2003).

Health care delivery

Health care activities during floods comprise actions to ensure that services continue to meet 'normal' public health needs, as well as actions to provide treatment for flood casualties and victims of flood-related disease. Besides the medical procedures themselves, they include technical and organizational activities designed to maintain services, supplies, communication and public access to health facilities, some of which may rely on effective inter-sectoral coordination. After Hurricane Floyd hit Pitt County in North Carolina, US, in 1999, for example, an emergency team ran the hospital command centre and the transportation centre to ensure continuous access to health care (Franklin et al, 2000). Teamwork between community physicians and university medical services secured health care provision. Family clinics offered 24-hour medical services (triage, treatment and referral), and medical staff were sent to community shelters to provide tetanus vaccinations, treatment of injuries and the management of chronic diseases (see Chapter 7). Where transport becomes difficult, health systems and relief agencies may establish extra emergency field hospitals or dispensaries. In China, the disaster response of health systems has included setting up replacement telecommunication facilities, the use of helicopters and steamboats as ambulances, and the use of mobile intensive care units (Xiaohong, 1993). Often, such emergency activities rely on help from the military.

Although there are many global commonalities in the pressures and problems posed for health care delivery during floods, broad disparities exist in population needs and response capacities between different regions and individual countries. The capacity to deploy and organize resources for crisis response is by no means solely determined by level of economic development. Nevertheless, the greatest challenges for health care delivery tend to occur in low-income countries exposed to severe flooding. In the worst cases, a disastrous flood in low-income countries may be marked by a temporary collapse of health care services owing to the destruction of facilities, disruption of transport and shortages of drugs. Nishat et al (2000) report on how the formal health system in Dhaka in Bangladesh was severely disrupted in this manner during the catastrophic flood of 1998 (see Box 3.2).

Box 3.2 *Health care disruption during the 1998 floods in Bangladesh*

The 1998 floods that overwhelmed much of Bangladesh were the worst on record, surpassing all previous events in scale and duration. Almost two-thirds of the country became inundated for up to two months and an estimated 18 million people required emergency food and health care (Ahmed et al, 1999). Facing food shortages, environmental health risks and emotional stress, many people had no ready access to treatment because local practitioners and pharmacies were forced to close (Shahaduzzaman, 1999). In Dhaka, the usual health system ceased to function effectively. According to Nishat et al (2000, p232), 'providers of the health care in the city were found almost unprepared for meeting the calamity', with poor levels of disaster management training and preparedness. With the normal system severely impaired, the main emergency response by government and non-governmental organizations (NGOs) was to extend opening times of un-flooded dispensaries, to set up field health posts, including diarrhoea treatment centres, and to establish 200 mobile health teams to bring services directly to communities. However, the resources of these teams were limited by insufficient manpower, equipment, medicines and transport.

Both Ahmed et al (1999) and Nishat et al (2000) strongly recommend a more systematic approach to disaster management and preparedness planning in the health sector within Bangladesh. Because of the limited effectiveness of mobile medical teams, one of the key suggestions is for a pre-established network of local emergency hospitals built above flood level and utilized for primary health care during normal times. Some of the other actions they suggest include mechanisms for training health cadres in emergency management and training volunteers in first-aid; provision for sufficient supply of medicines for common flood-related diseases; establishing anti-venom stocks to treat snakebite in rural communities; and provision of motorized small boats for use as ambulances during floods.

Yet, positive lessons for the delivery of health care during floods may emerge even from catastrophic events. Christie and Hanlon (2001) point to efforts in Mozambique to cope with the health impacts of the floods of 2000. Here, the formal public health system benefited from its close partnership with an NGO, the national Red Cross – Cruz Vermelha de Moçambique (CVM) – which carried out emergency preparedness and response activities in parallel with those of the government. As the floods deepened, CVM set up a network of emergency health posts to treat minor wounds and common ailments. In the capital, Maputo, the city health department cooperated with these efforts by sending visiting doctors to the posts and providing transport for volunteers.

Though much of the emergency effort in Mozambique in 2000 was carried out by national agencies, external support was also provided. The scale of health care problems during floods in lower- and middle-income countries often prompts a call for assistance and relief items from outside the country, from governments and international organizations (including specialist organizations such as Médecins Sans Frontières, or MSF, and Merlin). International resources mobilized for health care in major disasters commonly include drug and vaccine supplies, field health posts and personnel, as well as financial, organizational and logistical aid to domestic health systems. Beser et al (1991), for example, report that external help following a Turkish flood disaster consisted of financial support to the health sector, assistance in organization and planning, the setting up of an epidemiological surveillance system, and the provision of information and guidance through mobile health teams. Following floods in Kenya in 2003, UNICEF provided health care items such as re-hydration salts, drugs, mosquito nets and cooking sets, especially targeting diarrhoeal diseases, water-borne diseases and malaria to prevent avoidable deaths and disease, particularly among children (UNICEF, 2003).

One of the key lessons that emerge from evaluations of recent flood disasters is the need for careful coordination between agencies providing emergency health care, especially between in-country agencies and external relief organizations. Coordination was a major issue in Aceh, Indonesia, following the 2004 Tsunami disaster, where some 22 NGOs were working on health-sector relief, together with the Indonesian military and the Ministry of Health (WHO, 2005a). According to a Pan American Health Organization (PAHO) meeting report, external cooperation is usually valued, but it is best if medical relief efforts such as the establishment of field hospitals and the distribution of medical supplies are coordinated by local health authorities (PAHO, 1999). External agencies working on the ground may require logistical and technical support from agencies in flood-affected countries, which can sometimes place an extra burden on them during the critical emergency phase unless activities are carefully and jointly organized. Inappropriate material relief becomes redundant and may similarly create additional problems, such as the time and space needed to process and store unusable drug supplies (Guha-Sapir 1991). For donations of supplies, PAHO has developed a computerized Humanitarian Supply Management System to enable countries to coordinate incoming drug provision and distribution during disasters (Noji and Toole, 1997).

Mental health care

Psychosocial aspects of floods are increasingly highlighted in the literature, and it is useful to examine response in this area in a little more detail. As Chapter 2 shows, extreme stressors are a risk factor for mental health problems, and flooding can both create stress-related conditions and lead to the exacerbation of existing problems. Studies and reports following flood events now commonly call for raising awareness of the mental health impacts of flooding and related health care needs, especially in developing countries (e.g. Espacios Consultores, 2000; Herzer and Clichevsky, 2001; VanRooyen and Leaning, 2005). Health services need to be prepared to offer specific help to affected victims; but few national disaster plans explicitly address measures to identify or deal with psychosocial aspects of flood or other hazard events (PAHO, 1999). NSW Health (2000) stresses that mental health care in terms of psychological 'first aid', triage, assessment, referral and interventions needs to be part of an emergency health care response.

In all contexts, mental health care provision during emergencies may involve local volunteers and community-based organizations, as well as professional health personnel. Breo (1993) describes, for example, how the Red Cross provided mental health counselling to flood victims and caregivers through a voluntary team during the Midwest floods of 1993 in the US. However, key documents on disaster mental health stress the crucial importance of training and experience (NSW Health, 2000; WHO, 2003b). Well-trained disaster workers demonstrate not only good counselling and core psychological skills, but also establish cross-linkages with other organizations and individuals involved in relief work, and have comprehensive knowledge of policies and procedures that are in place to support flood victims (Chatterjee, 2005). Exposure to death, heavy workload and exhaustion are severe stressors that can also put the mental health of disaster workers themselves at risk. To mitigate these risks, specific training, working in teams, sufficient breaks, the distribution of clear roles and responsibilities, and professional follow-up and counselling for disaster workers is recommended (NSW Health, 2000).

Until recently, discussions of mental health aspects of flood risk and response have been confined mainly to industrialized countries (see Chapter 4 for the UK). Mental health issues seldom have gained high profile in the South; yet there may be tremendous risk factors during flood disasters in developing countries, related to the scale of suffering. Rashid (2000) portrays the level of stress from losses and disruption suffered by the urban poor in Dhaka, Bangladesh, during the 1998 floods. When MSF began providing medical relief in the town of Goinaves, Haiti – which was devastated by floods in September 2004 – they found that many of the survivors who attended their health centre required treatment for mental health issues alongside basic health care (MSF, 2004). Post-disaster psychological trauma has been particularly highlighted for children (Jabry, 2002) and, for rapid-onset hazards such as flash floods and tsunamis, often becomes manifest in fear of recurrence.

Gradually, the role for mental health care in such situations is becoming recognized. It was particularly prominent in efforts following the devastating 2004 Indian Ocean Tsunami: the Indonesian government, for example, trained over 150 community leaders and health workers in mental health intervention in order to extend emergency care provision in Aceh Province (WHO, 2005b). Kokai et al (2004, p110) argue that the increasing attention now being paid to disaster mental health in Asia is partly attributable to the growing 'acceptance of the notion of post-traumatic stress disorder (PTSD). This has allowed greater involvement of mental health professionals in providing ongoing support to survivors of natural disasters.'

The WHO document *Mental Health in Emergencies* (WHO, 2003b) describes principles and mechanisms for preventing and tackling mental health problems in emergencies in resource-poor settings. National preparedness plans need to include a coordinated system of adequate mental health response, including specialist training of health care staff and other local personnel. These activities should be guided by a focus on long-term development of community mental health services and other social interventions. Activities should follow national mental health programmes and national legislation and policy; but there should also be efforts to work in tandem with pre-existing coping mechanisms and traditional healers where applicable and feasible (WHO, 2003b). The guidelines divide mechanisms of response according to two phases of disasters – the acute emergency phase and the reconsolidation phase – and recommend that they include broad social and cultural interventions, as well as specific mental health care activities (for examples, see Table 3.2). To aid the emotional and psychological recovery of children, for example, Jabry (2002) notes that interventions may include talking through events, inclusion of children's perspectives in rehabilitation and future preparedness tasks, and restoration of routines (especially of educational activity).

Table 3.2 *Examples of social and psychological intervention strategies*

Acute emergency phase (short term)	Reconsolidation phase (medium to long term)
Improve the flow of information to the public on the disaster and the response, and on normal reactions to stress	Provide outreach education on psychological distress and available mental health care
Re-establish cultural/religious events, offer educational/recreational activities for children, and involve people in common-interest emergency activities	Facilitate community-based self-help support groups and encourage micro-scale economic initiatives
Organize non-intrusive emotional support by community workers, including provision of 'psychological first aid'	Train primary health care workers in basic mental health intervention, and educate community leaders in core psychological skills
Manage urgent psychiatric complaints within general primary health care	Ensure continuation or full reinstatement of treatment for psychiatric patients

Source: derived from WHO (2003b)

One important issue in mental health response is the question of 'targeting' services such as counselling and other forms of psychosocial aid. Tapsell et al (1999) and Tierney (2000) conclude that outreach and intervention efforts need to take risk factors into account and specifically target vulnerable groups of populations and areas that are especially hard hit. In large-scale disasters, Silove and Zwi (2005, p270) argue that limiting intensive psychosocial support to those with identifiably high levels of stress and grief (as well as to individuals with existing mental health disorders) 'allows scarce resources to be targeted at those at highest survival risk – a principle that is consistent with the overarching humanitarian mission'. To foster recovery for the majority of those affected by disasters they advocate offering the broader forms of social and cultural interventions noted above.

Protecting health infrastructure

Intact, functioning and accessible infrastructure is a cornerstone of effective health care provision for affected populations during flood emergencies. Yet, that infrastructure itself is often vulnerable to flood hazards. Hospitals, health centres and related facilities may become severely damaged or functionally disrupted by flood events (Menne, 1999), affecting access to health care and the quality of care. Any resulting breakdown of services thereby creates a situation of double jeopardy for client populations suffering from the health outcomes of flooding. Unless health agencies in flood-prone areas address the risk of damage to infrastructure, there is a danger that any preparedness planning for health care provision will be rendered meaningless by floods that prevent the system itself from functioning (PAHO, 2001).

Damage risks and response

Milsten (2000) summarizes the common infrastructural problems that may confront hospitals responding to disasters, including: physical damage to the health facility and on-site storage facilities; communication and power failures; water shortage and contamination; damage to equipment; and release of hazardous materials. In some cases, the physical damage to the buildings may be relatively minor; but the damage to non-structural electrical, mechanical and medical components may render services inoperable. In hospitals, such non-structural components may comprise up to 90 per cent of the overall cost of the facility (PAHO, 2000).

Serious disruption of public health services after severe floods has been reported in both industrialized and developing countries. Accounts of floods affecting health systems in high-income countries include closure and evacuation of hospitals and health facilities during flood and storm events in Germany and the US. In Saxony in eastern Germany, a total of 53 doctors' surgeries were destroyed or severely damaged during the Elbe floods of 2002. Their closure caused a loss of service that Orellana (2002) indicates reduced the capacity of the health system to respond to flood-related disease risk. The 1993 Midwest floods in the US had severe impacts on health care infrastructure and its accessibility. Axelrod et al (1994) describe the effect of the floods on primary health care services and their inability to respond to changes in health care demand due to damage to facilities, equipment, lack of drugs and supplies, and communication problems. Initial public health assessments of the disaster included analysis of impacts on the health system.

Floods caused by Hurricane Floyd in North Carolina, US, in 1999 placed major challenges on the public health systems (see Chapter 7). Disruption of hospital transport, electricity and water services was addressed through the provision of helicopters, emergency generators and alternative water sources, with assistance from the US army (Franklin et al, 2000). The consequences of damage to clinics and practices, equipment and medicines caused by the hurricane was also alleviated through voluntary efforts from physicians in the region, coordinated through the North Carolina Medical Society (Edwards and Schwartz, 2000).

Major damage to health infrastructure is often reported from extreme flood events in developing countries, linked both to the severity of events and to greater system vulnerability. Following severe floods in central Viet Nam in 2003, the WHO compiled a detailed health-sector report, noting how disruptions to the health infrastructure hampered effective response (Dang Van Chinh, 2003). Some health facilities were inaccessible for several days and significant physical damage to buildings was caused, especially those that had suffered repeated incidence of flooding during recent years. In the aftermath of the floods, insufficient resources for reconstruction and repair were available, particularly at a community level, as the focus was placed largely on district health centres. As well as damage to fixed assets, floods may cause loss of equipment and drugs – particularly in rapid-onset floods when there is little time to store items safely. Christie and Hanlon (2001) note that after the Mozambique floods of 2000, loss of drug supplies damaged by flooding of local health posts was substantial enough to prompt a specific appeal for new supplies.

A particularly useful body of literature on the impacts of floods and other hazards on health systems has emerged from the Americas, largely from a series of reports produced by PAHO. The region has experienced a number of damaging floods during recent years, including El Niño events in the central Andes in 1997–1998, the devastating 1999 flood in Venezuela and a series of hurricanes in the Caribbean. During the 1997–1998 El Niño, floods affected at least 34 hospitals and 485 local health centres in Ecuador and Peru (PAHO, 2001). Hurricane Mitch in 1998 had a particularly severe impact on the health care infrastructure in Central America, the rehabilitation and reconstruction of which required international support and major coordination of external aid resources (PAHO, 1998b; PAHO, 1999). An estimated 50 per cent of all hospitals in Latin America and the Caribbean are located in hazard risk areas and most are inadequately prepared for natural disasters (PAHO, 2003). Partly as a result of these risks, the protection of the health services network by reducing the vulnerability of existing and new hospitals, health centres and laboratories has become a policy priority for PAHO (see Box 3.3).

Box 3.3 *Protecting health facilities in Latin America and the Caribbean*

During the 1990s International Decade for Natural Disaster Reduction, protection of health systems began to assume a particularly high profile in international policy circles in Latin America and the Caribbean. Coordinated largely by the Pan American Heath Organization (PAHO), health ministries, scientists and architects began to exchange knowledge and ideas on strategies for improving the design of new facilities and for updating or retrofitting existing infrastructure to reduce the impact of hazards (Poncelet and de Ville de Goyet, 1996). Central to this strategic formulation have been economic arguments over cost effectiveness, as well as the potential to save lives. In hazard-prone areas, it is claimed that 'for each dollar invested in mitigation before a disaster strikes, enormous savings will be made in losses prevented' (PAHO, 2000, p4).

The process has continued since the close of the decade, with the publication of guidelines for protecting new health facilities from natural disasters (PAHO, 2003). The document argues that measures to ensure continuing functionality of key areas of hospitals when they are most needed should be part of every newly built facility. The guidelines suggest that mitigation work should begin in the pre-investment phase, when protection and specific performance objectives need to be formulated for the new facility. When assessing different site options, the choice of location should be informed as much as possible by existing risks from natural hazards. Facility design then needs to take an integrated approach to mitigating risks of both structural and non-structural damage: a process that requires coordination of expertise from different professions. During the construction phase, quality assurance procedures are then required to ensure that protection measures are implemented.

The guidelines compiled by PAHO for Latin America and the Caribbean could equally be applied to other regions where the need for integration of disaster mitigation in planning, construction and management of health facilities is just as pressing. For existing health infrastructure, a systematic analysis of both structural and non-structural components can point to priority upgrading measures to protect against flood risk (as well as to inform the facility's flood preparedness plans). There may even be a need for relocation or redesign of existing health facilities that are flooded on a regular basis. For new health infrastructure, mitigation of physical threat from floods should be integrated within all phases: planning, design and construction (PAHO, 2003). Wherever feasible, it should be built outside flood zones or designed to function effectively in a flooded environment. Guidelines and regulations on the design and construction of facilities may need to be revised and efforts undertaken to ensure that the new codes are effectively applied.

In the aftermath of floods, relief and recovery efforts may need to pay more attention to damage assessment and rehabilitation of health infrastructure (PAHO, 1999; Dang Van Chinh, 2003). A focus of intervention by governments, agencies and donors purely on emergency provision may impair prospects for addressing long-term health needs. As VanRooyen and Leaning (2005, p437) noted after the 2004 Indian Ocean Tsunami:

> *It is therefore essential that mobile medical programs and temporary field hospitals be converted rapidly into programs that rebuild and renovate damaged hospitals and health centres – rather than becoming parallel systems that might undermine the reconstruction of local systems.*

Water and sanitation: Protection and provision

Much of the communicable disease outcome of flooding events centres on the impacts of flooding on water supplies and sanitation facilities. Effects on both the supply and quality of water, and on the storage and removal of human waste, may bring serious health risks (see Chapter 2). Equally, actions in water and sanitation are among the most widespread of health-related coping strategies in the face of flooding. Hence, it is important to explore in detail the nature of risks and responses in this sector, as well as associated issues. Since water-borne and faecal-oral disease outbreaks during floods tend to be rare in higher-income countries, the discussion here deals primarily with studies undertaken in developing countries.

Once again, the focus here is less on technical matters, and more on how mitigation and emergency response actions are organized and the considerations that need to be made in ensuring that they have the desired effects on public health. We look mainly at interventions in this sector by state organizations and NGOs that are specific to flooding and flood risk contexts (though there is inevitably some reference to generalized principles of emergency water and sanitation). Although we do not cover them here, it is also important to note other actions relating to environmental health during floods that may need to be taken in parallel with water and sanitation measures. These include strategies to reduce solid waste and hazardous waste, and to enhance food safety and decontamination of homes, some of which are addressed most effectively via health education programmes.

Flood impacts on water and sanitation

Floods disrupt water supplies and sanitation through a combination of physical damage, inundation and contamination, placing both piped water and sewerage systems and household-level facilities at risk. At the system level, guidelines on the protection of water and sanitation infrastructure produced by PAHO note that floods can cause damage to virtually every part of a system, including intakes, dams, reservoirs, conduits, pipelines, chambers, valves, treatment plants, engine houses, pumping equipment and electrical installations (PAHO, 1998b). Components of the system are put at risk of displacement and rupture by erosion of protective soil cover, rising groundwater causing flotation, and excess water flow and wave action during tidal floods. Damage can also come from the submergence of electrical components and from excess sedimentation. Related disruption such as road blockages by flood debris can hamper efforts to repair systems.

According to Osorio (2003, p2), three-quarters of the population of Honduras was affected by disruption to water supplies after Hurricane Mitch in 1998 and the damage 'set the Honduran water sector back in its water coverage services to a similar level to that of three decades earlier'. McCluskey (2001) adds that flash or high-velocity floods are the most damaging for water systems because their physical force can knock out key components, such as treatment stations and pumping installations. Box 3.4 indicates the destruction caused by freak floods during the El Niño years in the central Andes.

Box 3.4 *Effects of El Niño floods on water and sanitation in Ecuador and Peru*

During late 1982 and early 1983, intense, prolonged rainfall associated with the El Niño–Southern Oscillation (ENSO) phenomenon brought severe floods and landslides to many coastal regions of Ecuador. Hederra (1987) described how the floods caused extensive damage to infrastructure across five provinces of Ecuador, affecting drinking water systems (damage to wells, elevating plants, pipelines and impulsions; interruption of service) and sewerage systems (damage to elevating plants, pipelines and impulsions, and sewer networks; obstructions caused by reflux of sewage). In the city of Babahoyo, discharges from the sewerage system (via inspection wells) directly into the standing floodwaters that lay across much of the city created a level of coliform contamination that 'corresponds to raw wastewater' (Hederra 1987, p304).

Freak floods caused by the same El Niño event also afflicted the arid coastal belt of north-east Peru. According to Maber (1989, p28), the floods destroyed the well system and pumping main for the town of Sechura, forcing the inhabitants 'to buy contaminated water from water-sellers using open wells several kilometres away'. The author reports how the impact of the flood led to a special community-based project called *Agua Para Sechura*, designed to give the town better-protected but also better-quality and more sustainable water and sanitation facilities.

It is not only networks of piped water systems and sewerage that are at risk of physical damage. Wells and latrines can also be vulnerable, although the structural damage caused to them may have less impact across space and time. In the 1991 Bangladesh cyclone, for example, tube wells were affected by the storm and tidal surge – official data reported that 38 per cent of tube wells in the affected areas were damaged (Hoque et al, 1993). According to the UNICEF Cyclone Evaluation Team (1993), however, much of the damage was not critical and most of the tube wells were quickly brought back into service after minor repairs to equipment, such as platforms and pump handles.

As well as suffering physical damage, though, water facilities are also subject to contamination that may be more cross-scale in its impact. Parker and Thompson (2000) regard large-scale contamination of drinking water as the most serious disease hazard from floods. Contamination may arise from animal cadavers near water intakes; high turbidity making purification difficult; floodwater entering well heads; flood levels higher than well head walls or water flowing directly over wells and other intakes; fuel/chemical pollution (fuel mixed with water also makes it more difficult to boil); and physical damage to water treatment plants (PAHO, 1998b; Caribbean Environmental Health Institute, 2003).

Even if the supply system itself is not interrupted, there can be cross-contamination from damaged sewerage systems. In the Bangladesh flood of 1998, Dhaka City's waste disposal system became almost completely ineffective (Nishat et al, 2000): many streets became flooded with water mixed with waste and sewage, the leakage of sewage contaminated most water supply lines, and the reserve water tanks of many houses became submerged and contaminated. Water level rise in sewer outfalls can cause contamination of groundwater supplies and can result in wastewater backing up and flooding through manholes in roads and the toilets and washbasins of homes and buildings (PAHO, 1998b; Caribbean Environmental Health Institute, 2003). Shut-off valves can prevent such back-flow; but in many cases in developing countries these are not installed.

In a report from Brazil on emergency environmental health, Philippi Junior et al (2003) state the prime importance of providing clean water and managing excreta after floods. This importance is reflected in the high priority accorded to water and sanitation in the risk reduction and emergency response efforts of many organizations across the world. In Mozambique in 2000, for example, 16.5 per cent of expenditure from a joint appeal by UK-based NGOs was spent on water and sanitation, compared with 8.4 per cent on 'health' (Cosgrave et al, 2001).

Mitigation and preparedness

Much of the flood response literature discusses strategies for emergency water and sanitation provision, and these aspects are discussed below. But emergency actions are only part of the water and sanitation story and may not be the most effective coping strategies against flood risk. It is important, too, to stress mitigation actions that protect system infrastructure and facilities in the home from becoming damaged or contaminated in the first place. Osorio (2003) argues, for example, that emergency response such as water distribution by tankers is logistically very difficult for Central American countries. Where feasible, the optimum solution, instead, is to design supply infrastructure to consider the geography of natural hazard risk and to incorporate measures to ensure that the system can continue functioning when floods occur.

In this sense, pre-flood protection and long-term flood recovery should ideally blend into one another. Indeed, action on water and sanitation can fit with all stages of the hazard cycle. Oxfam's River Basin Programme, covering the Ganges and Brahmaputra basins of South Asia, includes water and sanitation work in disaster preparedness – for example, the raising of tube-well heights prior to floods; emergency relief – for example, provision of sanitation kits and latrine repairs; and flood recovery – for example, the replacement or rebuilding of latrines (British Red Cross, 2001c). In the recovery phase from the El Niño floods of 1983, the project *Agua Para Sechura* in Peru involved reconstructing the water supply system and improving emergency wells to provide more adequate future protection of supplies (Maber, 1989). Dunston et al (2001) promote the benefits of moving from an emergency project approach to drinking water to a development project approach that emphasizes long-term safe water provision for communities at all times. As with most aspects of risk reduction, such an approach to water and sanitation protection is likely to require an ongoing commitment from agencies and tends to work best if grounded in broad-based community involvement in the design, construction, operation and maintenance of facilities (Dunston et al, 2001; Wisner and Adams, 2002; The Sphere Project, 2004).

As well as making systems more hazard proof, flood preparedness includes more temporary measures based on advance forecasts, such as the raising of tube-well heights to prevent inundation and precautionary measures to enable widespread treatment of contaminated water (Roger Young and Associates, 2000; McCluskey, 2001). Prior to the 2000 floods in Mozambique, provincial offices of the Red Cross (CVM) carried out preparedness planning from September 1999, when the first warnings of floods were issued (see Chapter 5). This involved advance distribution of basic kits, including chlorine for water treatment to strategic locations in flood-risk areas (Christie and Hanlon, 2001).

Emergency provision: Water supplies and purification

Provision of water is arguably the single most important measure for health protection of disaster-affected populations (Lillibridge, 1997). When floods strike, the agencies involved in response and relief have to consider several aspects of water supply and usage, including decontamination of supplies, providing sufficient quantities of water and hygienic collection, and storage and use of water by households (see Box 3.5). The Sphere Project (2004) stresses that insufficient water for drinking and hygiene can be just as harmful as contamination of water supplies and provides a minimum target for water supply of 15 litres per person per day, equitably distributed across an affected population. Wisner and Adams (2002) affirm that the first priority is to provide an adequate quantity of water, even if the supply is of low quality.

The Caribbean Environmental Health Institute (2003) recommends that an assessment of all sources of public water supply be undertaken after a flood, and priority accorded not only to drinking water systems but also to proper storage (to prevent contamination and breeding sites for mosquitoes). In the medium term, the next priority is to restore original sources. McCluskey (2001) stresses that recommissioning water supplies requires disinfection with super-chlorination rates, and that some sources, such as wells, may need physical cleaning first.

Box 3.5 *Sphere standards for water and sanitation*

Guidelines on disaster response developed by The Sphere Project (2004, pp63–73) establish three international water supply 'standards' (on access and water quantity, water quality, and water storage and use) and two excreta disposal 'standards' (on access to and number of toilets, and the design, construction and use of toilets). The five standards are worded as follows:

All people should have safe and equitable access to a sufficient quantity of water for drinking, cooking and personal and domestic hygiene. Public water points are sufficiently close to households to enable use of the minimum water requirement.

Water is palatable, and of sufficient quality to be drunk and used for personal and domestic hygiene without causing significant risk to health.

People have adequate facilities and supplies to collect, store and use sufficient quantities of water for drinking, cooking and personal hygiene, and to ensure that drinking water remains safe until it is consumed.

People have adequate numbers of toilets, sufficiently close to their dwellings, to allow them rapid, safe and acceptable access at all times of the day and night.

Toilets are sited, designed, constructed and maintained in such a way as to be comfortable, hygienic and safe to use.

The Sphere Project, 2004

Wisner and Adams (2002) note that where disruption or contamination of a water source happens, a number of immediate options may be considered. First, alternative sources nearby may be made available in emergencies, such as from unaffected wells or from supplies to food/drink factories. If these are unavailable, water may be trucked in by tankers, or existing contaminated sources may be chlorinated before consumption – at higher levels than may be normal. Priority for provision and treatment should be given to areas that do not have alternative sources, and special priority should be given to hospitals. The authors consider that household purification of untreated water should be a last resort.

During the 1998 floods in Bangladesh, one of the first responses was the raising of tube wells to prevent contamination (Roger Young and Associates, 2000). As the flood rose and many wells eventually became submerged, people waded through water or hired boats to access wells on higher ground. The supplies provided to designated flood shelters became very important. Agencies and the government also became involved in tankering water, especially in urban areas (Shahaduzzaman, 1999). As the flood receded, many agencies then provided bleaching powder and advice for cleaning and rehabilitating wells. Water supply was similarly a major issue immediately after the 1999 Orissa cyclone; but emergency decontamination was seen to have been a major factor in successfully preventing major epidemic outbreaks. As many as 68,000 tube wells were 'rehabilitated' by cleaning and bleaching within two weeks of the cyclone with support from the state government and external agencies such as Oxfam and UNICEF (INTRAC, 2000; Palakudiyil and Todd, 2003).

In many circumstances, local, state and international agencies may have little choice but to promote efforts to purify untreated water collected by households and to protect stored water around houses. Much of this centres on education (see earlier in the chapter); but it may also involve free distribution of purification kits and hygienic containers, as in the Bangladesh floods of 1998 (Roger Young and Associates, 2000). In Nicaragua, during Hurricane Mitch in 1998, the local NGO Madriz Community Movement 'mobilized their health brigades to prevent people drinking contaminated water and encourage them to chlorinate drinking water' (Richards, 1999, p5). Oxfam has designed and distributed special sealable water containers with taps to prevent environmental contamination (McCluskey, 2001).

Emergency provision: Sanitation

According to the Caribbean Environmental Health Institute (2003, p26), 'the importance of maintaining good sanitary conditions following a flooding event in order to protect public health cannot be overstated'. Inundation of latrines and lack of access to alternative toilets emerged as a major problem during the 1998 floods in Bangladesh, for example, and it is a problem especially heightened in congested urban areas (Roger Young and Associates, 2000). Wisner and Adams (2002) confirm that excreta disposal is of particular concern in urban areas because of the greater density of people and risk of contamination (whereas in rural areas the priority is likely to be protection of water sources). Indeed, as McCluskey (2001) notes, concentrating effort on providing supplies of clean water is not enough if parallel transmission routes for disease exist because of disrupted waste disposal systems.

Emergency provision of sanitation relates both to piped systems, where sewerage exists, and to household-level facilities (toilets and latrines). In terms of systems, the immediate response may include the isolation of sections still functioning and bypassing damaged or blocked sections (Wisner and Adams, 2002; The Sphere Project, 2004). This may be combined with sewage tankering services and the installation of septic tanks or containment tanks that can be regularly emptied. To ensure that people have access to adequate sanitation facilities in accessible locations, temporary or portable toilets may need to be provided, although Wisner and Adams (2002, p128) stress that first 'every effort should be made to allow people to use their existing toilets'. As for water, The Sphere Project (2004) establishes disaster response standards on sanitation facilities and their usage (see Box 3.5), emphasizing that people should have adequate numbers of toilets close to dwellings, and that these should be comfortable, safe and hygienic to use. Safety and cultural acceptability may be particularly important considerations for women. Nishat et al (2000) particularly emphasize that emergency shelter houses need to have adequate numbers of toilets – many people sheltering during the 1998 flood in Dhaka used open latrines.

Safe sanitation provision, like all aspects of preventive health, relies on more than just technical details. If emergency facilities are to provide protection, the people at risk need to be persuaded to use them through efforts such as hygiene education (Palakudiyil and Todd, 2003). However, attempts to introduce new types of toilet may be ill advised during the emergency phase. Cairncross et al (2003) emphasize that health promotion for safer sanitation may need to be more sophisticated than for water: there may be a need to 'market' use of new facilities. The International NGO Training and Research Centre (INTRAC, 2000) points out that efforts to change behaviour are unlikely to succeed in the immediate crisis period following a flood. A balance may need to be struck, with education and social marketing for new sanitation facilities perhaps best suited to long-term rehabilitation programmes.

Conclusion: Enhancing coping capacity

The foregoing discussion has drawn on diverse sources of existing information to set out the nature of responses to the health risks from flooding. The chapter has also highlighted some of the factors that are likely to shape their effectiveness and, hence, enhance both current coping capacity and prospective adaptation to future health risks. Here, we provide a summary assessment of the current state of knowledge on responses, picking out some of the key generic themes that have emerged from the review. Many of these topics re-emerge in the following case study chapters and are reflected upon further in Chapter 8.

Together with general measures designed to protect human systems from floods, the survey of literature has revealed various mechanisms and strategies that serve specifically to prevent or address mortality and morbidity impacts. Such responses exist in terms of health protection activity in the home and community; health, safety and hygiene education; disease surveillance and control; provision of health care; protection of health system infrastructure, and protection and provision of water and sanitation facilities. These coping mechanisms and strategies may take place before, during and after flood events; in practice, the delimitation between preparedness, emergency response and recovery phases of action is often blurred. The actors undertaking these responses include affected individuals, community organizations, medical teams, public agencies, non-governmental organizations and external agencies. A summary list of the types of responses identified is provided in Table 3.3.

There is little concrete information at present on which to assess the effect of such actions in reducing the health outcomes of floods (see 'Research needs'

Table 3.3 *A summary of health-related response mechanisms*

	Type of response	Examples
Actions by households	Avoidance of exposure to water	Raising furniture on bricks and creating raised walkways from planks
	Avoidance of waste contamination	Removing waste matter and unblocking drainage channels
	Reduction in vector abundance	Removing unused vessels where mosquitoes can breed after flooding recedes
	Treatment of water	Boiling; using alum crystals or disinfection tablets
	Coping adjustment to dwellings	Placing electrical wiring high up on walls in flood-prone environments
	Social support	Care and support for household members under stress
	Advance purchase of medicine	Ensuring household supply of treatments for common flood-related ailments
Actions by communities (with/ without external assistance)	Voluntary relief efforts	Distribution of food by richer families to poorer; setting up relief centres; emergency rescue
	Social support networks	Informal support networks to lessen negative emotional impact of floods
	Community citizen disaster preparedness programmes	Training and organization in reducing health risks; preparing emergency kits, evacuation plans, first aid and health care
	Community-based flood early warning system	Traditional warning mechanisms and new initiatives in local river monitoring
Actions by public/ private agencies relating to preventive health	Health, safety and hygiene education on floods	Dissemination of educational material and emergency information by various media and through outreach
	Disease surveillance	Activation of pre-planned surveillance system for selected flood-related diseases
	Disease control	Vaccination campaigns; vector-control mechanisms

in Chapter 8). However, the provision and organization of responses raises a series of issues relating to effectiveness; drawing on these, we distil here a set of generic themes for enhancing coping capacity of systems, organizations and individuals, and for avoiding maladaptive responses to the health risks of flooding. These themes are indicated in Figure 3.1 and are discussed, in turn,

Table 3.3 *A summary of health-related response mechanisms (continued)*

	Type of response	Examples
Actions by public/ private agencies relating to health care provision	Emergency planning	Disaster preparedness for health systems: practical drills; information and guidelines on availability of staff; decision-making channels; communication with media; supply and storage of medicines
	Needs assessment	Rapid needs assessment for directing health care response measures; monitoring health care needs among vulnerable groups
	Provision of emergency health posts and services	Field hospitals and mobile health care teams during emergencies; provision of boats for public access to health centres; coordinated distribution of medicines
	Prioritization of services	Rescheduling, admissions restrictions and continuation of essential care
	Mental health care	Provision of counselling and related support for affected populations
Actions to protect health infrastructure	Preparedness planning	Addressing issues of communication and power failure, physical damage to health care facilities, water shortage and contamination, etc.
	Flood-proofing	Appropriate design and construction of new facilities
Actions to protect and provide safe water and sanitation	Advance protection	Design supply infrastructure to consider the geography of natural hazard risk, and to incorporate measures to ensure that the system can continue functioning when floods occur
	Temporary protection measures	Raising tube-well heights; advance distribution of water treatment kits to strategic locations
	Emergency provision and restoration of water supplies	Emergency alternative water sources, e.g. tankers; decontamination and recommissioning of sources
	Emergency provision and restoration of sanitation facilities/systems	Portable toilets, emergency public latrines, sewage tankering services; isolation and repair of damaged sewerage sections piped systems

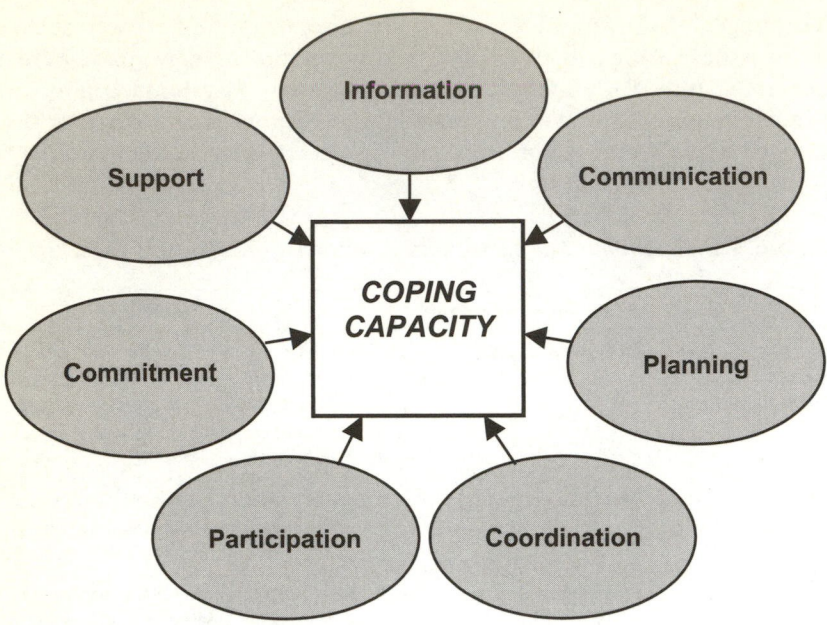

Figure 3.1 *Enhancing capacity to cope with health risks: Generic themes*

below. In the light of future risks associated with climate change and other drivers, we may also express these as key elements of adaptive capacity.

The chances of effective response to health risks are greatly enhanced by reliable *information* on the health needs of the population and the rehabilitation needs of health, water and sanitation systems damaged by floods. Good baseline data, for example, is a prerequisite for accurate disease surveillance during floods and needs assessment. However, the ideal of high-quality data has to be considered in context. In practical terms, there may be a trade-off between optimization of the accuracy of data gathering and the need to provide a timely response to health impacts.

The counterpart to reliable information is effective *communication*. The section on health education has highlighted the importance of genuine communication of information to the public in a meaningful and accessible manner. This applies to health promotion in general. Social differentiation in the perception of risks, together with cultural barriers to effective coping and take-up of interventions, highlights the need for health promotion activity to be tailored to local social contexts and to the differing needs and capacities of social groups. It is also crucial to recognize that education alone may not be sufficient. Use of unsafe water for drinking, for example, is caused often by lack of choice rather than lack of understanding.

Advance *planning* emerges strongly as a key message for the successful implementation of health education, emergency health care provision, infrastructure protection and other aspects of response to the health risks of floods.

It minimizes *ad hoc* decision-making during crises, and helps to ensure that response activities are comprehensive and coordinated. Preparedness plans, for example, are seen as crucial for health systems in flood-prone locations, covering how the system continues to function during flood events, as well as how the system responds to additional needs created by the flood. Plans, however, should not be too rigid. A planned approach requires a degree of flexibility, not just to cope with variability in the nature of flood events and their impacts, but also to enable reflexive incorporation of lessons from experience and from external examples of good practice.

Efficient response by agencies rests on effective *coordination* between sectors and organizations, and across scales of responsibility. Coordination helps to ensure that actions are mutually supportive and avoid gaps and overlaps in coverage. During flood emergencies where external assistance is forthcoming, for example, strong leadership by the internal health administration can help to ensure that the efforts of different organizations providing medical and other care for affected populations are harmonized. It can also make certain that external efforts are appropriate to local contexts.

Participation of local people in planning and implementing response strategies has emerged as another key theme, spanning most aspects of health protection. Community involvement presents many challenges and may not always be easy to foster, particularly if solicited in the immediate post-onset phase of floods. However, it may be a crucial factor in shaping the success of preparedness, emergency response and recovery activities. In many cases, inclusive processes may be built on existing community institutions, including neighbourhood flood committees; but where these are absent, ineffective or inequitable, there may be a need to foster development of broad-based social capital networks and decision-making institutions.

As for most aspects of hazards response, a key message from the review is that effective response requires considerable institutional *commitment* to preparedness and risk reduction, both in time and prioritization. Institutions in flood-prone areas need a long-term commitment to put strategies in place and to ensure that they are capable of functioning when emergencies arise. Wherever possible, investment in sanitation and water provision during the recovery phase from floods, for example, should aim to address long-term risks rather than merely covering immediate needs. Ideally, flood risk should be factored into mainstream health system planning. External agencies also need to consider providing a presence beyond the immediate flood relief phase, preferably with a long-term commitment to capacity-building and community involvement.

For low-income countries, in particular, strategic *support* for health risk reduction from floods may require an increase and/or a shift in emphasis in external funding assistance. A crucial change will be the move towards funding broad-based risk reduction measures rather than merely reacting to high-profile humanitarian crises. In terms of health protection, that means recognizing the importance of the burden of disease and other long-term health implications of floods; the importance of restoring primary and preventive care, as well as hospital facilities; and the potential cost effectiveness of health-sector flood mitigation and preparedness measures. It is important to recognize that many such long-term measures will have wider utility beyond the context of hazards: they have a synergy with broader public health goals. Most efforts to invest in health-related flood coping mechanisms, such as hygiene promotion, health system emergency preparedness and protection of water and sanitation systems, will provide ongoing health benefits – just as improvement in public health overall will help to reduce vulnerability to the specific health risks posed by floods, now and in the future.

4

The Mental Health Aspects of Floods: Evidence from England and Wales

Sue Tapsell and Sylvia Tunstall

Introduction

Until recently, floods in the UK have been typically small scale, short lived and shallow; but since 1998 parts of England and Wales have experienced frequent incidents of severe flooding. The flooding of Easter 1998 and the extensive floods of autumn 2000 (the wettest on record for over 270 years) raised the issue of flooding on the political agenda. More recently, the dramatic images of the severe flash flood in Boscastle, a small coastal village in Cornwall, in the summer of 2004 and extensive flooding in Carlisle, Cumbria, over the winter of 2004/2005, in which several people died, have highlighted the flood risk to people and properties. The predictions are that climate change could make extreme floods such as these a more frequent occurrence due to the projected wetter winters and more intense summer storms. The related human health impacts are therefore expected to increase over the next 50 to 100 years owing to the effects of global warming (McCarthy et al, 2001) and other factors, such as possible disparities in wealth and access to resources (Evans et al, 2004).

The increasing risk to health from flooding is partly due to increasing population exposure: an estimated 1.85 million homes and approximately 5 million people are now considered to be at risk from flooding in England and Wales (Environment Agency, 2001). A major problem is that many people do not expect to be flooded in an advanced industrialized country and are therefore unaware of the flood risk, particularly in urban areas. Figure 4.1 illustrates the extent of the autumn 2000 floods. Although over 10,000 properties were flooded in over 700 locations, in the majority of cases less than 100 or even less than 20 properties were affected, highlighting the localized nature of the flooding.

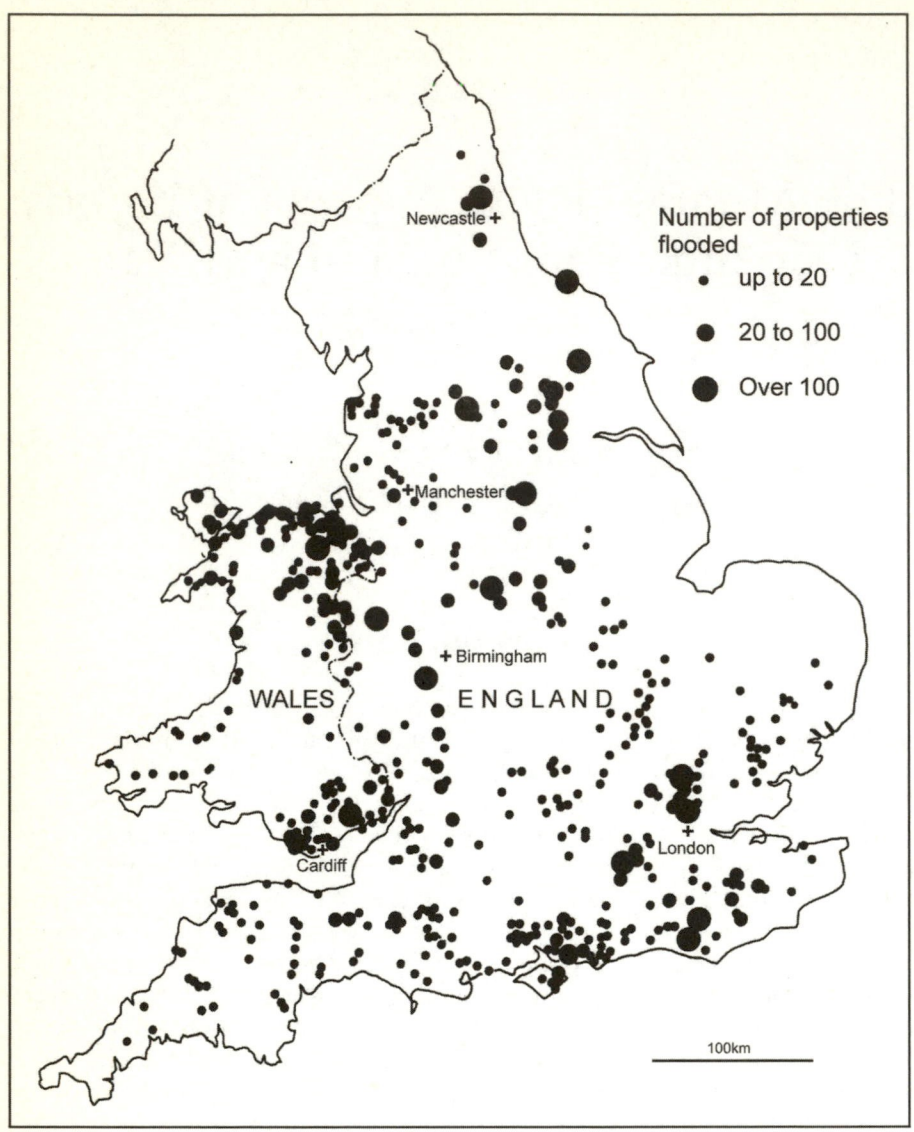

Figure 4.1 *Extent of the autumn 2000 flooding*

Source: based on map data in Environment Agency (2001)

Since the 1998 floods, there has been a growing awareness of the significance of the social effects that flooding may have on those affected – that floods are also about *people*. These 'intangible' effects, which include the impacts on both physical and psychological health, have until recently been effectively ignored by policy-makers. Assessment of the 'tangible' impacts of flooding, such as damage to property and financial and economic losses, has taken precedence over the intangible impacts, as these losses are better understood and more easily measured and valued. One consequence of this is a danger of emphasizing what can be valued in monetary terms as opposed to what is often more important to people, the effects of which may persist long after properties have been repaired. This is particularly true of the impacts of flooding on people's mental health.

The World Health Organization (WHO, 2001) has recently acknowledged that the mental health consequences of floods have not been fully addressed by those in the field of disaster preparedness or health service delivery. As discussed in Chapter 2, it is particularly these mental health impacts that are the most relevant in developed countries. In Europe and other parts of the developed world, few people die as a result of flooding thanks to increasingly sophisticated methods of flood forecasting and warning systems and improved preparedness planning. In addition, high levels of sanitation, good water supply systems and access to public health care mean that infectious diseases following flooding are rare.

The increased likelihood of future flooding has highlighted the potential of the risks to mental health and raised the question of how they can be addressed. Moreover, it is generally agreed that mental health is broader than a lack of mental disorders and includes people's general well-being (WHO, 2001). This chapter reviews the research on mental health and flooding in England and Wales. Drawing on recent evidence, it highlights the various mental health effects experienced by people whose homes have been flooded and the possible factors that may moderate these effects. Measures for reducing mental health effects are outlined and areas of further research are suggested.

Research in England and Wales on flooding and mental health

Despite being ignored at the policy level, the issue of flooding and mental health has not been entirely ignored by academics. A number of studies have been carried out from the late 1960s that have highlighted the various impacts of flooding on people's mental health in England and Wales, and have suggested that mental health impacts are potentially more significant than physical health impacts.

The earliest systematic study was that by Bennet (1970), mentioned in Chapter 2, which revealed significant psychological impacts following the Bristol 1968 floods. Parker et al (1983) approached 102 households believed to have been flooded in 1978 in Swalecliffe, Kent. Over 50 per cent of respondents reported that they had not yet recovered from the flood and that the tangible effects were less important than the intangible effects. The most significant flood impacts reported were (in order of importance):

- disruption to life of the household;
- loss of memorabilia and personal belongings;

- being evacuated from home; and
- the stress of the flood event itself.

A further study by Green et al (1985) focused on assessing the intangible effects of the tidal flooding of December 1981 at Uphill, Weston-Super-Mare. Three population samples were drawn: 101 flooded households; a control sample of 100 near-flooded households; a further control sample with no experience of flooding. Apart from demographic questionnaires, three main survey instruments were employed: an interview schedule (flooded households) and two self-completion (flooded and non-flooded households). The main instrument of the self-completion questionnaires was the Nottingham Health Profile (Hunt and McEwen, 1980), along with a short version of the Life Events score (Holmes and Rahe, 1967).

Consistent patterns of lower health status were found among those who had been flooded compared with the near flooded. For example, 75 per cent of flooded households reported mental health impacts, particularly depression and sleeping problems. Age was significantly correlated with more severe health impacts – the older the respondent the more likely they were to attribute some health effect to the flood. In the latter two studies above, key correlations showed that those reporting the greatest overall flood impacts also reported the most severe impacts from health effects and stress from the risk of future flooding, and that those suffering little damage in their homes also reported little effect on their health.

Green et al (1994), in analysing data for the EUROflood project of 1700 cases from different flood events in England and Wales, also found that the stress of flooding can result in both short- and long-term health damage, as well as increasing worry and anxiety about future flooding. The analysis used 500 different variables and focused on short duration floods that were relatively shallow (generally less than 1.5m in depth). The key findings were:

- The stress of the flood event was reported as being the most critical variable identified as important in determining whether health effects were reported.
- The stress experienced by the household was associated with the depth of the flood.
- Stress was significantly reduced if flooding occurred during daylight hours.
- Elderly people tended to report a higher degree of severity of health damage than did younger people.
- Evacuation was found to be particularly distressing.
- Financial losses were often less important than the loss of personal belongings.

Analysis also showed that individuals responded to a perceived threat by mobilizing personal and social resources, and that the availability of such support may serve to buffer or ameliorate the impacts of the threat.

Reacher et al (2004), in research following the autumn 2000 flooding in Lewes, Sussex, found flooded adults to have a fourfold higher risk of psychological distress. Flooding remained highly significantly associated with psychological distress after adjustment for physical illness. There was a strong indication that having to leave one's home during a flood was an important factor in psychological distress. Moreover, the authors suggest that psychological distress may explain some of the excess physical illness reported by flooded adults and possibly also by children. However, it was unclear if it was the flooding or events over the following nine months that were the reason for the increased rates of anxiety and depression.

Since the Easter 1998 floods, a number of qualitative studies have been conducted. These studies comprised a series of focus groups in five communities affected by inland flooding (Tapsell et al, 1999; Tapsell and Tunstall, 2000; Tapsell and Tunstall, 2001). Two of these communities (six focus groups) were followed up over a four-year period (Tapsell et al, 2003). The studies, which covered communities that had experienced flood events of varying characteristics and impacts, have helped to provide deeper insights into some of the important consequences of flooding on people's mental health and well-being.

The latest and most extensive study to date of the health effects of flooding was carried out in 2002–2003 (RPA et al, 2004) as part of a project for the Department for the Environment, Food and Rural Affairs (Defra) and the Environment Agency (EA), with a view to accounting for these impacts in benefit-cost appraisals for flood defence schemes. The study involved a series of focus groups and retrospective face-to-face questionnaire interviews with 983 'flooded' and 527 'at risk' respondents in 30 locations experiencing fluvial or surface water flooding of varying degrees since January 1998. The study was not based on epidemiological evidence such as that provided by Bennet (1970), but research conducted by social scientists based on retrospective data collection and respondents' self-reporting of symptoms; no control groups were used in the study. The rest of this chapter will discuss some of the key findings from this latest research, supplemented and illustrated by results from the authors' earlier qualitative research and findings from other industrialized countries.

Results from recent research

The RPA et al (2004) study confirmed the findings from the earlier research and clearly highlighted the significance of mental health impacts associated with the experience of being flooded. Stress was a key health effect reported in the early studies and was also a significant factor found to impact upon people's mental health in the latest research. The development of stress in disaster populations can be complex and the stress of a flood is not limited to the time it occurs. Parker et al (1987) suggested a 'multi-strike' model of flooding as a source of stressors – a flood being a multiple stressor that can produce three stress reactions of different intensities and durations:

1   stress of the event itself (short term, although it may be the most intense);
2   stress from the disruption caused by the flood (may last for many months);
3   stress from worry about future flooding (chronic stressor likely to fluctuate over time).

There are now an increasing number of studies that aim to examine the longitudinal impacts of disasters and trauma on people's mental health (e.g. Van Dyke et al,1985; Bravo et al, 1990; Steinglass and Gerrity, 1990; Bland et al, 1996; Smith, 1996; Becht et al, 1998; Waelde et al, 1998; Caldera et al, 2001). The general rule in the vast majority of studies reviewed by Norris et al (2001a) was that people's condition improved as timed passed. However, this trend was not always linear.

Three self-reporting survey instruments were used in the latest research: a checklist of psychological health effects developed from the earlier qualitative research; the General Health Questionnaire (GHQ-12) (Goldberg and Williams, 1988); and the Post-Traumatic Stress Scale (PTSS) (Scott and Dua, 1999). The GHQ-12, the PTSS and the health checklist were used in an attempt to measure the long-term psychological health effects associated with being flooded, while a Worst Time version of the GHQ-12 was used to measure the short- to mid-term effects. For a more detailed account of the methodology and results, see RPA et al (2004) and Tunstall et al (2006).

Self-reporting health checklists

Results from the health checklists showed that over 70 per cent of flooded respondents reported experiencing some mental health problems following flooding (Table 4.1) and 50 per cent of these reported multiple effects. This was a significantly higher figure than those reporting physical health effects during or immediately after flooding (54 per cent) or in the weeks and months following flooding (33 per cent). Many of the reported effects represent symptoms of common mental disorders associated with experiencing a traumatic event, with increased anxiety levels being particularly high. Moreover, there were significant differences between men's and women's reporting of effects. Significantly higher proportions of women than men reported all effects, with the exception of increased tensions in relationships (level of significance was measured at Chi-square $P<0.05$). Differences for increased anxiety levels, sleeping problems, flashbacks to the flood and nightmares were highly significant.

As with the Reacher et al (2004) study, findings also showed an association between reported physical and psychological health effects, although this needs to be explored in more detail. The psychological effects may partly explain some of the reported physical illnesses, such as increased blood pressure. In addition, the physical health problems experienced by people may themselves be stressors adding to the psychological effects. Around a quarter of the 983 flooded respondents reported consulting a doctor over the physical and psychological effects that they attributed to the flooding. This suggests that

Table 4.1 *Psychological health effects reported in the weeks or months after flood, by gender*

Psychological effects	Male – percentage (381)	Female – percentage (602)	Total – percentage (983)
Anxiety (e.g. when it rains or when the river rises)	42 (161)	64 (382)	55 (543)
Increased stress levels	31 (119)	39 (234)	36 (353)
Sleeping problems	18 (69)	29 (176)	25 (245)
Flashbacks to flood	11 (41)	21 (129)	17 (170)
Increased tensions in relationships	16 (61)	15 (91)	16 (152
Mild depression	10 (38)	17 (102)	14 (140)
Difficulty concentrating	9 (34)	15 (93)	13 (127)
Mood swings	10 (37)	15 (89)	13 (126)
Lethargy/no energy	6 (22)	12 (71)	10 (93)
Moderate depression	7 (26)	11 (66)	9 (92)
Panic attacks	4 (15)	11 (67)	8 (82)
Increased use of alcohol/drugs	5 (19)	8 (45)	7 (64)
Nightmares	2 (8)	9 (56)	7 (64)
Severe depression	3 (12)	6 (33)	5 (45)
Thoughts of suicide	0.3 (1)	2 (12)	1 (13)
Anger/tantrums	8 (32)	10 (59)	9 (91)
Suffered no psychological effects	42 (158)	20 (121)	28 (279)

Source: RPA et al (2004)

events such as floods may place an additional burden on health care systems that also needs to be considered (Ohl and Tapsell, 2000).

General Health Questionnaire (GHQ-12)

An attempt to measure respondents' current mental health was made with the use of the GHQ-12 (Goldberg and Williams, 1988). The GHQ is a commonly used survey instrument and is employed in the UK Health Survey for England. The GHQ-12 is a shortened (12-question) version of the longer GHQ and has been widely used to detect psychiatric disorders and disturbance in relation to a variety of natural disasters and is seen as a reliable and valid method of assessment. The disadvantage of the GHQ-12 is that it is not event specific and thus psychological problems detected may not be related to the particular event in question (in this case, flood). The GHQ also only considers symptoms experienced over the preceding few weeks, which if administered long after an event may result in the short- and medium-term effects not being captured.

There are two methods of scoring the instrument: the GHQ method (score 0–12) and the Likert method (score 0–36); for reasons of space, only the GHQ method is discussed here. Each of the 12 questions has four possible responses. To score the questionnaire, the first two response categories for each question are both given a 0 score (no symptoms), and the third and fourth response categories are given a score of 1 (some symptoms). Thus, this simply differentiates between those respondents within a sample who display symptoms of impaired mental health compared with those that do not. It does not take into account the degree of impaired health effects. The standard threshold for diagnosis of impaired mental health is a score of 4 or more out of the possible score of 12.

Table 4.2 shows the percentage of flooded respondents displaying symptoms of current mental health impairment compared with respondents who were at risk. Scores among those who were flooded were significantly higher for both men and women. Those at risk were drawn from the same areas as the flooded: some had been present at the time of the flooding but had not themselves been flooded; others had moved to the area after the flooding and had no direct experience of the event.

Table 4.2 *Results from General Health Questionnaire (GHQ-12) for current health in the last few weeks*

Population	GHQ-12 method – percentage showing impaired mental health (score of 4 or more)
Flooded – total (n = 814)	25
Flooded – women	26
Flooded – men	22
At risk – total (n = 485)	10
At risk – women	12
At risk – men	7

Source: RPA et al (2004)

Factors other than the flooding may be contributing to the current high scores among flooded respondents. Differences in age and stage in life cycle between the two groups could partly explain the different results. The mean age of respondents was 51, with flooded respondents being slightly older (mean 54.5 compared with 45.4 for those at risk). However, higher GHQ-12 scores were found among flooded respondents for all age groups apart from those aged over 60 compared with those at risk. Moreover, the differences in mental health by age group were not found to be significant within either the flooded or at-risk groups. Therefore, age is unlikely to account for the extent of the differences when compared with the at-risk population.

The results, thus, indicate that the experience of being flooded has resulted in continuing and long-term mental health impacts for some respondents in the study, despite the fact that for many people the flooding had occurred several years previously. Transcripts from qualitative research illustrate the mental health effects in a way that the quantitative statistics cannot, and highlight that the impacts are often long lasting:

> *...we just didn't think it would last this long [bursts into tears]... We're all upset but... I'm sorry, I'm just so tired. I don't sleep; I wake up and there's water round the bed every night. I see water round the bed; I just can't sleep any more... It was so frightening. I was on my own and I was so scared. And now I'm just tired.* (female five months after flood, 2000)

> *I still feel that, even today, even though I've got my house really nice and I've got everything. But what we went through... the emotional stress and if they paid us [compensation] I don't think that would cover it... I feel very strongly about all of this and I have never spoken to anybody about it and it would really help for someone to see that side of it, not just the insurance and house contents, and that's nothing towards what I went through.* (female 18 months after flood, 1999)

> *The house is back to normal, but we're not back to normal in the mind.* (male 18 months after flood, 1999)

> *It's the stress; I think if we had another [flood] it would kill me. With the way I've been this year, I think it would kill me... I'm on medication, which I wasn't before... I'm on anti-depressants.* (male 4.5 years after flood, 2002)

Worst Time health effects

One of the problems in the estimation of the longer-term prevalence of a disorder is that although people may be currently free of a symptom, a proportion may have experienced past episodes of impaired mental health (Power, 1988), and this was of concern in the latest study. There have been several attempts to devise both 'worst ever' and 'lifetime ever' modifications of self-report questionnaires (Schwarz and Zuroff, 1979; Bromet et al, 1986; Power, 1988). Power (1988) used an amended version of the GHQ-28 (Goldberg and Hillier, 1979) to construct a worst episode or a 'time I felt worst' version. Although some cautions were noted, Power concluded that the 'worst ever' GHQ-28 showed good overall test-retest reliability and that the sub-scales generally showed comparable inter-correlations with those for the standard GHQ-28. Power was able to use a six-month follow-up test to determine the reliability of the scale to take account of the problems associated with recall. At both times, respondents also completed the standard GHQ-28 to determine current health. However, cautions were noted that comparisons would have to be made with a clinical interview before any conclusions could be reached about threshold levels for determining impaired mental health.

A Worst Time version of the GHQ-12 was used in the latest study in England and Wales to measure the short- to mid-term psychological effects during or following the flooding. Results showed significant differences for both women and men compared to current GHQ-12 results, although re-testing to determine the reliability of the instrument was not possible. Two-thirds of flooded respondents (64 per cent) were found to have experienced significant mental health problems (Worst Time GHQ-12 score of four or more) at the time when their health was perceived as most seriously affected after the flood. For some respondents the worst time was reported as being during the first few weeks following flooding, while for others it was several months later. The median worst time was around one month after flooding.

There were significant differences between men and women with the Worst Time GHQ-12 method data, with 68 per cent of women displaying mental health effects compared with 55 per cent of men. These were significantly higher than the current GHQ-12 scores (Table 4.2) and indicate that women experience more severe effects in the shorter term than men, but that they appear to recover over time. Variations with age were not significant. However, the 65 and over age groups do appear different and, counter-intuitively, less affected. This is borne out by significant differences in the 'worst time' mean scores of the 65 and over age group compared with the rest.

To assess the intensity of mental health effects, the PTSS survey instrument was administered to respondents.

Post-Traumatic Stress Scale (PTSS)

There have been a number of studies focusing on post-traumatic stress disorder (PTSD) and flooding (e.g. Auger et al, 2000; Waelde et al, 2001; McMillen et al, 2002; Norris et al, 2002; Verger et al, 2003). A new survey instrument, the PTSS (Scott and Dua, 1999), was used with flooded respondents in the latest study in an attempt to measure PTSD. The PTSS is designed to measure the frequency, severity and duration of symptoms and is a tool to categorize whether or not subjects are suffering from PTSD. Unlike the GHQ, it focuses on a traumatic event (in this case, the worst flood people had experienced) and seeks information about respondents' current state of mind and symptoms. The PTSS poses questions on re-experiencing the traumatic event, numbing and avoidance, and hyper-arousal. A good method for interpreting symptoms is the PTSD Intensity Score, which is based on the sum of the frequency multiplied by distress scores for the symptom questions. The overall possible score can range from 0 to 272.

Results showed a small proportion of flooded respondents (15 per cent) to still be suffering from mild to more severe symptoms of post-traumatic stress as measured by the PTSD Intensity Score, despite the passage of time since the flood events. For the 747 flooded respondents (76 per cent) who completed the PTSS, the mean score was 21 (range from 0 to 121). However, the mean intensity scores varied considerably in the two pilot studies for the research and in the main survey, indicating that location may be a contributing factor.

Five symptoms featured very strongly in the results; these were:

1 being reminded of the flood by triggers;
2 feeling nervous/tense/having palpitations;
3 recurring memories of the flood;
4 difficulty falling or staying asleep; and
5 being overtly alert or watchful for no reason.

There were significant differences found when gender and age were considered. Women showed higher PTSD Intensity Scores than men, while those aged between 60–64 showed higher scores than older or younger respondents.

Although the PTSS has not been previously used in the UK, the findings are consistent with those found in the work of Scott and Dua (1999). While the general level of stress among flooded respondents was not as high as in other trauma groups, it was certainly higher than non-trauma groups in other studies (Scott and Dua, 1999) and it is clear that some people are severely affected.

Factors that modify the impact of exposure to flooding

A number of factors have been suggested as possibly contributing to mental health effects related to disasters such as flooding. These can include socio-demographic aspects of flooded populations which make them more vulnerable to the effects of flooding, aspects of the stressor event itself (flood), factors associated with post-event recovery, and individual psychological resources, characteristics and perceptions.

Vulnerability to the impacts of flooding

There has been much discussion during recent years on whether certain individuals are likely to be more vulnerable to adverse health impacts from disasters than the population in general (Gleser et al, 1981; Steinglass and Gerrity, 1990; Enarson and Hearn-Morrow, 1998; Fordham, 1998; Morrow, 1999; Buckle et al, 2000). Evidence indicates that vulnerability to the health effects of flooding is more likely in individuals such as women; the elderly and infirm; the very young; those with low incomes; ethnic minorities; and those with pre-existing health problems. This was confirmed in some of the findings from the research. However, there could be a number of explanatory factors and some caution is needed in interpreting the results.

In the recent study, whichever health measure was used, women were found to be more affected at the time of the flood than men. This is normally attributed to women's role as homemaker and carer, a role that is particularly affected by flooding but which continues during recovery from the event. Research also suggests that strong marital ties can exacerbate the negative psychological consequence of disasters for women who have experienced flooding (Gleser et al, 1981; Solomon et al, 1987). Solomon et al (1987) found that although excellent spouse support attenuated men's symptomology, its presence was associated with an exacerbation of symptoms in exposed women. This is not always the case and there was evidence from the qualitative research that the experience of being flooded had strengthened some relationships. However, strong family ties may be more burdensome than supportive for women in times of extreme stress, adding to their responsibilities. The chair of a local flood action group in one flooded location echoed these sentiments:

> *Because of this... 'I'm supposed to cope' attitude ... it's the women, isn't it, you know this... it's the women... regardless of the circumstances, I am supposed to prepare a meal, I am supposed to deal with the shopping, I am supposed to have the food available for my family, I am supposed to cope with the ironing and the washing, even though I don't have a washing machine or an iron, it's sort of ... what's been drilled into them... the women deal with the children and food and the cooking.* (female five months after flood, 2000)

However, findings from the research indicate that women's mental health improves over time, possibly once the home is back in order and normal life is resumed.

Findings on age as a factor affecting the impacts of disasters are mixed (Huerta and Horton, 1978; Gleser et al, 1981; Ticehurst et al, 1996). In the latest study, those aged in their early 60s and, in some instances, in their 50s were generally shown to have been affected more than those of older or younger ages; the relationship between effect and age is therefore non-linear. Although the very elderly and infirm may suffer more effects, there is also evidence that elderly persons cope quite well with disaster situations. They tend to report fewer adverse emotional effects and feelings of relative deprivation than younger people who may be more at risk because they have greater burdens before the disaster strikes and they assume greater obligations afterwards. This was evidenced in both the qualitative and quantitative research findings.

One age group that has often been ignored in disaster studies, despite often being among the most affected, is that of children (Flynn and Nelson, 1998). Fifty-six per cent of children (271) within flooded households in the study were reported by parents to have experienced psychological impacts. These effects were lower in most cases than those reported by adult respondents for themselves and may be because of difficulty in assessing impacts on other members of the family; the data should therefore be treated with caution. As with the adults, anxiety during rainfall was reported for the highest percentage (29 per cent), followed by increased stress levels (11 per cent) and sleeping problems (10 per cent). Nightmares, bedwetting, behavioural changes and tantrums were commonly reported in the qualitative studies, and children were particularly distressed at losing their possessions:

> *...he was telling his friends at school what had happened; [he had lost his] play station, Pokemon cards, you know, to us they sound petty and pathetic, but to him it meant the earth, just like my photographs and personal possessions meant to me.* (female five months after flood, 2000)

Findings from qualitative research following flooding in north Wales and the north-east of England found some significant impacts on children, which some parents thought had been ignored (Hill and O'Brien, 1999; Tapsell and Tunstall, 2001). One important impact can be the disruption to their familiar daily routines. This may mean having to miss out on regular activities because of temporarily living elsewhere, because the activity is cancelled due to the flooding, or because parents can no longer afford to pay for activities due to the financial impact of the flooding:

> *It's like my little boy, he keeps saying about Christmas and I said, you know, this year you're going to have to ... not do without ... but not get as much as you normally do, I said, because ... you know, I need things for my house.* (female five months after flood, 2000)

Allen and Rosse (1998) also suggest that children are highly sensitive to post-disaster distress and conflict within the family. On a similar note, Deering (2000) suggests a strong role for parents in conditioning children's response – for example, in restoring routines and in providing reassurance. Interestingly, in the latest study, analysis showed that the presence of children in the house was associated with greater self-reported psychological health effects for all adults. Results from the qualitative research indicate that this is possibly due to parents' responsibility for and anxiety about their children's safety and well-being.

Factors influencing health measures

In analysing the data from the latest quantitative survey, the degree of health impact was associated with a wide range of factors: socio-demographic; flood characteristics; and post-flood characteristics/events. Table 4.3 shows the significance of key factors identified in multivariate analysis as influencing the health measures used in the study.

Gender and age have already been highlighted as being potential factors affecting flood impacts. There was also evidence that factors such as depth of flooding, prior health and evacuation were also significant in affecting health measures. However, dealing with insurance claims was one of the most significant variables affecting the health measures.

Flood insurance is available in England and Wales as a standard feature in household policies, which is an unusual arrangement compared with many European countries and North America. In the survey, 93 per cent of respondents had flood insurance; the mean value of insurance claims paid to households was around UK£27,000. Delayed settlement of insurance claims was frequently cited as a stressor in the qualitative research:

> *... every time we contacted them, 'oh that's not our department', 'that goes to so and so', and 'it's been an absolute nightmare of phone calls'; it took them weeks to sort anything out.* (female five months after flood, 2000)

Table 4.3 *Significance of key factors identified in multivariate regression analysis as influencing health measures used in the study*

Significance	PTSD Intensity Score as Ln (P+1)[b]	Current GHQ-12 Likert	GHQ-12 Likert at worst time
Highly significant P<0.001	Problems with insurers Prior health Gender	Prior health	Problems with insurers Gender Prior health
Significant P<0.05	Evacuation Flood depth Warning time Time to get back to normal Vulnerable housing Contamination of floodwaters Aged 65+	Time to get home back to normal Area house price Problems with insurers	Uninsured losses Evacuation Time to get back to normal Contamination of floodwater Rented accommodation Warning time Aged 65+
Less significant P<0.10		Support received	
Overall R^2	0.26	0.34	0.26
Adjusted R^{2a}	0.24	0.33	0.24
Number of observations	629	733	507

Notes: See Tunstall et al (2006) for a more detailed discussion of these factors.

[a] The adjusted R^2 indicates the proportion of the variance in the health measure explained by the listed factors.
[b] The PTSD intensity score with 1 added (PTSD + 1) was converted through a log 10 transformation (Ln).

Moreover, those people with lower socio-economic status may have few resources to pay for flood insurance and are therefore at greater risk of losses, and the potential health implications resulting from such losses, than those who have insurance cover.

In many disaster studies reviewed by Norris et al (2001a), other factors identified as modifying the impact of disaster exposure included troubled interpersonal relationships; family strains; social disruption; and occupational and financial stress. These factors and others which affected the recovery process and impacted upon the longer-term well-being of flooded respondents were evidenced in the England and Wales studies, as illustrated in Table 4.4.

Table 4.4 *Factors identified as modifying flood exposure and recovery impacts*

Factors	Evidence	Illustration
Interpersonal relationships and family strains	Marital stress has been found to increase after disasters – strains in relationships were reported by 152 out of 982 respondents (16 per cent) following flooding (RPA et al, 2004). However, the experience of flooding may strengthen relationships and partners may provide strong emotional support (Tapsell et al, 2003)	'I'm honest, I'm very surprised there aren't ten divorces at least...Yes, very surprised. I mean you want to live here and hear the arguments going on between man and wife, and the kids' (male five months after flood, 2000) 'I go and look at the river, there's a row... what price husband and wife rowing just because you were flooded five years ago and nobody's done a thing about it' (female 4.5 years after flood, 2002)
Financial stress and obligations to provide financial and social support to others	Evidence from the 1990 Towyn and 1993 Aberconwy floods in north Wales (which directly affected some 9000 people) indicates that personal and family finance was one of the greatest concerns to the people affected (Hill and O'Brien, 1999)	'The value of the house – gone...The value of everything that was in the house had gone. About UK£100,000 gone. I'm 50, you know, and I don't want to start again after 50' (male five months after flood, 2000) 'Financially, it drains you. You don't realize it, it's slowly, it drains you all the time because you're needing things all the time – for the children' (female, 18 months after flood, 1999)
Occupational stress	Problems of coping with flood recovery while working full time are common. For some, the stress is doubled by their work premises also being flooded, which may result in job losses (Tapsell and Tunstall, 2001)	'A lot of people couldn't work initially. Many people [reported] sick and not for the physical illness. They couldn't cope with what was happening and they couldn't face going to work, and a lot of employers weren't sensitive to that' (female five months after flood, 2000)
Isolation	Lack of understanding by employers, work colleagues and even those living nearby who had not been flooded can lead to many people feeling isolated (Tapsell et al, 1999)	'There's no way anybody that hasn't been through it can fully understand... Everything, really from the panic of not knowing what to do, to lack of communication with other people. You feel terribly isolated to start with because you've got nobody to talk to' (male 18 months after flood, 1999)

Table 4.4 *Factors identified as modifying flood exposure and recovery impacts*
(continued)

Factors	Evidence	Illustration
Impacts upon personal identity and the sense of 'self' and 'place'	Flooding of homes is said to undermine people's individual sense of identify (Fullilove, 1996; Sime, 1997). Eighty-nine per cent of respondents in the latest study reported losing some irreplaceable items or items of sentimental value (RPA et al, 2004)	'Seeing all my home just covered in rubbish... everything just completely rubbished, it's like you feel as if your life as been turned into rubbish, it was really horrible' (female five months after flood, 2000) 'Well, you saw years of your life just disappearing under the water. And you didn't know what to do. That was it – gone, all that you'd worked and saved for, and everything else, was just going' (male seven months after flood, 1999)
Attachment to home and possessions	Possessions within the home can also assume considerable significance to people as attachment objects, helping to define who they are and who they care most about (Keene, 1998). Flooding can also lead to people losing this attachment (Tapsell et al, 1999)	'My mother's sewing box my father made her, it went somewhere down through the floor and you know, OK, maybe we'll get a new sewing box, but it won't be my mother's box' (female five months after flood, 2000) 'We lost interest in the house when it flooded; we lost interest in it as a home. It wasn't a home anymore' (male seven months after flood, 1999)
Loss of security in home	Homes are often conceived as emotional and physical sanctuaries from the outside world. The experience of being flooded may lead people to redefine their concept of 'home' (McCarthy, 2004)	'...but if you haven't got your home, you haven't got that sense of security and the fundamental sense of well-being and being alright' (female five months after flood, 2000)

Psychosocial resources

The most frequently reported mental health effect from the self-reporting health checklists mentioned above was increased levels of anxiety, which was reported by 55 per cent of flooded respondents. This anxiety was also evidenced in results of the PTSS and GHQ-12. Some of this anxiety was severe and persisted for several years following flooding. According to Beck

(1976), the factors involved in the occurrence of more severe and persistent anxiety can be divided into two categories:

1 factors that lead people to experience relatively greater levels of anxiety (in this case, the experience of being flooded); and
2 factors involved in the maintenance of high levels of anxiety (e.g. subsequent heavy rainfall and anxiety about future flooding, and lack of confidence in the responsible authorities to provide protection from flooding or a flood warning).

In psychology, cognitive theory proposes that people experiencing anxiety *believe* that they are threatened with either physical or social harm. Whether or not the harm they fear is objectively present is immaterial to the *experience* of anxiety (Salkovskis, 1996). One of the hallmark symptoms of PTSD is physiological reactivity to traumatic reminders, which in the event of flooding might be heavy rainfall (evidenced in the PTSS scores). Beck et al (1985) describe a useful conceptualization of the cognitive component of anxiety that appears relevant to flooding:

$$\text{Anxiety} = \frac{\text{Perceived probability of threat} \times \text{Perceived cost/awfulness of danger}}{\text{Perceived ability to cope with danger} + \text{Perceived 'rescue factors'}}$$

Perceived probability of threat
Studies have shown that worry about the risk of future flooding is extremely important. Worry is closely associated with perceived risk, being a function of beliefs as to the likelihood of the event and its consequences (Green et al, 1987). An increased perception of likelihood of danger would therefore result in an increase in anxiety, as illustrated by many focus group respondents:

> *The anxiety is still very much there... It's just this awful sense of menacing foreboding that keeps happening every time there's heavy rain... we're still as we were before, except that now we expect it, whereas before [we didn't].* (female 18 months after flood, 1999)

> *It's just the sort of tension of waiting for it to happen ... to be quite fair ... I don't think it will ever happen again. But it's ... it's the fear of the fear.* (male 4.5 years after flood, 2002)

The maintenance of the anxiety can result in selective attention – that is, the noticing of stimuli consistent with the perceived danger. This noticing of danger signs may then erroneously be interpreted as a sign that the danger has really increased, thus increasing concern and reinforcing the interpretation. For example, those people who have experienced their homes being flooded frequently report observing high river levels after the flood (which they then associate with the threat of further flooding), when they had not associated high river levels with flooding before the flood. Moreover, the experience of being flooded leads many people to adopt behavioural responses, such as constant monitoring of river levels. Safety-seeking behaviours, such as staying up all night during heavy rainfall, can also reinforce the perceived threat:

> *Well, I keep watching the river. I even stand on the chair near the window and then I can see the bridge and see how far up the waters are.* (female five months after flood, 2000)

> *Well, I just think it's so sad that you get up to go to work on a morning and before you go to work you walk round and check on the river ... I mean, I would never have dreamed of it [before the flood].* (male five months after flood, 2000)

Perceived cost and awfulness of danger

The level of flood impacts and perceived cost and awfulness of these impacts (e.g. levels of damage to property and contents, household disruption, and risk to life and injury) can multiply the perceived threat. Disruption of normal household and community life and activities were found in the research to be a key factor in affecting mental health impacts from flooding. Much of the disruption related to returning the house to normal (cleaning, repairing and refurbishing) and was often associated with having to live for months in damp and dusty conditions, often on upper floors of the property or in rented accommodation. In the latest study, the mean length of time for households to return to normal was 31 weeks and the mean length of time until all those living in the household had returned (for the 64 per cent who had moved out of their homes after flooding) was 23 weeks:

> *I think we've lost a year of our lives... Just totally blotted; we might as well forget about it.* (female five months after flood, 2000)

The perceived probability of the threat of future flooding multiplied by the perceived costs and impacts therefore serve to increase levels of anxiety.

Perceived ability to cope with danger

The combination of risk and cost may be modulated by the extent to which people perceive that they would be able to cope or not cope with the danger, and the extent to which factors external to themselves would be involved, such as support from others. Perceptions of coping capacity vary depending upon many factors, including individuals' psychological characteristics:

> *I couldn't cope with another flood; I've had enough this time. I would walk away; I would walk away from the whole lot. I mean, I've got a mortgage, I can't afford to, but I would, I feel like doing that now because I've just had enough.* (female five months after flood, 2000)

> *I felt like a robot. I cried but it was all more a dream; it was just like, I just didn't have any emotions... I just wanted to forget. We were all a bit traumatized; it was all strange, very strange, but it didn't get emotional or uncontrollable, it was all more... we'll cope.* (male five months after flood, 2000)

With flooding, people's anxiety may result partly from the perception that they have no control over being flooded. This 'loss of control' may be a stressor in its own right and can explain the high levels of continuing anxiety and worry expressed by residents. Losses in psychological resources (such as sense of control) may exacerbate the impact of flooding on psychological distress. Increasing coping strategies and psychological resources could therefore help to moderate the mental health effects of flooding.

Perceived 'rescue factors'

Rescue factors such as systems of post-flood social support may also prove to be important in moderating some of the mental health effects resulting from flooding. Findings from the qualitative and quantitative studies showed that most support received was from neighbours or family. According to Norris et al (2001b), those who believe that they are cared for by others, and that help will be available if needed, fare better psychologically than those who believe they are unloved and alone.

However, there is some confusion about the effectiveness of different types of support received following disasters. Although there is a need to provide some form of early intervention and crisis support (Eyre, 2002), conclusions drawn from studies on psychological debriefing are mixed (NCPTSD, 2001). Kaniasty and Norris (1993), Lutgendorf et al (1995) and Haines et al (1996, 1999) all found that social support moderated the impact of a disaster on psychological distress. However, there is little evidence as to which forms of social support are the most effective. Green (1988) found that the extent and type of social support received by people who had been flooded seemed to have no effect on their reported stress or extent of disruption caused during a flood event.

After the 1993 Aberconwy flooding in Wales, social workers called on houses to ask if people needed any support. This gave people the opportunity to talk through their experiences and to seek counselling, something the majority would not have proactively sought (Hill and O'Brien, 1999). In England, the Lewes Flood Aftercare Group was formed by various statutory and voluntary-sector organizations following flooding in the town. The group was seen as a success in providing emotional, informational, practical and social support to over 250 people (Lewes Flood Aftercare Group, 2001).

There does appear to be evidence, therefore, that aiding people's capacity to cope and providing appropriate, adequate and timely support may serve to moderate mental health effects and to reduce levels of anxiety. This might include therapies such as cognitive restructuring to help people in reassessing their perceptions about flooding and their ability to cope with potential future flood events.

Responses and policy implications

Any possible increase in the occurrence of future floods is likely to have implications for human mental health, as well as implications for government policies to address potential impacts. A number of pre- and post-disaster strategies and measures can be implemented to increase coping capacity and reduce vulnerability, and thereby minimize the effects of flooding on people's mental health.

It is a given of emergency management that self-reliance, individual and local preparedness, and awareness of the risks faced are all elements that are important in reducing vulnerability to flooding. The nature of action at the local level to protect against floods depends fundamentally upon awareness of flood risk and of how people perceive the risk. In England and Wales the Environment Agency has been increasing public awareness of flood risks through annual awareness campaigns at both national and local levels. This is particularly crucial in locations where flood risk awareness is low. Preparedness planning is also essential alongside the provision of information on effective prevention and protection methods, and education on the potential mental health risks and impacts from exposure to flooding.

To reduce the human health impacts, it is important, where possible, to prevent human populations from exposure to floods either by providing structural flood defences or other non-structural measures designed to reduce exposure and consequences. Ways need to be found to help people adapt to living with the risk of flooding. In England and Wales, adaptation to living with the increased risk of future flooding is currently being considered by those government agencies responsible for flood risk management. With the realization that it is no longer feasible to be able to offer protection from all floods (Environment Agency, 2003), recent years have seen a policy shift in emphasis from focusing on defending against floods to managing the risk of flooding. A consultation document for developing the future flood risk management strategy in England highlighted the importance of non-structural measures, such as improved flood forecasting and warning systems, flood insurance and effective land-use management (Defra, 2004).

At the household level, self-help measures to reduce the damage to property and the stress caused by flooding are encouraged, thereby alleviating some of the negative consequences on people's mental health. These measures include promoting flood insurance and flood-proofing of properties. At the community level, improved flood warning and evacuation systems, community and flood action groups, voluntary associations and religious institutions may provide emotional and practical support and advice. The National Flood Forum in England has campaigned for grants to be made available to those living in at-risk areas for the flood-proofing of properties, as awareness and take-up of these products are currently low.

Health-related responses and policies to promote population resilience to flooding must include practical support for individuals who are flooded and provision of adequate psychological support (Reacher et al, 2004). Yet, few national disaster plans explicitly address measures to deal with psychosocial aspects of flooding (PAHO, 1999). NSW Health (2000) in Australia stresses that mental health 'first aid' (in terms of psychological first aid, triage, assessment, referral and interventions) needs to be part of an emergency health care response. Outreach activities may include psycho-education, revisiting pre-existing ways of coping, ensuring medication of psychiatric cases and creating self-help groups.

What is interesting from the current research is that many of the key factors that appear to influence the mental health effects of flooding are those which are susceptible to human intervention and management (Tunstall et al, 2006 press). Notably, measures such as having adequate insurance cover and, more particularly, the way in which insurance companies process flood claims can have a highly significant impact on health outcomes. Much, therefore, depends upon the efficiency and professionalism of insurance company personnel and building contractors, as well as help made available within communities by local authorities and emergency services. This suggests that the management of post-flood response by community and professional agencies can have a significant impact on mental health outcomes and needs to be more seriously addressed by all those involved. Imposing a legally binding 'duty of care' on insurance companies could be one measure for facilitating and aiding post-flood recovery.

Future research needs

There are a number of areas where further research in the UK and other developed countries is needed to help understand the mental health effects from flooding and how to address them. First, there is still a need for much better information, particularly of a quantitative nature, on mental health impacts and appropriate interventions. Good evidence in the form of more extensive prospective and longitudinal studies (including clinical interviews) is needed with those who experience flooding to confirm the results reported in this chapter and elsewhere. In particular, direct research on the impacts on children, rather than relying on reporting by parents, is needed.

Although the levels of explanation offered by the statistical analyses in the case study discussed in this chapter were reasonable by social science standards, much of the variance in the health effects of flooding remained unexplained. Therefore, further research to investigate other factors such as personality, life history and community organization is needed.

Data is also needed on the impacts upon medical services through increased hospital admissions and consultations following flooding. The health economic costs in terms of time taken off work, inefficient working, and the costs of prescriptions and medications also need to be assessed. These costs could run into millions of pounds in the long term and increase the argument for the emphasis on preventive measures. More research is also required on whether mental health impacts, where they are unavoidable, will respond best to psychological and/or pharmacological interventions delivered through health services, or whether the interventions would best be targeted at providing financial or other assistance. As 50 per cent of prescribed medication is not taken (L. McKenna, pers comm, 2005) and medicine that sedates may contribute to making people less able to respond to any future flooding, indications point to increased emphasis on other types of assistance.

There is a further need, therefore, for evidence of the benefits of mediating or moderating roles for coping and social support. The distribution of post-disaster help is often dependent upon network size or political influence and is not necessarily allocated by need. As a result, access to social support needs to be further explored and it is crucial to understand the processes that influence the receipt or mobilization of such support – for example, through awareness of levels of social capital and social networks, and membership of flood action groups.

A better understanding of how the responses of insurance companies and other professionals may influence mental health effects is crucial with a view to making improvements in respective standards of service. Finally, there is an ongoing need for better understanding of vulnerability and resilience factors in relation to flood risks and impacts, and in providing more appropriate and better-targeted measures to mitigate these.

Conclusion

Results confirm that even in developed countries where floods may be relatively small scale and shallow, the impacts on people's mental health can be significant and are not only restricted to the immediate post-event period. Mental health problems identified include increased levels of stress and anxiety and other symptoms of common mental disorders, and, for a minority, post-traumatic stress disorder. Differences were also identified in levels of impacts according to gender and age.

The findings show that the measures of health used were able to differentiate between current health status and people's perception of their health during and after the flood. They also show that the current health status of respondents is linked to the health effects experienced at the time of the flood and its aftermath. The GHQ-12, if applied retrospectively to the 'worst time' following the flood, provided a reasonable measure of the short-term psychological effects, while the PTSS provided a reasonable measure of the long-term effects. Results from the GHQ-12 and the Worst Time version both suggest that better long-term psychological support systems need to be in place following flood events.

The factors that moderate the impacts of floods on human mental health are many and complex, and more investigations are necessary before a better understanding of these can be reached. If future predictions of more frequent flooding are to be taken seriously, actions need to be taken now to prepare for and address the potential mental health impacts on flooded populations. Although not all flooding can be prevented, more can be done to reduce people's vulnerability and increase their resilience and capacity for recovery, thereby helping to prevent or reduce the mental health impacts.

5

The Mozambique Floods of 2000: Health Impact and Response

Sandy Cairncross and Manuel Alvarinho

Introduction

In this chapter we document what is now acknowledged to have been a relatively well-managed response to unprecedented catastrophic flooding in a very poor country. Using government health surveillance data, we derive approximate estimates of the burden of disease-associated mortality attributable to the floods of 2000 in Mozambique, and compare it with the long-term impact of the disruption that the floods brought to the national economy. We then place the discussion of health impacts within the context of overall preparedness, emergency response and recovery activities, and discuss prospects of future mitigation of flood impacts in the country.

Flooding in Mozambique

Mozambique is perhaps the most flood-prone country in Africa. In addition to the Limpopo, Save and Zambezi, a number of other rivers bring water from neighbouring countries in the west and discharge into the Indian Ocean. Roughly one third of the country's land area is floodplain or at least below 100m in altitude. Tropical storms frequently build in the Indian Ocean; when they move westwards with the prevailing trade winds, Mozambique is their first landfall.

As a result, the country is no stranger to flooding (Bolton, 1983). Soon after independence, the Limpopo floods of 1977, the worst on record, were followed in 1978 by serious flooding on the Zambezi and Licungo. Both events killed scores of people and affected hundreds of thousands more. In 1984, floods followed famine in the south, submerging the Maputo City waterworks, 90 years old and never flooded, under 2m of water. In early 1996, all the rivers in the south of the country, from the Zambezi down, flooded again. One year later, severe flooding of the Buzi, Púngoè and Zambezi rivers in central Mozambique cut the east–west road connection between Mozambique and Zimbabwe for a fortnight. In 1999, there were serious local floods in Sofala and Inhambane provinces, which severed the country's main north–south road artery for a similar period. After the 2000 floods that form the main focus of this chapter, there were again severe floods in central Mozambique in 2001, caused by the Zambezi, and in 2003, by the River Save.

The 2000 floods and their extent

Heavy rains in December and early January 2000 caused the Incomati, Maputo and Umbelúzi rivers to burst their banks; but the damage this caused was local and not unusual. By the end of January, the flood levels were falling; but in early February Cyclone Connie passed slowly over southern Mozambique and then continued to drop record rainfall on the neighbouring countries upstream. The Incomati River washed away the hydrological gauging equipment at the South African border and flooded the main road north from Maputo, cutting the capital off from the rest of the country. The Limpopo swelled to the level of the record-breaking 1977 flood, which had killed 300 people.

As if that was not enough, on 22 February, Cyclone Eline hit the coast of Mozambique halfway between Maputo and Beira, and moved inland towards South Africa and Zimbabwe, dumping more rain on already sodden land to drain into rivers that were already overflowing. When the third flood wave on the Limpopo reached Xai-xai, capital of Gaza Province, it was 3m higher than the highest previous flood level. Reaching a maximum flow of 10,000 cubic metres per second, it was the worst flood in at least 150 years. Four other major rivers – the Save (whose peak flow equalled that of the Limpopo), the Buzi, the Umbeluzi and the Incomati – were now flooding simultaneously. Indeed, the Limpopo overflowed onto the Incomati's floodplain, creating a vast unified flood that was 120km across at its widest point and covered an area of 30,000 square kilometres – nearly as large as The Netherlands (see Figure 5.1).

Health impacts

Immediate impacts

The government estimated that 700 people died in the floods, mostly by drowning. Remarkably, an estimated 45,000 people were rescued and taken to places of safety, roughly half by Mozambican military and civilian boats, and half by South African and Malawian helicopters. Without these efforts, many of these would have died. An additional 500,000 people were forced to leave their homes, and 140,000ha of fields under crops were lost. Altogether some 2 million people, or more than 10 per cent of the country's population, were affected by the floods. In Gaza, the province through which the Limpopo flows, it was estimated that 300,000 were affected out of a population of 1.1 million.

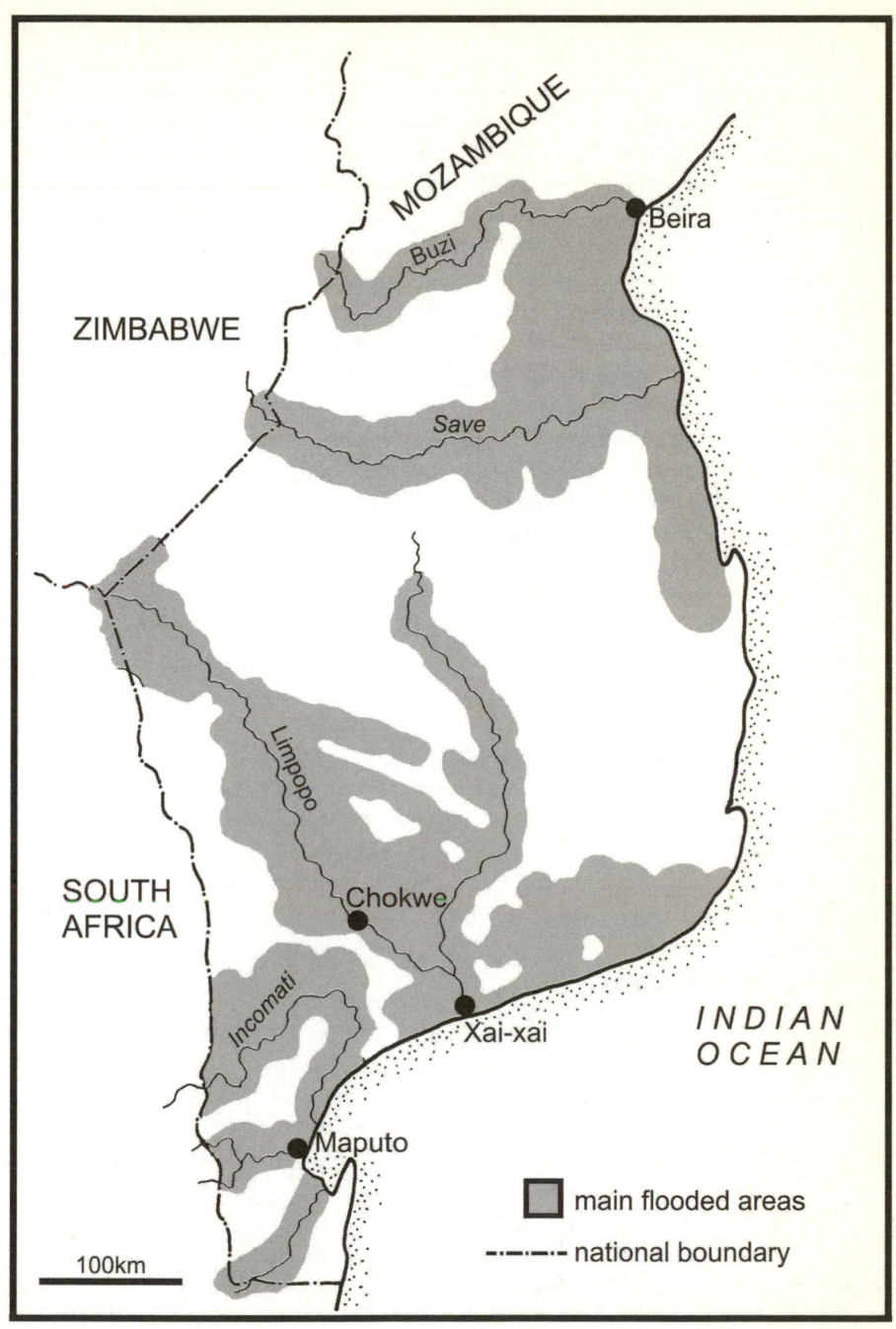

Figure 5.1 *Southern Mozambique, showing the areas flooded in 2000*

Source: adapted from Government of Mozambique (2000)

More than 100,000 of the displaced people were accommodated in three centres. However, a doctor with experience of the camps for refugees from Mozambique's civil war in the 1990s commented on the very different mood of the flood victims, who in spite of their material losses were relatively cheerful and eager to return to their houses and farms (J. Cliff, pers comm, 2004).

Damage to infrastructure included more than 200km of electrical power lines and 300km of roads (Government of Mozambique, 2000). The Health Ministry reported that one major hospital had been partially destroyed, in addition to the total or partial destruction of 4 rural hospitals, 39 health centres and a number of stores for medical supplies. Needless to say, the medical supplies and equipment in those health centres and stores were also lost. The Ministry of Education estimated that 1300 classrooms were damaged, mostly in primary schools.

In Gaza Province alone, over 300 rural water points, mainly hand pumps on wells or boreholes, were damaged out of a total of 800. Over 40,000 of the province's 100,000 pit latrines were destroyed by the flood. In the urban areas, not only were the cities of Chokwe and Xai-xai flooded to between 2m and 4m in depth, causing 3000 septic tanks to overflow, but the piped water supplies in eight smaller towns were damaged.

The total cost of loss and damage to assets, inventories and infrastructure, as well as lost output and earnings, was estimated at more than US$0.5 billion (World Bank, 2000), or some 15 per cent of the country's US$3.4 billion gross domestic product (GDP).

A recent literature review on flooding and health (Ahern et al, 2005) has noted that the most important health impacts of major flood events are usually related to diarrhoeal diseases, including cholera and dysentery, and to vector-borne diseases, particularly malaria in settings where it is already endemic. The existing literature and their own previous experience led the Mozambican authorities to expect these, and the actual impacts are considered below.

Diarrhoeal diseases

Figures 5.2 to 5.4 show the annual incidence (in cases per thousand population) of cholera, dysentery and diarrhoeal diseases, in general, during the years before and following the floods, as reported in the Chokwe area (the city and the surrounding rural district), in the Xai-xai area and in the rest of Gaza Province by the routine communicable disease surveillance system of the Ministry of Health. All three figures show increases in incidence for Chokwe and Xai-xai, in the epicentre of the flood zone, which are greater than for the province as a whole and which are followed by decreases to lower values in the following years. The timing of the increase in incidence in 2000, first recorded during late April as health services were gradually returning to normal, also supports the hypothesis that it is a consequence of the floods. There is certainly no reason to believe that the increase was due to improved reporting in the immediate flood aftermath since no additional surveillance system was set up at the time.

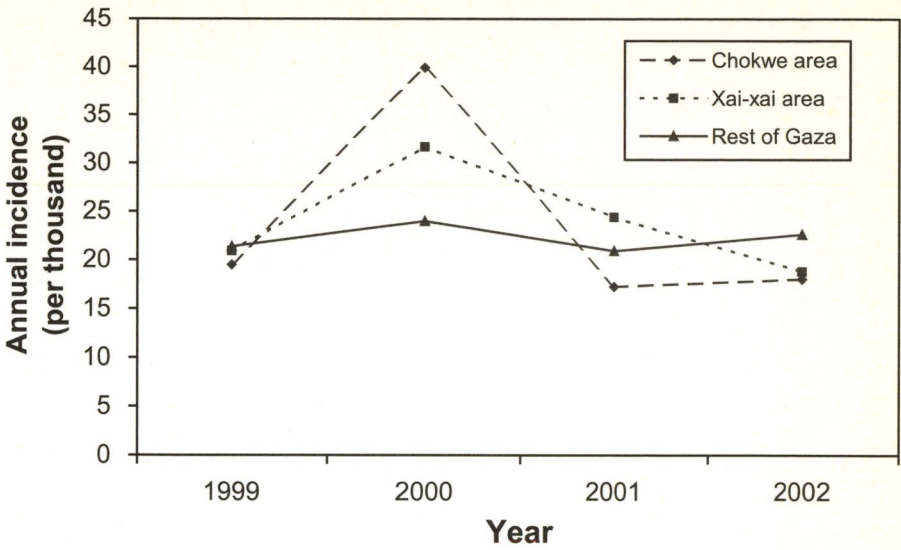

Figure 5.2 *Diarrhoea reported in Gaza Province, 1999–2002*

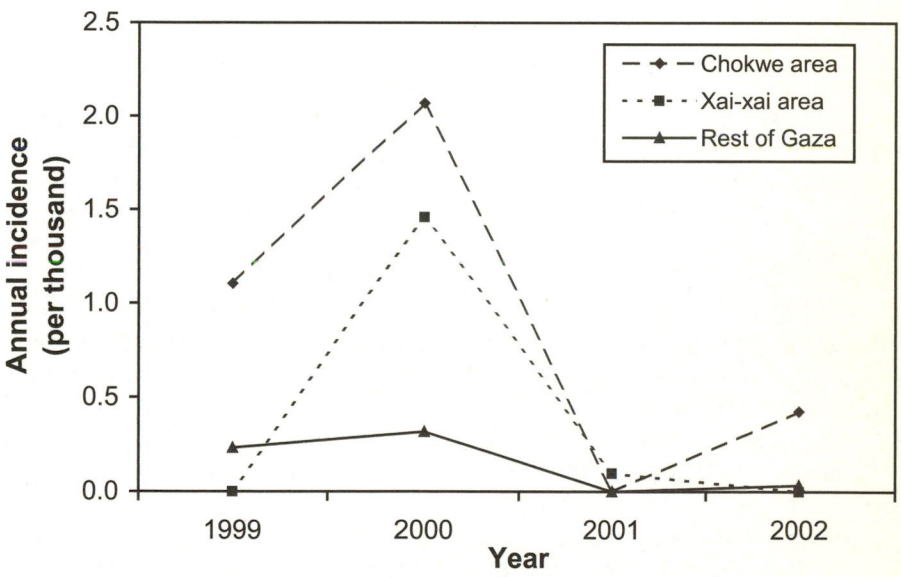

Figure 5.3 *Cholera reported in Gaza Province, 1999–2002*

Attributing a precise number of cases to the floods is not so easy, however. Only a proportion of cases are reported to a health centre, and this proportion is likely to have been smaller during the disruption caused by the floods, when health centres were inaccessible or submerged. Moreover, the differences in incidence between 1999 and 2001 illustrate the variations between years which

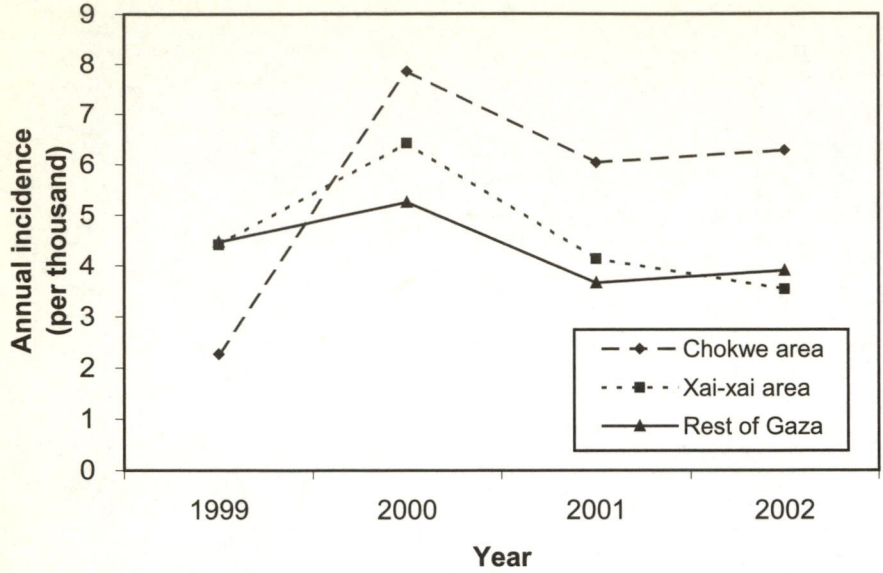

Figure 5.4 *Dysentery reported in Gaza Province, 1999–2002*

occur in the normal course of events. Taking as a baseline the means of the incidences in 1999 and 2001, the floods appear to have caused, at the very minimum, the numbers of cases shown in Table 5.1.

One might think that the cases of diarrhoea which are reported would be likely to be the more severe and life-threatening ones, with a higher case fatality ratio than that in the community at large. Nevertheless, Kotloff et al (1999) estimated from Gambian and Bangladesh data that the number of deaths from diarrhoeal disease in the community was of the order of six to eight times greater than in health facilities. Unfortunately, such studies comparing hospital deaths with mortality rates in the community at large are very rare; one such study in Lesotho (Feachem et al, 1978) found that only 1 in 15 deaths of children under five was recorded in a health facility. In the calculations below, we follow Kotloff et al (1999) and vary this 'community multiplier' from four to ten.

The most authoritative case fatality ratio identified by Kotloff et al (1999) for bacillary dysentery in developing countries is that of 11 per cent, published by Bennish and Wojtyniak (1991), which is based on 14 years of data. Excluding accounts from individual communities, where the research team's intervention is likely to have depressed the case fatality ratio, values reported from epidemics range from 4.5 per cent in Zimbabwe (Nathoo, 1997) to 13 per cent in northern KwaZulu-Natal, South Africa (Chopra et al, 1997).

Case fatality ratios reported for cholera during recent years have varied between 1.7 per cent for a flood-related outbreak in West Bengal (Sur et al, 2000) to 2.5 per cent in Uganda (Legros et al, 2000) and 5.1 per cent in an urban outbreak in Zambia (CDC, 2004a). The higher rates in Africa may be due to relative unfamiliarity with the disease and its appropriate management. Brown et al (2002) also point out that cholera fatality ratios are high in settings of social disruption, such as refugee camps, where they can exceed 5 per cent.

With regard to other diarrhoeal diseases, mainly occurring among children, the review by Kosek et al (2003) could find case fatality ratios for paediatric diarrhoea in developing countries from only two studies: 0.11 per cent for children under five in New Guinea, and 1.27 per cent for children under three in India. In the latter case, the mothers had received training in the home management of diarrhoea without which, according to the study author, the ratio would have been higher. On the other hand, the figure for other ages would be lower. Bearing in mind that most diarrhoea episodes and deaths are among children under three years' old, we extend these ratios to all ages.

Taking clinical case fatality ratios and multiplying by four or ten to give deaths in the community suggests a total attributable mortality from all diarrhoeal diseases of between 200 and 4000 deaths (see Table 5.1). Most of these deaths, like the mortality from diarrhoea at other times, would be among children below the age of five years.

Table 5.1 *Reported cases of diarrhoeal disease attributable to the 2000 floods in Gaza, and estimates of the number of deaths in the population due to this cause*

	Cholera	*Dysentery*	*Other diarrhoea*	*Total*
Chokwe area	304	536	4308	5148
Xai-xai area	381	581	2429	3391
Rest of Gaza	127	955	1778	2860
Total cases	812	2072	8515	11,399
Case fatality ratio:				
Low estimate	1.7%	4.5%	0.11%	
High estimate	5.1%	13%	1.27%	
Community multiplier:				
Low	4	4	4	
High	10	10	10	
Hence, estimated deaths:				
Low	55	97	37	189
High	414	2694	1081	4189

Malaria

Apart from the diarrhoeal diseases, it was malaria which the Mozambican health authorities expected to result from the floods. Malaria was considered likely to result from the creation of new mosquito breeding sites as the water receded, and the bringing together of large numbers of people, which would favour transmission. Early reports from the National Disaster Management Institute and in the media (Christie and Hanlon, 2001, pp30, 45) suggested that a malaria epidemic might have been occurring. However, the Ministry of Health's statistics show no increase in the number of malaria cases reported to health facilities in Gaza Province during the floods (see Figure 5.5). The lack of a malaria epidemic may be due to the concerted action of the Ministry of Health, the United Nations Children's Fund (UNICEF) and non-governmental organizations (NGOs) which promoted insecticide-impregnated mosquito nets, sprayed some accommodation centres and switched the drug used for treatment from Chloroquine (requiring several doses) to single-dose Fansidar, which is more expensive but has more effect on transmission.

It has been suggested that the continuing increase in the incidence of malaria after the floods of 2000 was due to the formation of numerous small and permanent ponds in the area that had been flooded. Natural depressions in the sandy soil were sealed by sedimented silt so that they retained water

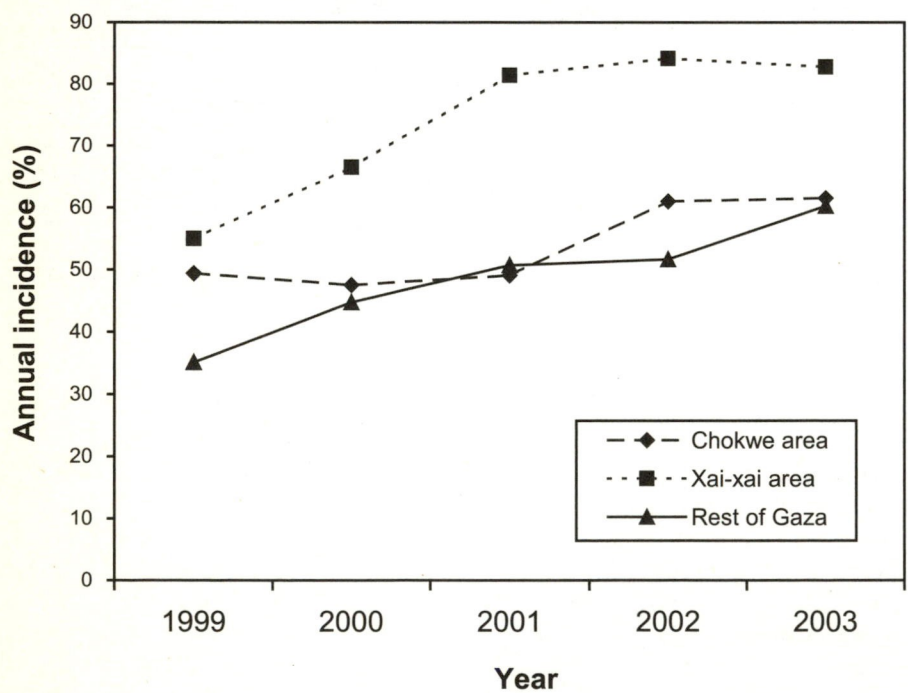

Figure 5.5 *Reported malaria in Gaza Province, 1999–2003*

after the floods receded. Many of them have persisted for several years since the floods and have altered the appearance of the landscape in areas such as Vilankulo when seen from the air. However, other explanations for the gradual and continuing increase in malaria cases are more plausible; they include increasing resistance of the malaria parasites to prophylactic antimalarial drugs in the area, and the increasing prevalence of AIDS (Craig et al, 2004).

Economic disruption and long-term health impacts

Unusually, gross domestic product data were published for individual provinces of Mozambique in the 2002 *Human Development Report* of the United Nations Development Programme (UNDP, 2002). Table 5.2 shows the figures for annual change (growth or decrease) in GDP, broken down by province, for 2000 and for the three years preceding the floods. The difference between the provinces affected by floods and the rest of the country is shown graphically in Figure 5.6. The impact of the floods on GDP can be seen in four of the five affected provinces.

For Maputo Province, the exception, the data for 2000 are distorted by the start of production at the MOZAL aluminium smelter, which boosted the province's manufactured production by 182 per cent and accounted for a 20 per cent growth in manufacturing industry at national level during that year. The GDP growth for Maputo Province in 2000 is therefore omitted from the following analysis.

Although the growth in the Mozambican economy had been gradually declining during the late 1990s, mainly due to the economic collapse in

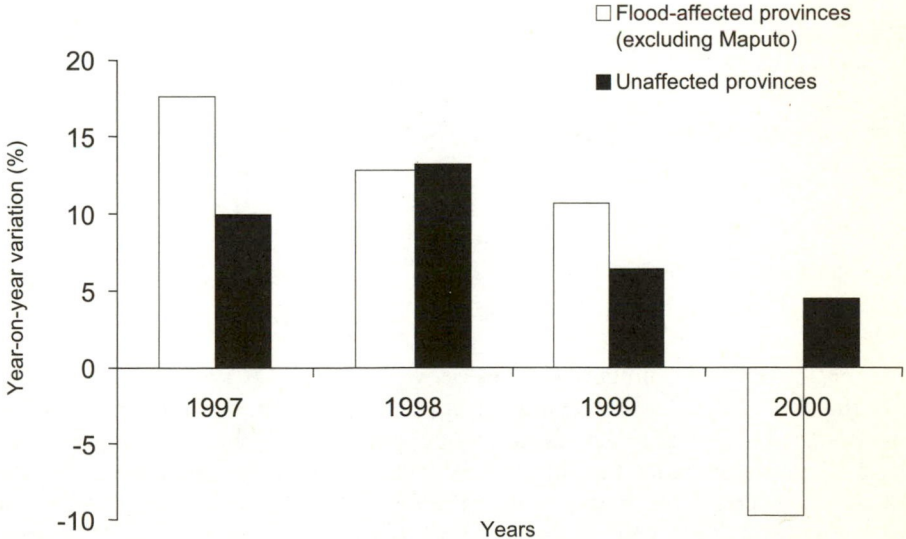

Figure 5.6 *Annual growth in GDP, Mozambique, 1997–2000*

neighbouring Zimbabwe, the provinces which were affected by floods in 2000 had been performing as well as, or better than, the others. In 2000, however, there was an absolute decline in GDP in those provinces by nearly 10 per cent, while the rest of the national economy continued to grow. The difference in growth between the flood-affected provinces and the others was statistically significant (p = 0.014).

Table 5.2 *Annual change in GDP by province, Mozambique, 1997–2000*

Province	Contribution to GDP[a] (percentage)	Annual change in GDP (percentage)			
		1997	1998	1999	2000
Not affected by floods:					
Maputo City	37	3.5	20.5	6.8	5.9
Niassa	3	18.7	3.9	11.5	6.9
Cabo Delgado	5	1.5	23.4	3.9	−1.3
Nampula	14	25.9	7.6	1.9	0.5
Zambezia	9	7.7	−3.4	8.1	0.8
Tete	5	19.8	1.1	12.5	16.6
Weighted average		9.9	13.3	6.4	4.5
Affected by floods:					
Manica	5	21.9	28.1	11.9	−11.1
Sofala	9	4.3	10.3	10.2	−10.5
Inhambane	5	8.3	8.4	10.0	−1.3
Gaza	4	19.1	14.1	9.5	−17.1
Maputo Province	5	45.3	5.6	12.2	26.5
Weighted average		17.6	12.8	10.7	−9.8[b]
National total	100	11.1	12.6	7.5	1.6

Notes: [a] In 1997.

[b] Excluding Maputo Province.

Source: adapted from UNDP (2002)

Taking the difference in growth rates between the affected and the unaffected provinces as a measure of the impact of the floods, it follows that the effect of the floods in 2000 was to depress the economic growth of the affected provinces by 14.3 per cent. Since the economies of these provinces (including Maputo Province) account for 28 per cent of the national GDP, this corresponds to a reduction of 4.0 per cent at national level – which explains most of the drop of 5.9 per cent in the national growth rate from the previous year (see Table 5.2).

Such a devastating effect is likely to have had a substantial impact on mortality, particularly infant mortality, which has long been known as a powerful indicator of the effect of poverty. Recent research on the association between gross domestic product and infant mortality rates (Jamison et al, 2004) suggests that much of it is attributable to heterogeneity in technical progress between countries. This leads to a figure for the elasticity of infant mortality rate with income that is less than had previously been thought, with a high estimate of −0.326 and low of −0.071. Since the damage wrought by the 2000 floods in Mozambique will have affected other sectors, particularly education and health care, which contribute to the model of Jamison et al (2004), the high estimate is more appropriate.

Taking elasticities of −0.071 and −0.326, respectively, the drop of −14.3 per cent in GDP for the flooded areas corresponds with increases in infant mortality rate of 1.01 per cent and 4.66 per cent – that is, from the existing Mozambican rate of 134.6 per 1000 live births (Macro International, 1998) to 136.0 and 140.9, an increase of 1.4 and 6.3 per 1000. Given Mozambique's birth rate of 44.4 per 1000 and a population of 5.982 million for the five flood-affected provinces (INE, 2004) these increases correspond to a low estimate of 364 and a high estimate of 1673 infant deaths attributable to the *economic* damage caused by the floods.

The true figure is likely to be larger than this. Assuming that the effect of income on mortality at other ages is similar to its effect in infancy, it follows that the total number of deaths likely to have resulted in 2000 from the economic effects of the floods is of the same order of magnitude as the total due to drowning and injury (700) and to enteric infections (200 to 4000), as discussed above. Moreover, the full cost of the floods, as noted earlier, was nearer to 15 per cent of national GDP than the 4 per cent derived here. Recovery from these losses must have had a depressive effect on economic growth and, thus, a continuing impact on nutrition and mortality over several succeeding years. For example, Prime Minister Pascal Mocumbi warned parliament in December 2000 that the rice harvest in 2001 was expected to be 20 per cent below normal because of damage to irrigation systems and a shortage of seed.

The economic damage was not a diffuse effect averaged out among the population; it took the form of the loss of specific crops and property belonging to more than 200,000 individual households. We can only speculate on the effect of these losses on the morale and mental health of the people concerned. Recent research in the UK (Reacher et al, 2004, and the work reported by Tapsell and Tunstall in Chapter 4) have found that physical illness associated with flooding is likely to be accompanied by a far greater burden of psychological distress.

Response to the flood

It is important now to set the discussions of health impact within a broader understanding of flood preparedness, emergency response and reconstruction efforts before, during and after the 2000 floods in Mozambique.

Pre-existing preparedness

Since the 1980s, there had been a government department in Mozambique to manage natural disasters and the associated relief efforts; but in July 1999 it was replaced by the National Disaster Management Institute, under the oversight of a coordinating council chaired by the prime minister and including the ministers of foreign affairs, public works, transport, health and agriculture. In 1999, for the first time, contingency planning for disasters such as floods was built into the planning process at national, provincial and district level. Each district was asked to produce a contingency plan, though the quality of these plans varied widely. Many districts provided little more than details of their early warning systems and assembly points, if any. The institute's National Contingency Plan was launched in November 1999.

Meanwhile, the institute organized workshops and training exercises. Fire brigades and the police were involved in these, as well as boy scouts, the Red Cross and religious bodies.

The technical committee of the institute normally meets just four times a year; but by September 1999, following a general warning of high rainfall from local meteorologists, it was meeting fortnightly. In the following months, the warnings grew a little more specific and the pace of preparations quickened. The Red Cross was invited to join the committee and began its own preparations. In November, the Ministry of Health instructed provincial health directors to prepare for possible floods and cholera epidemics; to assist them, medicines due for distribution in 2000 were distributed in late 1999. Senior health officials were sent out to the provinces to motivate staff and to ensure that enough tents were available for cholera treatment centres.

In order to raise awareness, the institute produced a calendar for 2000 with photos of the damage caused by the 1999 Inhambane floods and distributed it to local leaders. However, the institute had only very limited resources (for example, only seven boats in the southern half of the country) and organization in the affected provinces was weak. Its preparations appear to have made little impact on public awareness, although the institutional set-up and the training were probably helpful in the emergency phase. However, nothing in living memory could have prepared people for what was to come.

Immediate response and coordination

The immediate response of the international community was massive. By early March, 9 foreign air forces with 56 aircraft, and 2125 foreign military and paramilitary personnel were involved in the rescue and relief operations. Maputo airport saw four times the usual number of aircraft movements – a total of 10,000 during the floods – and ten times the volume of cargo.

After the initial rescue operations, most of which were accomplished by Mozambicans and which involved hundreds of boats, including 218 donated for the purpose, the first priority was the distribution of food, followed by medicines and doctors. The volume of food carried dwarfed all of the other relief supplies.

Coordination of this effort was a huge challenge. The foreign minister chaired the daily coordination meetings of the international agencies involved and established a Joint Logistics Operations Centre. Often, one agency took the lead in coordinating the others in a particular domain: the World Food Programme for food distribution, UNICEF for water and sanitation, and the Malawian air force for Beira airport. Gradually, they handed over coordination to the corresponding Mozambican government agencies. A similar pattern was found at local level. For example, displaced local government officials from Chokwe District took over much of the management of Chiaquelane accommodation centre.

Coordination was not easy. The US and UK air forces refused to use the aircraft parking spaces allocated to them at Maputo airport and drove vehicles onto the runway, disrupting the landings. Not a single NGO returned the questionnaire distributed by the National Disaster Management Institute in an effort to coordinate their work. One representative said: 'I am not here to tell you what we are doing. I am only here to listen.' One sector that was neglected, partly because no specific agency was responsible, was shelter; as a result, many families in the accommodation centres were not issued with tents or plastic sheeting (Simkin, 2000). Eventually, the Red Cross and other NGOs stepped into the breach.

The measures taken to prevent malaria epidemics in the accommodation centres have already been mentioned. Thanks to these and to the food distribution, a study of mortality in the centres found death rates of 1–3 per 100,000 per day, less than the normal rate for that population (Gaza Directorate of Health, 2000). The Nutrition Department of the Health Ministry also found that 'moderate' malnutrition was less prevalent among children in the centres than it normally was when the children were at home. This is the opposite of the common experience of relief workers in other disasters – that people in emergency camps tend to have *worse* health, largely because of the high population densities.

There is no contradiction between the relatively healthy condition of the displaced people in accommodation centres and the increase in incidence of enteric infections. The health of the population who were *not* accommodated in such centres, but who took refuge on isolated areas of high ground, was, no doubt, substantially worse. Moreover, the excess incidence of diarrhoeal diseases was noted only from mid April (Lucas, 2000), by which time the floodwaters were receding and increasing numbers of people had returned to their homes.

Reconstruction

The government put together an estimate of reconstruction costs and presented it to a meeting of donors, which it convened in Rome with the help of the United Nations in May 2000 (Government of Mozambique, 2000). These estimated costs are listed in Table 5.3. Note that the total does not include the cost of rebuilding damaged family homes nor, as the World Bank pointed out

Table 5.3 *Estimated costs of reconstruction after Mozambique floods
(US$ million)*

Sector	Cost	Sub-total
Education	36.0	
Health and social services	54.3	
Sub-total: Social sectors		*90.3*
Water and sanitation	27.1	
State buildings and equipment	26.6	
Roads and bridges	58.8	
Railways, aviation and communications	60.3	
Minerals and energy	16.4	
Support for population resettlement	24.5	
Sub-total: Infrastructure		*213.8*
Agriculture and livestock	63.4	
Fisheries	22.1	
Industry	12.0	
Trade and tourism	26.1	
Sub-total: Productive sectors		*123.6*
Meteorology	7.1	
Environment	5.3	
De-mining	7.0	
Strengthening disaster management	2.4	
Sub-total: Vulnerability reduction		*21.9*
Grand total		*449.6*

Source: Government of Mozambique (2000)

in a parallel estimate (World Bank, 2000), the cost of relief operations (US$65 million), or the value of lost output and foregone earnings (US$211 million).

If only health-sector costs, water and sanitation, and de-mining are considered as directly related to health and the prevention of injury, health-related costs account for about 20 per cent of this total. However, we argue above that, measured in terms of mortality, the health impact of the *economic* damage caused by the flood was comparable to the directly caused health effects. From that perspective, the entire budget is health related.

The immediate response of the international community to Mozambique's appeal was positive, and a total of US$453 million in aid was pledged. However, a number of donors, including the UK, the European Union and Japan, included money which had already been given under other schemes for other purposes. The government found that only US$10 million of the US$45 million pledged by the UK was actually new money. Moreover, most of it was slow in coming. The government had hoped to spend three-quarters of it by the end of 2000, but only one quarter of the money was made available by then, and some of it was still trickling in during 2004. The government had requested, in the interests of transparency, that the funds should be deposited untied into a special bank account; but only 5 of the 22 donor countries at Rome agreed to do this, so that it was not generally possible to channel the money to the sectors with highest priority.

One sector of direct importance to health that did receive the full amount pledged to it was water supply and sanitation. Once the water had receded and the displaced population returned to their homes, attention turned to the piped water supplies in the towns. By July 2000, the water supply in Chokwe was working again, and UNICEF was concentrating on improvements to the system. The Xai-xai and Inhambane water supplies were also upgraded with new boreholes and pipelines. It took longer for the benefits of this work to reach individual households; only half of the 4000 damaged water supply house connections had been repaired by 2002, and less than half of the 3000 damaged septic tanks.

In the rural areas, 211 wells and boreholes with hand pumps had been installed or reinstated by July 2001. By 2002, a total of 400 such rural water points had been restored or built in Gaza Province, more than the 300 damaged in the floods. The proportion of the rural population with access to water supplies, which had fallen from 42 per cent to 30 per cent as a result of flood damage, had thus been increased to 53 per cent in 2001, and was estimated at 65 per cent in 2002.

Future mitigation and preparedness

The water sector also repaired 140km of damaged flood protection dykes for Xai-xai and Chokwe, involving the placing and compaction of more than 0.8 million cubic metres of soil. However, more was clearly needed than restoration of the *status quo*. Some possible mitigation measures were discussed at an international conference in Mozambique in October 2000 (see Box 5.1).

It needs to be borne in mind that Mozambique is one of the world's poorest countries, and that investment in increased preparedness for floods as exceptionally large as those which occurred in 2000 would divert resources from other urgently needed development projects. Donor funding for such investment proved harder to obtain than funding for reconstruction. For example, of the money requested by the government to upgrade its network of meteorological and hydrological observation stations, only 15 per cent was offered by the donors in Rome.

Some mitigation measures that may save lives and prevent injury cost practically nothing. Marking evacuation routes and flood refuges, and designating those responsible for passing on flood warnings and organizing evacuation, is hardly expensive. President Chissano suggested at the conference that teachers might play this role.

Box 5.1 *Living with future floods in Mozambique*

An international conference held after the floods in Maputo during 27–28 October 2000 generated a number of recommendations for future flood mitigation and preparedness. These included the following:

- All planning must involve local residents.
- Mobilize local leaders to review and update preparations with people's participation.
- Accept that many people will live on floodplains, as they are fertile.
- If the state wants their productivity, it must also help the residents in time of need.
- Flood defences are mostly unaffordable, so the stress should be on evacuation of people in major floods.
- Flood levels of 1977 and 2000 should be painted on buildings and signposts.
- Link flood warnings to these benchmarks – for example, 'below 1977'.
- Flood warnings must be clear and simple, but not cause panic.
- Ensure that people understand that there will be some false alarms.
- Provide clearly defined escape routes and safety zones – for example, roofs of strong buildings.
- Ensure safety zones are clearly marked with respect to the 1977 and 2000 floods.
- Provide facilities for people to bring and store their valuables in safety zones – for example, set schools aside for this after flood warnings.
- Provide safety zones for cattle.
- Build escape roads, not parallel but perpendicular to river courses.
- Train teachers as flood watch monitors and escape route wardens.
- Use radio for flood warnings, including mobiles.

Other mitigation measures can be built into the reconstruction effort at little extra cost. For example, most buildings of cement blocks were not seriously damaged; most of the homes that were destroyed were built of mud (wattle and daub) or reed matting. There was a strong case for constructing any public buildings of materials solid enough to resist future floods. With regard to houses, however, there were tensions between agencies seeking to maintain high standards in the reconstruction effort, even if this meant that they could only help a few families, and those keen to provide a minimum of help to the many.

Locating public buildings such as health centres and schools on high ground, and providing them with load-bearing roofs upon which people could take refuge, would also help. Many people refused to heed flood warnings and move to higher ground because they were fearful of leaving their cattle and belongings, lest they be stolen. Designated flood refuges, such as school buildings, should be designed and managed such that cattle and movable property can be kept there during floods.

For many people living in Mozambique's floodplains, there is no suitable high ground near them that could serve as a refuge, and the fertility of those floodplains means that people will continue to live there. If floods in Mozambique continue to grow more frequent and more severe, there may be a case for building artificial refuges in the form of earth mounds analogous to the traditional *bari* of Bangladesh.

Mozambique is one of the few countries to have integrated contingency planning for natural calamities into its annual economic planning process. The Mozambicans realize that the international response to their calamity in 2000 was exceptionally large, partly because of the intensive media cover it received. They understand that they may not always be so lucky.

Acknowledgements

In preparing this chapter, we have drawn heavily on the excellent book on the Mozambican floods of 2000 by Christie and Hanlon (2001), and readers seeking the source of any unreferenced statements in the factual account are referred to their book in the first instance. Two medical colleagues, Dr M. Lucas and Dr J. Cliff, provided invaluable epidemiological information. The interpretation of this information and responsibility for any mistakes are our own.

6

Coping with Floods in the Mekong Delta, Viet Nam

Pham Gia Tran and Roger Few

Introduction

This chapter examines local-level responses to extreme floods in the Mekong Delta of Viet Nam – a setting where annual floods are part of the normal environmental and social fabric, but where abnormally high seasonal peaks have occurred repeatedly in recent years. To date, there has been little published analysis of health issues relating to flooding in Viet Nam despite mounting alarm over current and future risks, and, in particular, the impacts of floods on children (Pham Thi Lan, 2000; Jabry, 2002). Here, we make a small contribution towards addressing that gap by reporting on an initial scoping study on health risk and coping mechanisms in two flood-prone urban centres in the Mekong Delta region, where low-income communities, in particular, are often exposed to high water levels.

The chapter first introduces the flood problem situation in the Mekong Delta, before discussing the study and its findings on how local state agencies, health clinics and community-scale organizations perceive, prepare for and react to mortality and morbidity risks from flooding. The account pays particular attention to the vulnerability of children in the region, discussing related research work on the high proportion of child deaths from drowning during floods and associated safety initiatives. It then relates the study findings to the broader policy context within Viet Nam, where non-structural state responses to flooding are re-emphasizing the traditional 'living with floods' culture that is longstanding in the region.

Flooding in the Mekong Delta

Viet Nam is one of the world's most severely flood-prone developing countries. Wickramanayake (1994) reports that flooding caused by monsoon rains, typhoons and coastal storm surges constitutes the principal form of natural disaster in Viet Nam. Major flood-prone regions include the river plains of the Red River Delta in the north and the Mekong Delta in the south, as well as the coastal lowlands and upland valleys in the central provinces of the country (Government of Vietnam, 2001). Moreover, an official report on climate change risks underlines the danger that extreme flooding may become more frequent in the country in the future (Ministry of Natural Resources and Environment, 2003).

According to government sources, the recent history of flood disaster has been most severe in the Mekong Delta (Government of Vietnam, 2001). Compared with the Red River Delta, the channels of which have long been contained within an extensive dyke system (Le Minh Nhat, 2003), the ramifying channels of the lower Mekong are relatively unconfined, allowing seasonal peaks of water to inundate and fertilize much of the agricultural land in the delta (Sneddon and Nguyen Thanh Binh, 2001). Seasonal flooding has therefore generally been perceived as beneficial, though punctuated by the occasional catastrophic flood event. However, some studies suggest that during recent years the pattern has become less predictable, with both extreme high and extreme low water levels becoming more frequent (Dao Xuan Hoc, 2003). From 2000 to 2002, severe flooding occurred for three years in succession, with disastrous effects. In the 2000 floods, more than 480 people lost their lives, over 58,000 houses were evacuated and economic losses were estimated at US$280 million (IFRC, 2000).

The Mekong Delta is located in the south of Viet Nam (see Figure 6.1). It covers around 39,600 square kilometres and has a population of 16.1 million – equivalent to one eighth of the land area and one fifth of the total population of Viet Nam. Seven of the 12 Mekong Delta provinces experience flooding, and the flood-prone areas cover around 20,000 square kilometres, or about 50 per cent of the delta (Adam Fforde and Associates Pty Ltd, 2003). Flooding in the Mekong Delta affects both urban and rural settlements, and, as in most countries, its impact is perceived to fall most heavily on the poor (Esposito, 2002). Although poverty tends to be lower among city dwellers in Viet Nam, there are increasing concentrations of urban poverty in flood-prone sites. In recent research, the poor in Ho Chi Minh City, for example, consistently ranked regular flooding among their more critical problems (Thai Thi Ngoc Du et al, 2002).

The few studies to date that have been carried out on health issues during floods in the region suggest that local populations have significant concerns. As well as fears over child mortality (Save the Children, 2003), concerns surround disease risk associated with environmental contamination and disruption of water supplies and sanitation, as well as indirect health effects, such as those

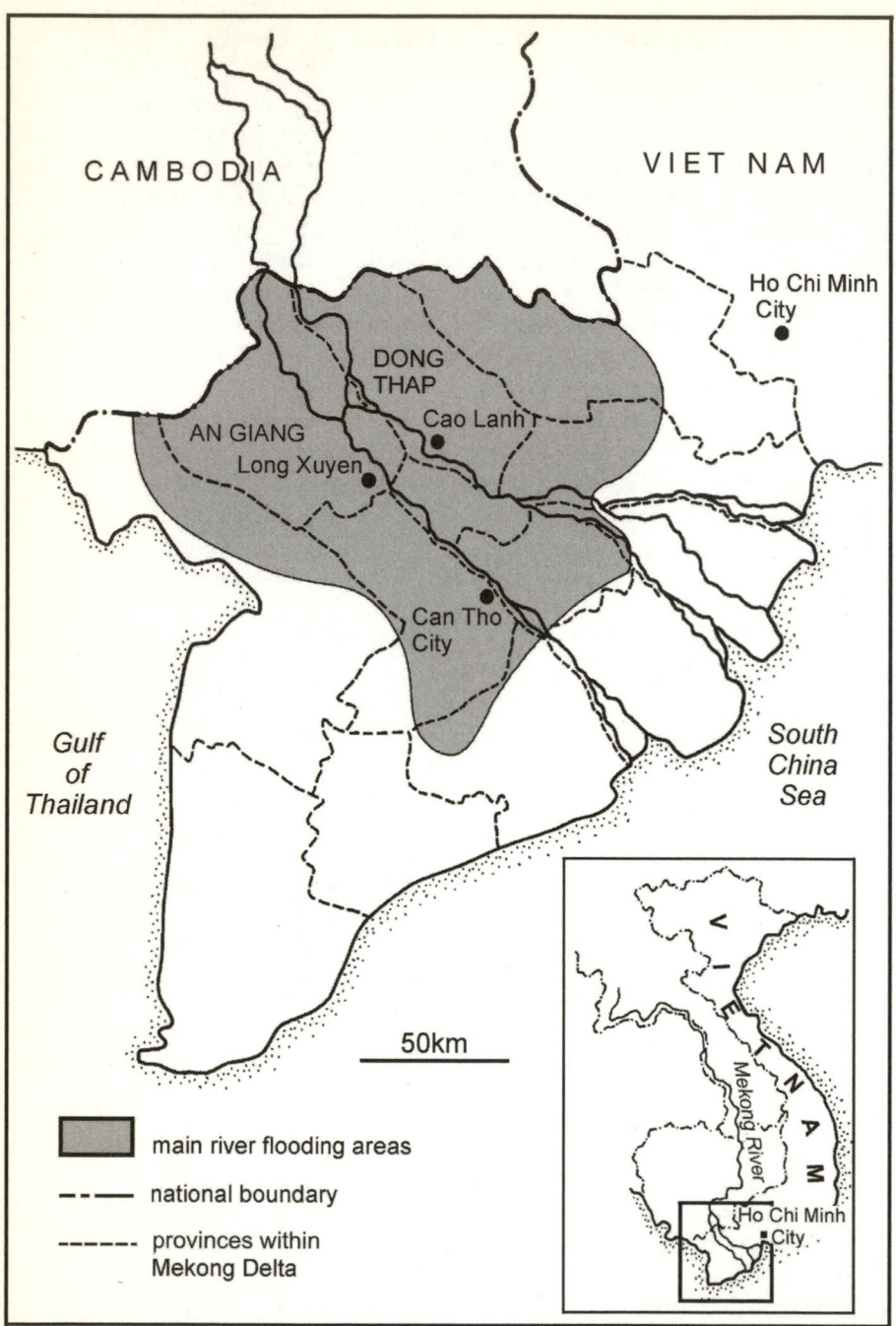

Figure 6.1 *The Mekong Delta, Viet Nam, showing the main flood-prone areas*

Source: based on mapped data from Department of Environment and Natural Resources Management, Can Tho University, Viet Nam (2004)

stemming from disrupted access to health care facilities and from economic losses (Esposito, 2002).

Methods and study sites

The purpose of this preliminary study was to gather initial information on the scope of health risks and to develop an understanding of the range of health-related responses associated with flooding in the Mekong Delta in order to build a foundation for larger-scale future work. However, given the relative paucity of published work focusing on health issues associated with floods in Viet Nam and in developing countries, in general, the collation and analysis of material from key informants and secondary sources is valuable in itself. The study entailed two main components, both undertaken in early 2004:

- *Literature review and national-level interviews*: review of secondary materials (reports, papers, policy documents) and interviews with key informants (in national government, aid agencies, non-governmental organizations and the academic community) in Hanoi and Ho Chi Minh City. These activities set the context for the study (providing national and regional information on floods and flood mitigation, health, environmental health, community development and disaster response).
- *Field studies*: the main qualitative data gathering by the project team took place in two urban locations within the Mekong Delta – in Cao Lanh (capital of Dong Thap Province) and Long Xuyen (capital of An Giang Province). Three wards were selected within each city, and one administrative block within each ward. Interviews were then carried out at three levels – city/province, ward and block – together with collection of secondary data and field observation. Table 6.1 provides a list of the interview meetings for each city. Several of the interviews at ward/block level were group interviews, with up to eight participants in attendance. All interviews were semi-structured, guided by a flexible question schedule, designed to elicit interviewees' perceptions of flood events and attendant health risks and information about the forms of coping response in the community at both household and communal level. Where feasible, interviewees were also asked for their perceptions about the role of external policies/interventions in shaping local flood mitigation and resilience.

The cities of Cao Lanh and Long Xuyen lie in the heart of the Mekong Delta (see Figure 6.1), each located on one of the two main branches of the Mekong that flow south from Cambodia, splitting further into a maze of distributaries as they progress towards the sea. Seasonal flooding affects many parts of the cities from July to October – with depths of up to 1m reported by interviewees in the highest recent floods. Some urban areas are protected from flooding by earth or concrete dykes; but many peripheral and some central areas have incomplete structural defences, as well as deficient drainage systems. In both cities, large

Table 6.1 *Local-level interviews*

	Cao Lanh	**Long Xuyen**
City/province level	Cao Lanh People's Committee	Long Xuyen People's Committee
	Cao Lanh Health Centre	Long Xuyen Health Centre
	Dong Thap Health Department	
	Dong Thap Red Cross	An Giang Red Cross
Ward level (three wards in each city)	Ward People's Committee Ward Health Station	Ward People's Committee Ward Health Station
Block level (one block in each ward)	Block leaders	Block leaders

sectors of the population do not have access to piped water and sanitation systems, though figures for piped water access tend to be lower and official poverty rates higher in the study wards in Cao Lanh. Although the pressure of urbanization in these cities is not great, the process of transformation of land use, from rural land to urban land, is increasing. This creates a need for the construction of new urban infrastructure systems. At present, urban facilities and services are mainly distributed in the central areas.

The roles of local actors

Before describing the study's findings on local risk and response perspectives, it is necessary to briefly underline the roles of different actors at the local level in terms of flood preparedness and health-related emergency response. Together with the self-protection mechanisms undertaken by households themselves, relevant actions are also undertaken by local state agencies, health systems and mass organizations.

Key among the state agencies are people's committees – local executive branches of government organized at the provincial, district and commune (rural) or ward (urban) levels. The Vietnamese Communist Party has a similarly tiered structure. Below ward level in urban areas, neighbourhoods are also divided into blocks, each of which has an elected management board. The overall shape of the political and administrative system in Viet Nam has remained little changed during the country's *doi moi* reforms, although, as noted below, new governance processes are now being instituted within that system (Mattner, 2004).

Local health systems are also organized in three tiers below the central Ministry of Health and consist, essentially, of provincial-level hospitals, district health centres and commune/ward health stations. Each tier offers curative and preventive health services. Both the district- and commune/ward-level facilities are under administrative authority of the equivalent people's committee, but are supervised technically by the health system tier above (Segall et al, 2000).

A special feature of Viet Nam is also the network of mass organizations that can be mobilized to provide public assistance during crises, including branches of the Viet Nam Red Cross Society (VNRC), youth organizations and women's organizations. Key among these is the VNRC, which again has a tiered structure from national to local level, has close links with the state and constitutes the core human resource for humanitarian work in the country, with a total membership of more than 7 million people (NDM-Partnership, 2003).

These sets of actors come together to plan and coordinate flood mitigation, preparedness and relief activities, with a Committee for Flood and Storm Control (CFSC) typically established at province, district and commune/ward levels (Jabry, 2002). Members of CFSCs include representatives of people's committees, functional agencies and mass organizations. According to an assigned task or their own normal function, each member of the committee organizes and deploys their activities in cooperation with other members. Volunteers from the mass organizations, for example, may work in conjunction with the people's committees and health facilities on a variety of health-related activities in response to floods. As the study reports, in the Mekong Delta these activities include running emergency rescue boats, undertaking health monitoring, distributing drugs, improving water sources, cleaning drainage channels and undertaking post-flood clean-up operations. Such cooperation among various social actors promotes the decentralization of management tasks, pools resources and assists the locality in enhancing capacity to cope with floods. However, it requires appropriate mechanisms for cooperation and sufficient participatory capacity from each partner. In this context, it is important to take note of emerging national policy on state–public partnership and public involvement.

The Grassroots Democracy Decree, introduced in 1998 and revised in 2003, sets out a basis for sharing responsibility between the government and the people, and highlights the types of actions in which communities should become involved (Government of Vietnam, 2003). The decree allows for processes of consultation, approval and, in some cases, supervision of local government actions by residents and local non-state organizations (Mattner, 2004). In general, when it comes to practical policies such as flood mitigation, for example, it is still central government that tends to provide guidelines for agencies to follow, as well as financial support. However, in implementing the policy, the local authority is now expected to seek contribution from social organizations and the public, both in terms of mobilizing their resources and giving them a share in decision-making on the design and implementation of improvement activities. The process of applying the provisions of the decree at the local level is at an early stage, and progress, to date, in developing the policies and mechanisms to secure popular participation remains uneven. Although the initiative has considerable political significance, it is difficult, at present, to predict its long-term implications for governance (Mattner, 2004).

No specific government health policies exist relating to floods, although the Ministry of Health has its own flood response committee that meets before the flood season and during flood events to coordinate actions, such as distribution of drug supplies. However, a number of central policies in health promotion and flood preparedness, some targeted specifically towards the Mekong Delta, are closely linked with reducing the health impacts of flooding. They include strategies for local-scale emergency preparedness (Government of Vietnam, 2001), the construction of new housing sites (residential clusters) on high ground (Adam Fforde and Associates Pty Ltd, 2003), and initiatives to protect children during floods (see Box 6.1) – all of which involve local state–public partnerships.

Health risks of flooding

The first element in our discussions with local key informants was a description of the chief health impacts they perceived as associated with severe flood events. Specific health risks related to flooding were reported by interviewees from all levels and sectors, including representatives of the formal health sector. Such risks appear to be of widespread and genuine concern to the local population. The Department of Geography of the University of Social Sciences and Humanities, Viet Nam National University, Ho Chi Minh City, is currently investigating perceptions of environmental health in three provinces within the Mekong Delta (with results due for publication in 2006). In a household survey carried out in Cao Lanh as part of this project, 75 per cent of respondents identified an impact of flooding on the prevalence of disease and ill health.

Drowning, injury and stress

During severe floods in the Mekong Delta, the physical existence of floodwater in and around human settlements causes deaths and injuries. Unlike flash floods or tidal waves, which bring rapid and violent surges, the seasonal riverine floods that affect the delta are slow-onset hazards associated with gradual accumulation of water. Many of the deaths therefore arise from incidents in which vulnerable individuals become immersed in floodwaters that are already present in their living environment. As Table 6.2 reveals, the great majority of the drowning deaths during recent years in the region have been of children, most aged under six (Save the Children, 2003). Indeed, recent research has revealed that drowning (both during floods and in non-flood times) is now the leading cause of child deaths in Viet Nam (UNICEF Vietnam, 2004). Ward-level interviewees noted at least four cases of local children drowning during floods during recent years in the study sites. The head of one ward health

Table 6.2 *Deaths from floods in An Giang and Dong Thap provinces*

	1994	1996	2000	2001
An Giang				
Total deaths	166	35	134	135
Deaths of children	134	32	94	104
Dong Thap				
Total deaths	–	–	150	41
Deaths of children	–	–	116	37

Source: Adam Fforde and Associates Pty Ltd (2003)

station in Cao Lanh also mentioned the risk of injuries from living and working in standing waters, such as cuts received from submerged objects.

Stress and mental health impacts of flooding are seldom reported in developing countries, although evidence from North America and Europe suggest that the psychological disturbance created by the presence and effects of flood hazard can be significant (see Chapter 2). No local-level interviewees in this study proposed stress as a major flood risk factor, although two did refer to worries about transportation and livelihood and one ward official in Long Xuyen reported a recent reduction in fears and concerns among residents following completion of a local dyke system and other flood preparedness activities. In another recent study, Tran Thanh Tung et al (2005) found that 76.5 per cent of the 115 residents they surveyed from two rural sites in An Giang Province reported 'having anxiety and fear' at the arrival of the flood season. Reasons given for this concern included danger to children, fear of inundation of the home, damage to local infrastructure and disruption of economic livelihood. Those who reported 'having no anxiety or fear' cited familiarity with flood conditions, stability of livelihood and reliable house construction as reasons for lacking major concern.

There is a strong possibility that stress-related health impacts were underreported in our scoping study. Part of the problem is how 'health' is defined, and respondents generally talked in terms of narrow 'physical' health (injury and disease) rather than a more holistic conception of health and well-being. As research by CARE International in Viet Nam (Esposito, 2002) suggests, the lack of formal identification of stress issues during disasters probably also reflects the low level of provision for mental health care within Viet Nam, a situation common to many developing countries. Indeed, their report and emerging evidence from other sources suggest that anxiety and depression following disruptive floods can be a contributory factor towards mental health problems in Viet Nam. UNICEF Vietnam (2002) particularly draws attention to the potential impact of child drowning on the victims' relatives.

Infectious disease

Disease outcomes of flooding may result either from exposure to floodwater or from changes in hygiene behaviour caused by the disruptions that flooding brings. The list of diseases associated with floods in Esposito (2002) broadly corresponds to the findings of our study. Interviewees from health agencies and people's committees at all levels consistently reported a series of infectious diseases that they perceived were more prevalent during the presence of floodwaters in the local environment, although there was often considerable variation in perceptions of their prevalence and precise cause. The field studies highlighted three main categories:

1 *Diseases related to disruption of normal hygiene behaviour and the spreading of contamination by floodwaters*. Floods can contaminate drinking water sources and inundate latrines, spreading pathogens in the environment and causing people to resort to unsafe water sources and toilet practices. Several interviewees also blamed disease transmission on careless practices of waste disposal, including the dumping of dead animals in water. Diarrhoea is by far the most commonly reported ailment resulting from contamination, and in most study locations the number of diarrhoea cases was reported to rise during flood times.
2 *Mosquito-borne diseases*. Concerns over mosquito-borne diseases relate to changes in the distribution of breeding sites for mosquito larvae during floods. Although malaria exists in the region at background levels and potentially threatens to re-emerge, the principal local fear is of dengue haemorrhagic fever. Incidence of dengue fever was commonly thought to rise in the flood season, possibly caused by people's increased use of open containers for treating and storing drinking water (the *Aedes* mosquito that transmits dengue requires clean water for breeding sites).
3 *Other infections caused by bodily exposure to water*. Local interviewees strongly associated flooding with increased incidence of fungal skin disease, eye infections, gynaecological infections and respiratory disease. Skin disease from contact with contaminated water was a consistent complaint raised in all but one of the ward- and block-level interviews. Some people implicated the spread of agricultural pesticides by floodwaters as the cause of skin and eye complaints, although others perceive that they may result from micro-organisms rather than chemicals and waste pollutants.

In most cases, the disease patterns reported during recent floods in the region have not taken the form of outbreaks or epidemics, but simply an increased incidence above normal background levels. Most of the pathogens are already endemic in the population and/or the environment. Floods may exacerbate them, but the causality is not always clear. Dengue fever is the most clear-cut example of this problem. Dengue incidence may be related more to high rainfall than to floods per se – with rainwater collecting in containers and discarded vessels close to human habitation. If floods and rainfall coincide, then it may be reported as a flood consequence rather than a rainfall consequence. In the Mekong Delta, the link is confused even more by an apparent connection between drought and high incidence of dengue (possibly related again to the need to store water for domestic use). It has been suggested that floods may initially wash away mosquito larvae from breeding sites. Indeed, some interviewees argued that flooding was beneficial for health in that it washed away sources of disease from the local environment, although dykes in urban areas could negate this benefit.

In one national-level non-governmental organization (NGO) meeting, it was suggested that disease incidence in floods tends to rise about one month after the initial flood event for a combination of reasons. Once waters become still or recede, it was argued, pollutant concentrations increase, people tend to move around more and become more exposed to contaminants and pathogens, and by that time immediate flood relief may have declined.

Local responses to health risks

In general, the study found that a wide and varied range of measures exist to counteract the health risks of floods – reference to many of them were repeated in several of the study sites; but the coverage of all of them is by no means universal. Unfortunately, the limitations of this research mean that no assessment can be made of the extent and effectiveness of these measures. Instead, we concentrate here on setting out the range of responses to health risks that exist at the field sites, grouping them under the following broad headings.

Safety precautions

One of the most striking health-related responses in the Mekong Delta is the present drive to protect children from flood risks. Prompted by the high proportion of young children in the recent death tolls from flooding, actions are under way to improve child safety by several agencies, including local government and mass organizations, as well as NGOs. Box 6.1 describes some of the measures that have been implemented.

The interviewees from ward and block levels in Cao Lanh and Long Xuyen also discussed actions taken by households that serve to enhance the safety of family members. If they have the means to modify their home in advance, people often invest in raising the floors of their homes on concrete platforms or on stilts. In other cases, emergency sandbagging is common during the early onset of seasonal floods. In homes that are flooded but still occupied, people commonly avoid exposure to the water by raising furniture on bricks and creating walkways of raised planks in and around the home. If flooding conditions become too severe in low-lying dwellings, it is common for households to evacuate their homes and make emergency shelter in open space on higher ground, such as roadside embankments.

Box 6.1 *Action to reduce child drowning deaths*

Extreme seasonal flooding in the Mekong Delta has recently caused the deaths of hundreds of children, the majority of whom have been young children drowned in the high floodwaters. A total of 400 children died during the catastrophic floods of 2000, and a further 300 lost their lives in the floods of 2001 (UNICEF Vietnam, 2002). In 2002, total deaths were 106; but, of these, 99 (93 per cent) were of children (Dang Quang Tinh, 2003). A specialist study on child drowning in the region coordinated by Save the Children reported that most deaths were among children aged under six from low-income families (Save the Children, 2003). Although strong currents from rapidly rising river floods may put infants at special risk, many of the child victims died when floodwaters were already well established. According to the study, many of the children were from families of small household size who had been left at home without adequate supervision for long periods while parents were out earning their livelihood (Dan Quang Tinh, 2003).

Since 2000, a number of responses have been made to tackle child drowning in floods. Initiatives by government agencies, NGOs and mass organizations have included provision of free swimming classes, safety training for primary school teachers and the distribution of pamphlets for children and their parents (MARD, 2003; NDM-Partnership, 2003). As key among the recommendations of their study, Save the Children (2003) advocated strengthening policies to develop a more accessible and affordable system of kindergartens for pre-school-aged children. Since 2002, the government has created a network of emergency 'flood kindergartens' in the Mekong Delta, some of which have their own medicine supplies. During flood crises, these are opened to young children, many of whom do not normally receive childcare services. To date, independent assessment of the effectiveness and usage of these centres is not yet available. However, Dang Quang Tinh (2003) claims that the 918 emergency kindergartens set up during the severe floods of 2002 helped to reduce the number of children drowning that year from the level in previous years, and there have been widespread calls for continued expansion of the initiative (Neefjes, 2002).

Health and hygiene education

The importance of health and hygiene promotion, both before and during floods, was emphasized repeatedly by interviewees from all levels and agencies. In Viet Nam, much of this work is undertaken through conventional propaganda channels such as the local government loudspeakers sited throughout communities, distribution of leaflets, meetings and campaigns of mass organizations, and direct visits to vulnerable community members, such as pregnant women and the elderly. Key public information needs identified by interviewees relate to the use of clean water, boiling and disinfecting of water from untreated sources, food hygiene, safe sanitation, the use of coils and bed nets to avoid mosquito bites, and the removal of mosquito breeding sites through the use of lids on water containers and by turning empty vessels upside down.

As underlined by several ward-level interviewees, an important prerequisite of effective education is the training of networks of community health promoters in avoiding and treating common flood diseases. The success of health and hygiene education also depends upon the frequency of visits by health promoters to households. Regular visits are important to follow up on education activities and assist people in how to practise what they have learned within the home. It is questionable whether the quantity and quality of this service is necessarily adequate, especially in Cao Lanh, where there was a reported one to two voluntary health promoters for each residential block (approximately 700 households). Most health promoters had received only short and narrowly focused training courses, and there was little supervision of their work.

Household health care

Results from interviewees at block and ward levels suggest that when avoidance of disease is unsuccessful during flood conditions, poor households in the region make use of a variety of both modern and traditional medicines. Commonly used modern products include cough medicine, antibiotics, eye drops, diarrhoea medicine, ointment for skin disease and eye drops, while traditional remedies include oil from boiled plant leaves and fruit to relieve skin infections. Few people, however, mentioned deliberately purchasing medicines in advance of the flood season as a precautionary measure – access to drug stores was not generally raised as an issue in these urban locations where pharmacies are widely distributed. However, some families benefited from free distribution of medical kits by external agencies. As an example, such a kit might contain bandages, cotton wool, paracetamol, cough medicine, eye drops, diarrhoea tablets, antibiotics and skin ointment.

Formal health care

Flood risk responses noted by representatives of the formal health sector – city health centres and ward health stations – included actions to maintain health services during flood times, as well as to provide for special health needs of the population. In areas where health clinics themselves were affected by floods, efforts were made to keep the services in operation. As a World Health Organization (WHO)-funded study of the impacts of floods on health systems in central Viet Nam found (Dang Van Chinh, 2003), accessibility of health facilities can become a problem during floods. Staff in Cao Lanh and Long Xuyen reported that they had provided walkways or boats to enable the public to gain continued access. In some cases, clinics were protected from floods by sandbagging or patients' beds were chocked up to raise them above standing water. The flood threat in the cities, however, was not considered great enough for emergency medicine stores to be set up within each block.

One aspect of health care emphasized by health staff was the need to undertake monitoring for common flood-related diseases, such as the fungal gynaecological infections frequently contracted by women wading through waist-high water. Clinics stated that they undertake regular check-ups for such infections during floods, including household visits, which in some cases have to be made by boat. Another important activity of the formal health sector during the flood season is to heighten disease surveillance. A disease-monitoring network is established from the ward level to the province level to detect the incidence and prevalence of diseases; follow-up occurs to prevent outbreaks in the locality, especially of dengue haemorrhagic fever and other serious infectious diseases.

Environmental health

Improvement in environmental health conditions, including water and sanitation in households, was generally seen as a crucial response to flood risk before, during and after inundation. Key preparedness actions described by ward- and block-level interviewees include measures to improve and protect water sources and sanitation facilities (such as provision of piped water from deep wells and improved latrines), clearing of waste matter from drainage channels, removal of stagnant water and unused vessels where mosquitoes can breed, and mosquito spraying. Some of these actions are undertaken by households, some jointly by community members and some by external intervention from organizations such as the United Nations Children's Fund (UNICEF).

During floods, when normal water sources are compromised, people commonly treat river water by boiling, cleaning with alum to remove particles and/or disinfection with Chloramin B tablets. Agencies such as the VNRC may distribute water treatment substances, water storage containers and water filters to poor households. In some areas, after floods, volunteer groups carry out environmental cleansing.

In both cities in the study, the most severe problems of environmental health occur primarily in the urban periphery and the inner slum areas. The main environmental problems here include pollution of waterways and drainage channels by wastewater and solid waste, and blockage and inundation of channels due to insufficient solid waste collection and deficiencies in the drainage system. To solve such problems, besides projects wholly funded by the state, residents can upgrade their local environment through infrastructure credit programmes provided by the state, mass organizations and NGOs. However, apart from the building of roads on dyke systems, there was little evidence of involvement in such participatory upgrading activities in the study localities.

Living with floods: Policy, culture and health

It is useful now to set the above findings on perceptions of health risk and local response within the broader context of flood management in Viet Nam. As in many hazard-prone countries, the Vietnamese government has historically concentrated on structural mitigation and flood relief efforts, rather than integrated social and technical programmes that incorporate flood preparedness and non-structural mitigation (see Chapter 1). But repercussions of the severe floods of 2000, together with recent involvement of the United Nations Development Programme (UNDP) in disaster risk reduction in Viet Nam, have helped to prompt a change in policy. Since 2000, a Living with Floods policy has been promoted in the Mekong Delta: an approach that recognizes that flooding cannot be, nor should be, completely controlled, and that efforts should also go into ensuring that communities can cope with, co-exist with and perhaps even exploit floods (MARD, 2003).

The Living with Floods policy is associated closely with another key initiative, the Second National Strategy and Action Plan for Natural Disaster Mitigation and Management in Viet Nam (Government of Vietnam, 2001). In the Mekong Delta, this strategy has defined the objectives of disaster mitigation and management up to 2020 as:

- protection of lives and property of people, ensuring sustainable and secure shelter for local people;
- protection and stabilization of agricultural production and increase in aquaculture activities;
- protection of infrastructure projects; and
- protection and maintenance of the environment and ecology in the Mekong Delta.

Although national-level interviews suggest that technical and engineering preparedness responses such as the construction of dykes and residential clusters still predominate in the new approach, they indicate that more investment is now being put into 'softer' aspects, such as education, income-raising, health promotion, environmental health and child safety. Discussions with local-level officials suggest that the Living with Floods policy message is circulated, acknowledged and widely understood at the grassroots of state structures in the region. Given the natural environment of the region, the limitations of large-scale flood control are widely recognized, and the focus, instead, is mainly on local-scale mitigation and preparedness efforts. One local Communist Party official argued that because flood avoidance is impractical, it is therefore very important to focus attention on coping with floods and especially on coping with its health impacts.

Historically, of course, people have always co-existed with floods in the Mekong Delta (MARD, 2003). Riverine flooding created the very fertile, flat land that has long sustained a high population in the region. Regardless of any policy directive, people do, in reality, 'live with floods' as part of their seasonal environment and have developed traditional dwellings, transportation and livelihoods to suit the conditions. From the tone of the interviews, flooding events or *lũ* in the Mekong Delta are generally perceived as variable (in scale and duration), but regular, episodes. Even the extreme floods of 2000 and 2001 are not necessarily perceived as 'disasters'. They are seen as distinct from unpredictable, rapid-onset and devastating events, as can be the case with flash floods or *lũ quét* in the central provinces of Viet Nam and cyclonic tidal waves on the coast.

The custom of living with floods may help to explain some aspects of health risk and flooding in the region, and such cultural aspects could be a fruitful area for further research. Several respondents at local and provincial levels, for example, suggested that mental health issues connected with flooding are absent in the region precisely because people are accustomed to coping with floods. In a sense, they are seen to be pre-adapted to flood risk compared with populations who might experience flooding unexpectedly. It is notable that traditional festivals were still maintained in the region during flood events. Such a positive outlook, together with the long-term adaptive experiences of people, may considerably mitigate the negative perceptions about flood risk to life and livelihood. However, as noted earlier, lack of identification of stress and mental health issues connected with flooding may also be because of lack of attention: authorities may not have carried out monitoring for such impacts, which are methodologically difficult to detect. Meanwhile, concern is now emerging from a range of sources over the risks of anxiety and depression connected with floods events (Esposito, 2002; Tran Thanh Tung et al, 2005).

The processes of urbanization and rural–urban migration may add a further dimension to the cultural aspects of flood response and health in the Mekong Delta. In-migration into the study cities was possibly connected with some of the cultural/attitudinal claims made about barriers to improved health and hygiene behaviour. Several national and local interviewees suggested that many poorer households retained a 'rural' culture in relation to their flood-prone environment that was not suited to higher density housing conditions of the urban or peri-urban environment. This, they claimed, was manifest in the continued use by many poorer households of river water for drinking and fish-pond latrines for sanitation. However, other informants suggested that these habits were followed less out of choice than out of necessity: poverty itself constrains people's ability to respond to health education and to change their practices (such as paying for piped water or constructing raised toilets).

Conclusion

It would be premature for us to provide concrete, practical recommendations for enhancing response to the health risks of flooding in the Mekong Delta, owing to the preliminary nature of the study. However, in addition to the 'scoping' discussions of health risks and current responses, we also sought perspectives on future intervention needs, and it is useful to record those perspectives here. The following list of priority actions were identified primarily by local-level interviewees:

- Ensure that health promotion activities are timed and organized so as to reach all vulnerable households, and strengthen the training of local health volunteer groups.
- Improve the supply of medicines for flood-related illness and of water treatment products.
- Assist people in accessing information on both common modern and traditional medicines for the treatment of water-related diseases.
- Emphasize the key importance of environmental health risks.
- Extend clean water, sanitation and solid waste removal services to all households.
- Provide low-interest credit to households for sanitation improvements.
- Provide central/external investment in partnership with local communities for further construction of dyke systems.

The call for greater support in these areas was strongest in the more vulnerable low-income residential areas of the two cities, located in both the outskirts and the central areas. These sites are characterized by deficiencies of clean water, drainage systems and waste collection. In general, the priority actions identified by the local actors we interviewed match those reported in other studies and assessments of flood management in the Mekong Delta. Reports prepared by Esposito (2002), Neefjes (2002) and Le Van Tuan (2003) emphasize a need for further investment in health promotion, training and sanitation, although there is also a call for improved preparedness within health systems in terms of disaster planning and management of health care during emergencies.

The study also highlighted broader aspects of societal response to flood risk in relation to health. Interviewees recognized the cross-sectoral dimensions of health protection, emphasizing the importance of a comprehensive approach to flood risk reduction that includes measures related to employment creation, poverty alleviation and infrastructure improvement, as well as preventive health. Implementation of these actions cannot be merely by government, but must be the responsibility of all social actors. Local authorities and mass organizations currently play a major role in coping with flood crises, and it is important to build their capacity further. Mobilization of the contribution of other local actors will also increase resources available to cope with the health risks from floods; but the sustainability of such contribution is likely to rest on a genuine commitment to implementing the grassroots participation in decision-making now enshrined in legislation (Esposito, 2002; Government of Vietnam, 2003). This initial study has raised positive examples of how local state and non-state actors, including community volunteers, can work together on projects such as health promotion, provision of swimming lessons for children and the creation of flood kindergartens. However, levels of community involvement and participation differed between localities, depending, in part, upon the awareness, capacities and experience of local authorities in participatory ways of working. Identifying and supporting effective mechanisms of cooperation between local actors may therefore play a crucial part in reducing future health risk from extreme floods.

Acknowledgements

This study was funded by the British Academy Committee for South-East Asian Studies. The authors were greatly assisted in the fieldwork by Bui Thi Thuy Hong and Nguyen Thu Cuc of the Centre for Research on Poverty Reduction and Social Development (CRPRSD), University of Social Sciences and Humanities, Ho Chi Minh City. We would also like to express our thanks to Luong Quang Huy of the Centre for Environment Research, Education and Development, Hanoi, who arranged the meetings in Hanoi, and to all the people in Cao Lanh, Long Xuyen, Ho Chi Minh City and Hanoi who participated in the study.

7

Flooding in the US: Responses from Government and the Medical and Public Health Sectors

Christopher A. Ohl

Flooding and its health impact in the US

Like much of the world, the US regularly experiences flooding. Because of its geographic and climatic diversity, a result of its large size traversing several climatic zones, all types of flooding occur. As well as riverine floods (both flash and slow onset), the US has floods caused by snowmelt, coastal storm surges (usually coincident with tropical storms and hurricanes), urban storm drain overflow and tsunamis.

Depending upon the climatic and geographic elements of the region, flood events may be regular and frequent. In some of these areas the human population has largely abandoned settlement in high-risk flood zones, or in some instances has constructed flood control structures such as dams, reservoirs, dykes and levees to protect rural dwellings, city structures and their inhabitants. In other instances, including some large population areas, inhabitants have remained in high-risk zones because of economic reasons, their desire to reside in an aesthetically pleasing location or denial that flooding will recur. Many communities along the Florida and Gulf coasts are at high risk from recurrent flooding associated with hurricanes and tropical storms; yet they rebuild following each event and the population of these regions continues to increase (Union of Concerned Scientists, 2003). In other areas, flooding is rare and unexpected, and catches the affected population totally unprepared. This was the case in the 2003 Houston, Texas, flood that resulted from an overwhelmed urban storm sewer system during Tropical Storm Allison (Nates, 2004).

Some large population areas have been thought to be at high risk for a catastrophic flood, but have done little to prepare for such an event. For instance, many experts had predicted that large-scale flooding would occur in the largely below-sea-level city of New Orleans, Louisiana, following a major hurricane (*The Times-Picayune*, 2002; Laska, 2004). Despite this, both local and federal governments largely ignored these warnings and had done little to mitigate for such an event. Consequently, over 80 per cent of the city's residents were devastated by the flood following Hurricane Katrina in 2005.

While many flooding events are minor, affecting only agricultural or undeveloped land and small numbers of people, others are catastrophically large, in some cases overwhelming flood control structures (e.g. the 1993 Mississippi River floods in the Midwest and the 2005 urban flooding of New Orleans) (Larson, 1996; Charatan, 2005). Of the top ten natural disasters ranked by disaster relief costs that occurred in the US during the later half of the 20th century, nine were due to a primary flooding event or to tropical storms and hurricanes associated with major flooding (FEMA, 2005a). Figure 7.1 shows flooding disasters from 1980–2004 that have incurred damage costs of over US$1 billion. Fifty-two per cent of the most costly weather disasters during this period were due to primary flooding or to hurricanes and tropical storms. These events incurred over US$197 billion in relief costs (NOAA, 2005a). Hurricane Katrina and its associated flooding have been estimated to have

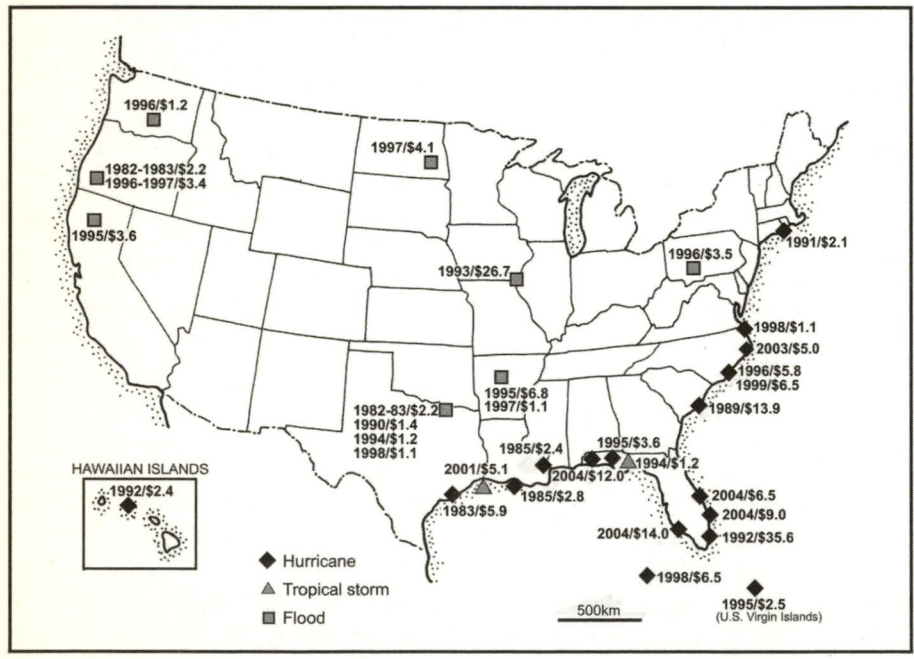

Figure 7.1 *US$ billion flooding disasters, 1980–2004*

Source: based on mapped data from NOAA National Climatic Data Center, US, www.ncdc. noaa.gov/oa/ncdc.html

caused between US$100 billion and US$200 billion in property damage and relief costs, and it is by far the US's costliest natural disaster to date (Wolk, 2005).

Worldwide, the health consequences of flooding vary depending upon the type and scope of the flood, underlying economic and public health conditions of the afflicted area, and baseline frequency of contagious and chronic diseases of the population (Noji, 1997). With the exception of Hurricane Katrina-related flooding, which caused over 700 deaths in New Orleans, flooding in the US seldom results in catastrophic loss of life or significant direct health-related morbidity. Flooding is, however, the leading cause of death among weather-related natural disasters in the US. (Noji, 1991; Ohl and Tapsell, 2000). Eighty-six deaths were caused by flooding in 2003, with 78 per cent due to flash floods and 12 per cent due to river floods (NWS, 2005a). Forty-five per cent of the deaths that were due to drowning were attributed to attempts to traverse flooded roadways in motor vehicles, a common finding in flood-related mortality statistics (Jonkman and Kelman, 2005). US tropical cyclones have caused an estimated 600 deaths since 1970. Fifty-nine per cent of these were due to flooding – a figure that rises to 78 per cent for children (NWS Southern Region HDQS, 2003; FEMA, 2004a). Hurricane Floyd, a 1999 category 2 hurricane that resulted in severe inland coastal flooding in eastern North Carolina, was responsible for 77 deaths, the majority due to drowning (over half in motor vehicles) (CDC, 2000). Other causes of death included burns, electrocution and carbon monoxide poisoning – all noted as causes of small numbers of deaths in previous floods (CDC, 1993b, 1993c, 1994; Daley et al, 2001). Although many flood-related deaths in the US occur during flash floods, slower onset events are also associated with mortality. The 1993 Midwest floods resulted in 47 deaths, 27 of them in Missouri (CDC, 1993c). Of these, 41 per cent were due to non-flash riverine flooding.

Flood-related morbidity is also observed in the US. Emergency department surveillance in North Carolina during a six-week period following Hurricane Floyd in 1999 showed that 67 per cent of visits were due to disease and 33 per cent due to injury (CDC, 2000). Regarding injuries, orthopaedic and soft tissue injury predominated, although hypothermia, dog and insect bites and carbon monoxide poisoning (due to gasoline-powered generators and pressure washers) were also reported. Most injuries were noted during the first week after hurricane landfall. Furthermore, a statistically significant increase in respiratory, minor gastrointestinal and cardiovascular diseases was noted compared with a seasonally matched baseline period. Perhaps most notable was a considerable increase in emergency department visits for chronic medical needs, such as oxygen tank and medication refills, dialysis and vaccines. This increase was, for the most part, due to a lack of access by afflicted persons to their usual medical providers or services. An increase in psychiatric maladies was also reported, including an increase in visits due to suicide attempt or injuries resulting from violent crime or abuse. This data is arguably the most comprehensive report of flooding-related morbidity in the US during recent times and shows similar findings to other surveillance following floods (CDC,

1993a, 1993d, 1996). Such data is important for the US, as it would be for any geographic or political region, in order to shape and direct public health and medical-sector responses to significant flooding events.

Before Hurricane Katrina in 2005, it was thought that because of a well-developed pre-disaster public health and utilities infrastructure, and adequate supplies of food, water and shelter, that US society was relatively well equipped to cope with the health impacts of flooding (Ohl and Tapsell, 2000). Large-scale or long-term population migration had been rare from floods prior to Katrina (over 500,000 people were left homeless and displaced by this storm and subsequent flooding). In addition, because of sufficient sanitation, vaccination programmes and a well-developed medical system, baseline rates of serious communicable diseases are extremely low in the US (Noji, 1997). The threat of communicable disease outbreaks following a flood therefore tends to be minimal and pre-existing medical care facilities are usually able to attend to the medical needs of afflicted populations. The New Orleans flood following Hurricane Katrina (in part because of its large scale and catastrophic nature) brought out several weaknesses, however, in US responses to massive floods and other natural disasters, and illustrated striking inadequacies and disparities in baseline public health measures, particularly for the poor and racial minorities (*The Lancet*, 2005). It also brought to our attention in the extreme that despite a lack of communicable disease outbreaks, flood-related mortality and morbidity is most intense in the elderly, chronically ill and infirm, and that during a large flood the greatest challenge to the health care system is to continue to provide medical care to this population (Greenough and Kirsch, 2005). In addition, this flood highlighted how government and its response agencies at all levels, national, regional and local, can fail to provide for its citizens during a major disaster because of slow, inadequate, misdirected and poorly planned and coordinated public health responses.

Responses to flooding

In the US, health-sector response to flooding includes interventions and public education designed to diminish drowning deaths and acute injury or disease, as well as to provide medical care to those acutely ill or injured. Acute medical care facilities also need to expand their services at these times in order to accommodate large numbers of persons with chronic infirmity or disease who are unable to access their usual health care resources. Because flooding in the US disproportionately affects the economically disadvantaged – a segment of the population more likely to suffer from chronic disease or disability – shelters, emergency medical services, hospitals and chronic care facilities need to adapt to the increased needs and numbers of such patients during floods (Noji, 2005).

Similar to almost all disaster responses, the public health- and medical-sector responses to floods in the US can be broadly classified according to the date of onset of the disaster. These include pre-disaster planning and mitigation, emergency phase responses and recovery phase responses. These responses are shaped by the intrinsic organization of health care, public health and emergency services in the region and are dependent upon internal and outside economic and human resources. Flooding, like other large-scale natural disasters, will often affect the infrastructure of existing health care services, which may limit the ability of these facilities and medical providers to care for the acute and chronic health needs of the population. Thus, assistance from outside the disaster area is often required and is provided or coordinated by government and non-governmental organizations (NGOs) at the state and, to some extent, national level.

The public health and medical sectors' responses to flooding in the US occur in parallel at the individual, local, regional and national level, and, in general, follow standard procedures developed for response to a disaster. Historically, these responses have not been well coordinated between various public health agencies and medical care facilities. It had been assumed that planning and restructuring of disaster response in reaction to homeland security concerns had addressed these shortfalls. However, the New Orleans flooding of 2005 showed that many inadequacies still exist in the coordination of disaster responses in the US. In fact, it has been suggested by many that an overemphasis on bioterrorism and other terrorist threats at the federal level actually weakened the ability of public health and safety agencies to respond adequately to the needs of a large flood-afflicted population in this city (*The Lancet*, 2005).

Individual or family level

The most fundamental level of action for coping with floods is that of the individual or family unit. US citizens who reside in areas prone to disaster have historically been encouraged to plan and prepare for such events, including hurricanes, floods, earthquakes and tornadoes. Since the World Trade Center and mail-associated terrorism events of 2001, there have been governmental attempts to amplify and extend individual and family readiness for natural disasters to human-initiated incidents that threaten homeland security

In preparation for a disaster, individuals and families have been instructed by local, state and federal agencies, as well as by NGOs, to prepare evacuation routes and alternative shelter, as well as pre-position supplies of food, potable water, medications, blankets, first-aid materials, insect repellents and battery-operated radios or televisions (DHS, 2005a). In addition, homeowners in flood-prone areas are encouraged to make alterations to their dwellings, such as raising the structure, securing fuel tanks and procuring flood insurance (FEMA, 2004a). Citizens are reminded of these measures yearly via posters, flyers, mass media presentations and advertisements, and workplace education during National Hurricane Preparedness Week, National Flood Safety Awareness Week and other community disaster preparedness initiatives (DHS, 2005a; FEMA, 2005b; NOAA, 2005b). The Federal Emergency Management Agency (FEMA) has developed a training course entitled *Are You Ready*, an in-depth guide to emergency and disaster preparedness that is administered by local community action leaders (FEMA, 2005c). This training includes the establishment of local citizen corps and community emergency response teams composed of citizens who have received this basic training in order to assist first responders and other governmental emergency teams during a disaster (FEMA, 2005d, 2005e). Specifically related to flooding, a current education effort targeting motor vehicle operators is termed *Operation Turn Around, Don't Drown* and is designed to educate individuals not to drive across flooded roadways and, thus, hopefully reduce vehicle-related drowning (NWS, 2005b).

In addition to pre-disaster preparedness, individuals are called upon during the emergency and recovery phase of the event to act independently to protect their health. These measures are outlined in health education materials distributed by posters and fliers, through the mass media and over the internet. Examples of such self-directed actions include disinfection of possibly contaminated drinking water; ensuring food safety; avoiding floodwater and flood-contaminated materials; use of personal protective equipment and clothing during clean-up; proper methods for decontaminating or disposing of flood-contaminated belongings or building materials; and proper use of gasoline-powered equipment to avoid carbon monoxide poisoning (CDC, 2004b). Recently, special health protection information has been made available from environmental health agencies and the Centers for Disease Control and Prevention (CDC) on the health risks of mould, which is often found in structures several days after floodwaters have receded (CDC, 2004c).

Despite such education and encouragement, individual preparedness in the US for disaster, including flooding, is grossly inadequate. This is evidenced by a survey that showed that individuals who survived Hurricane Andrew in Florida were no more prepared for a future tropical cyclone one year following the hurricane than they were during the time period immediately before it (Rincon et al, 2001). In addition, the 2005 New Orleans flood showed that large segments of the population of this city had not made any preparations for Hurricane Katrina despite mass media saturation about the storm's path, size and potential for flooding for several days before its landfall. Potential reasons for such a lack of individual or family preparedness include a lack of awareness or denial of potential hazard; procrastination; poverty and a lack of resources for supplies and equipment; disenfranchisement by segments of society with government and leadership; language barriers; and, perhaps most importantly, inadequate implementation and mass population penetration of existing education and prevention messages by government.

Flood disaster individual responses for the elderly, infirm and the disabled require special preparation, and leaders within the disability community have attempted to make special educational materials available for these persons (FEMA, 2004b; The Center for an Accessible Society, 2005) The 2005 New Orleans flood, however, showed that disaster planning at the level of the individual is woefully inadequate for special needs populations at all levels. Many of these individuals are not capable of individual action and are dependent upon family, friends or long-term care facilities for their daily living. Thus, special planning is necessary for these people for transportation and evacuation, special needs shelters and for the provision of access to higher levels of medical care. It is likely that the majority of communities across the US are unprepared to meet this population's need at the time of disaster.

Local public health agencies

Perhaps the most fundamental and important response to the health effects of flooding in the US occurs at the local level. Figure 7.2 shows the various elements of response to floods provided by local-level agencies relating to both public health and medical care. In general, during the first few hours of minor disasters and the initial three to four days of major large-scale disasters, it is the local government and, to some extent, private agencies and NGOs that are responsible for the disaster response.

Local water, sanitation and electrical utilities, together with transportation departments, shoulder much of the responsibility for re-establishing the infrastructure that is the foundation of public health. Some of these utilities, such as water, are owned by the local community, while electricity service is usually owned and operated by private companies and corporations. If these services cannot be readily restored before or after floodwaters recede, evacuations will be prolonged and emergency and medical responses severely hampered (Noji,

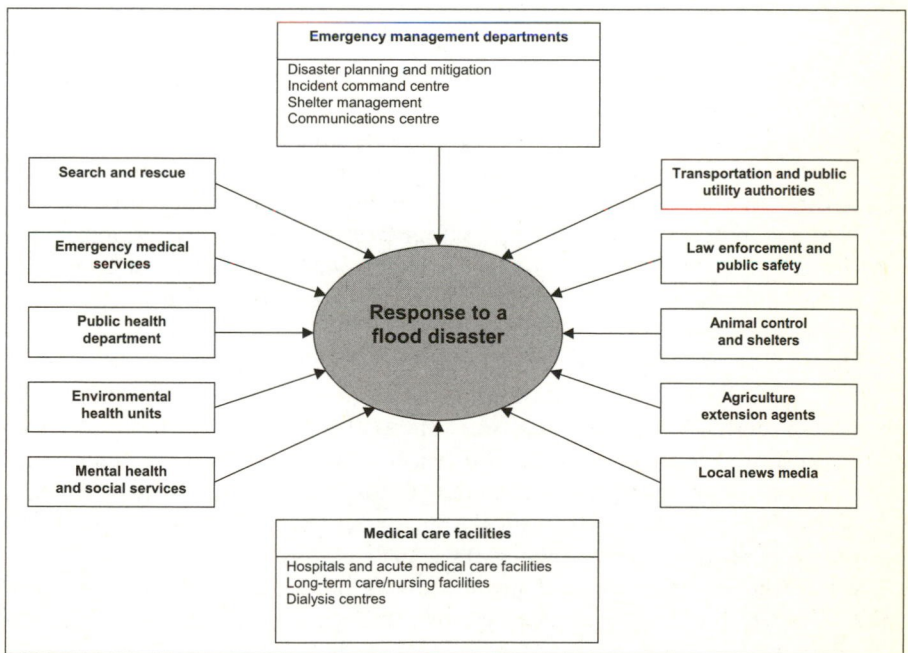

Figure 7.2 *Health-related elements of local-level response to flooding*

1997). Restoration of utilities and transportation networks usually requires assistance from construction and repair crews from outside the affected area. For large flooding disasters, this support often comes from other states or US regions, as seen following the 2004 Florida hurricanes (*Sun–Sentinel*, 2005). Privately owned utilities from other regions often cooperate to assist in such efforts.

The local health authority in the US is the city or county public health department. During a major flood, these agencies operate under the provisions of the county disaster plan under the leadership of the local health director. They serve to coordinate health care services across the area and, with the assistance of NGOs – typically the American Red Cross – provide basic health care and limited disease surveillance in county- or city-operated emergency shelters, which are usually located in schools or other public buildings (Leitheiser et al, 1997). They are particularly involved in staffing local shelters designed for special needs populations: pregnant women, the elderly and infirm, or those with serious chronic underlying diseases that usually require home nursing care (Clinton et al, 1995). In addition, local health departments coordinate local NGO and health care volunteers, disseminate health education materials to the population and assist with county-wide surveillance for injury and illness (Leitheiser et al, 1997). They are also responsible for providing emergency immunizations to the populace (vaccinations are seldom needed in the US following a flood, with the possible exception of tetanus vaccination for those with an out-of-date immunization who are directly involved in flood clean-up). During the recovery phase, the county health department usually offers testing of potable water wells for contamination and participates in insect-vector control. Their environmental health officers also assist in inspecting dwellings to ensure their inhabitability.

The city or county disaster plan functions under an incident command structure and ideally integrates with local hospital disaster plans. The local health director reports to the county or city incident commander and generally is positioned in the county incident command or emergency operations centre. The local health director will often be called upon by the print or broadcast media for information on the community's health or as an expert interviewee for public information.

Depending upon the particular county or local government's resources, county health departments and other agencies will attempt to respond to their populace's mental health needs during a flood (Leitheiser et al, 1997). During and following a flood, county mental health clinics and other social service agencies will often set up telephone assistance lines, mental health provider appointments, counselling and local support groups. City or county social service agencies often participate in these efforts.

While the oversight of the community's health rests within the local health department, the responsibility for public safety resides with local law enforcement. They are responsible for closing impassable or flooded roads, enforcing curfews and disaster perimeter security, and respond to accidents and selected medical emergencies. In the US, the local fire department or freestanding county emergency medical services division is responsible for first response medical assistance and emergency medical transportation (Jezierski, 1998). These local agencies are also responsible for search and rescue operations. If responding to a large-scale flood, they will often request assistance from state, federal or military sectors for additional manpower and advanced equipment, such as helicopters.

In addition to responses to protect human health, local and county authorities are also responsible for emergency assistance for animal health. Flooding can affect large populations of food-producing animals, causing significant mortality and morbidity (Schmidt, 2000). Not only is there an agricultural and economic aspect to protecting food-animal health, but sick or dead animals are a reservoir for zoonotic diseases that can potentially be transmitted to people. County agricultural agents, with assistance from the state department of agriculture, are responsible for farm animal welfare and carcass disposal. In addition to farm animals, family pets are affected by flooding and their owners will often risk their own life or health for their protection (Heath et al, 2001). This was speculated to be one reason for people failing to evacuate New Orleans on the approach of Hurricane Katrina (Nolen, 2005). The rescue and shelter of pets requires additional planning and resources from emergency service and animal control units (FEMA, 2004c).

It can be seen that while local government and public health agencies have many responsibilities and tasks during a flood disaster, for some communities their level of financial, human and material resources and pre-disaster planning may be inadequate to provide an effective response for more than a few hours. In such circumstances, the responsibility to augment or take over disaster operations falls upon regional or national government agencies.

Medical facilities

The health care system has responsibility for meeting both the acute and chronic medical needs of patients affected by flooding. In the US, the health care system is based on local medical providers (individual doctors or group practices), community hospitals that generally offer inpatient and emergency care for uncomplicated diseases or injuries, and larger regional 'tertiary' medical centres and hospitals that care for patients with more complicated medical conditions. Table 7.1 provides examples of some of the challenges that these various facilities are likely to face during severe floods.

Individual health care providers or group practices that provide health care in the outpatient setting often lack the resources to care for their patients during a large flooding event (Axelrod et al, 1994). Disruptions in power, water and transportation infrastructure, and ancillary services such as pharmacy, limit their ability to examine and treat chronic or acute illness. In addition, some providers are preoccupied with their own families' needs and thus are unavailable to attend to their patients. Therefore, much of the medical needs of persons affected by flooding will fall on the local or regional hospital, particularly the facility's emergency department (Ogden et al, 2001).

Table 7.1 *Typical problems faced by health facilities during flood disasters*

Local medical providers	Hospitals and medical centres
Lack of integration within disaster plans	Current disaster plans may fall short
Often disabled by infrastructure disruptions, including loss of power and water supplies	Often disabled by infrastructure disruptions, including loss of power and water supplies
Lack of planning for resident evacuation (long-term care facilities)	Lack of planning for patient evacuation in case of system failures
	All but emergency surgery becomes of low priority
Difficult to coordinate/communicate with other medical and public health sectors	Patient and staff transportation to and from the facility is difficult
Inability to provide usual outpatient care	Larger hospitals become the fallback for both outpatient and inpatient care
Inability of patients to access usual outpatient pharmacy and nursing services	Inability to discharge flood-affected patients with ongoing outpatient medical needs
Medical providers may lack knowledge on typical flood-associated diseases and injury	Medical providers may lack knowledge on typical flood-associated diseases and injury
Staff may be overwhelmed by own family concerns	Staff may be overwhelmed by own family concerns

Unless the flood is massive or the hospital facility is inoperable due to flood-related disruptions in utilities or building infrastructure, patients will be brought to the emergency department by private, public or ambulance transport rather than the hospital attempting to dispatch medical units to the field. In some instances, helicopter air ambulance is necessary due to extreme injury or illness, or the inability to access the patient by ground transportation due to flooded roadways. In rare instances, such as in the recent New Orleans flood, boat transportation may be used. In order to care for the increased numbers of patients, hospitals will often need to implement disaster plans that provide for increased manpower and resources available to the emergency department.

Non-essential or elective surgery and routine hospital admissions are usually deferred until the acute phases of the emergency are over.

During most flood disasters, US hospitals will operate under their disaster plans, which provide for a chain of command, organizational structure and logistics for natural or human-initiated disasters (Schultz et al, 2003; Thomas et al, 2005). The Joint Commission for Accreditation of Healthcare Organizations (JCAHO) requires all hospitals to have such a plan and to conduct disaster drills semi-annually (JCAHO, 2005). When the disaster plan is executed, a hospital-based emergency operations and command centre is established and control over much of the hospital's medical operations are delegated to the incident commander, traditionally an emergency medicine or trauma physician with special expertise and training in disaster medicine. Representation from the hospital's administrative and medical staff leadership is almost always available in the command centre, as are other members of the facility's disaster committee. Phones, two-way radios, computer terminals with internet access and televisions are usually pre-positioned in the command centre. Frequent communication with the city or county emergency operations centre is essential. Because many large-scale floods can be predicted or are in conjunction with large forecasted storms, the disaster plan may be implemented and command centres established before the actual flood begins.

Some of the special challenges and demands that US hospitals have faced during past large-scale floods and the response measures that they used to confront them have been published (Ramsey, 1994; Clinton et al, 1995; Peters, 1996; Reed, 1997; Franklin et al, 2000; Gay, 2002; Nates, 2004). Two studies focus on Pitt County Memorial Hospital in eastern North Carolina, a 731-bed regional university hospital that provides tertiary medical care to 29 counties. During the severe inland flooding associated with Hurricane Floyd, the hospital was charged not only with meeting the usual acute and chronic medical needs of the population it serves, but with treating patients normally cared for in other smaller hospitals or clinics that were knocked out of operation due to the flood (Franklin et al, 2000; Gay, 2002). In addition, because of severe disruptions in road transportation and a lack of city power and water, it struggled to meet its own operational needs. In response, the hospital established a transportation centre to triage transportation of patients and health care staff, and brought in three additional helicopters and flight crews from across the nation to increase its air transportation capabilities. Assistance was also provided by helicopters from the North Carolina Air National Guard and US Coast Guard. These air services also air-lifted the hospital's medical, ancillary and support staff between their homes and work, allowing them to provide for their own families' needs, as well as the hospital's. To meet a greater than expected hospital demand for electricity, extra generators were procured. One of the most crippling events for a hospital is the loss of community water. This occurred for approximately one week at Pitt County Memorial Hospital. Water was trucked from other communities in order to supply an initial 100,000 gallons to pressurize its water system, and an additional 200–600 gallons per minute for cooling of equipment and function of sanitary facilities. The hospital's rehabilitation centre swimming pool was used as a reservoir and settling tank. Bottled water was used for drinking and cooking. Other hurdles facing this hospital during the flood included operation of a dialysis centre for approximately 1000 patients using trucked-in water; staffing special needs shelters established on the hospital grounds; procuring and transporting pharmaceuticals to patients cut off from their usual pharmacies (special pharmaceutical dispensing centres were established); and assisting the state health department with disease and injury surveillance.

Smaller medical facilities and hospitals may be quickly overwhelmed by the loss of infrastructure and utilities that occur during large floods, and are forced to evacuate patients and emergency medical services to other regional hospitals (Sternberg et al, 2004). It is unusual, however, for tertiary-care regional medical centres to have to evacuate patients because of floods (as opposed to earthquakes, where hospital structures may become unsafe for patient or staff inhabitation) (Schultz et al, 2003). One exception occurred during Hurricane Allison, which caused catastrophic urban flooding in Houston in 2001. Memorial Hermann Hospital in Houston was forced to evacuate all patients after more than 40 million gallons of water inundated the basements of the Texas Medical Center. This urban flood cut off all electricity, internal transportation, such as elevators, and the communications systems – including paging and internal and external phones (Nates, 2004). Emergency generators were also rendered inoperable. Patients, including those in intensive care units, were carried down stairwells using backboards and stretchers to a waiting vehicle or air transport.

During the flooding in New Orleans following Hurricane Katrina, all but one of the city's major medical centres were severely disrupted by flooding, power and communication outages, loss of water and sanitation, and medical and nursing staff shortages (Berrgren, 2005). It was necessary to evacuate all patients and medical staff at both university-affiliated regional medical centres in the city – a task made extremely difficult because of a lack of ground, helicopter and long-range air transportation. An exact count of the number of patient deaths that occurred in New Orleans due to the lack of high-acuity medical care resulting from a lack of electricity and water, as well as from extreme heat in patient rooms lacking air conditioning and ventilation, has not been determined. It is likely, however, that the number of attributable deaths is well over 100 (Davis and Johnson, 2005).

In cases of widespread disruption of hospital services, such as occurred during the 2001 Houston and 2005 New Orleans floods, field hospitals are often established and staffed by the military or other federal or state medical response teams in order to continue emergency medical care in the community (D'Amore and Hardin, 2005). In the case of the New Orleans flood, several days passed before this could be accomplished due to the scope of the disaster and slow federal relief responses.

The above examples show that ingenuity and improvization by a hospital's engineering and medical staff are needed in order to continue to care for patients during a flood. Case studies of such scenarios also show that hospital pre-disaster planning for floods is inadequate. Unfortunately, many US hospitals have historically not devoted many resources to disaster planning and do not have provisions in their disaster plans to provide for the 'internal disaster' (i.e. loss of operational infrastructure) or to meet the physical and mental health needs of its employees and staff (Aghababian et al, 1994). The 2005 New Orleans flood shows that an emphasis on disaster and mass casualty response in hospitals since the terrorist events of 2001 has not necessarily improved this planning, nor has recent New Environment of Care standards from JCAHO that require hospitals to perform a hazard and vulnerability analysis for their facility (JCAHO, 2005). Some hospitals, however, have recently increased their manpower and equipment resources devoted to mass casualty care during disasters (largely funded by federal grants), and these facilities now take their required semi-annual disaster drills much more seriously. Training for hospital personnel in disaster response is available from the Department of Homeland Security (DHS) at their Noble Training Center (FEMA, 2005f). This centre is a simulated hospital facility specifically designed to train hospital-based emergency managers and health care professionals in a realistic environment to enable them to manage a mass casualty event resulting from natural disasters, technological incidents and acts of terrorism. Funding for such training is provided by the DHS. In addition, it is likely that the lessons learned from Hurricane Katrina, Tropical Storm Allison and Hurricane Floyd will be analysed in the future to improve hospital engineering mitigation for flooding and their responses to internal hospital disaster.

Other medical-sector responses to flooding apart from hospitals include volunteer medical, nursing and pharmacy professionals who will often self-organize to provide medical care in makeshift clinics, shelters and nursing homes, or via home visits for homebound patients (Kappedal, 1997). Mental health providers might also make themselves available for counselling and refer the acutely depressed or mentally ill for more advanced services. The importance of volunteer efforts by local citizens with medical skills cannot be overstated during a flood emergency.

Schools of medicine and public health

Academic medical training and research campuses have traditionally not been thought of as a component of disaster response. However, because of their role in teaching health care and public health professionals and their research-oriented staff and resources, they can make an important contribution to flood disaster planning, emergency response and recovery.

An important aspect of planning or responding to a disaster is for the involved personnel to be knowledgeable and well trained in all aspects of emergency response, including disaster types and their associated public health threats. Other areas of required knowledge include epidemiology and surveillance, rapid needs assessment, risk mitigation and incidence command structure. Many schools of public health now offer courses of study or certificate programmes in these topics, some of which can be taken through distance learning over the internet (UNC Chapel Hill, 2005a). In response to the terrorism events of 2001, the North Carolina School of Public Health established the North Carolina Center for Public Health Preparedness (UNC Chapel Hill, 2005b). Although the primary mission of the centre is to improve the capacity of the public health workforce to respond to terrorism and other emerging public health threats, much of the curriculum and subsequent development of expertise will also improve the public health response to flooding. Since 2001, medical schools have begun to develop and implement curricula for their medical health professions students that instruct students in the fundamentals of public health response to disasters and terrorism. The National Center for Disaster Preparedness at the Columbia University Mailman School of Public Health, together with the various schools of medicine and nursing at the Columbia Health Sciences Campus, have developed a curriculum with learning objectives and core competencies for teaching health professions students about emergency management, bioterrorism, and disaster and public health preparedness (Markenson et al, 2005). Several schools of public health and medicine also offer lectures or print material that provide continuing medical education credits in disaster preparedness for practising physicians and nurses.

Academic medical centres are involved in flood disaster response in matters outside of education. During the emergency and recovery period, their resources and infrastructure can be valuable for assisting public health authorities to conduct surveillance for disease and injury, provide immediate education to the public and medical care providers, and respond to requests from the news media. Faculty at medical and nursing schools may also assist with clinical patient care (Benedict, 2003).

Schools of medicine and public health have the potential to conduct important research on the long-term health effects of flooding. Similar to other regions in the world, quality research is much needed on this topic in the US, particularly on the potential diseases related to exposure to floodwaters and the pollutants and toxins that they contain. Other important areas of necessary study include the health effects of toxic moulds that grow in recently flooded structures and the impact of flooding on mental health and overall physical well-being. US academic medical centres have undertaken some research on these topics in the past; but such studies have traditionally been woefully under-funded and few quality studies exist. Recent increases in research funding for disaster preparedness and response may potentially be directed at selected areas of flood-related research in the future, particularly towards those aspects that could be applied to general disaster relief.

Response at the state level

Large-scale floods often encompass geographic areas greater than that of the local community or county. In addition, many catastrophic floods will often overwhelm local public health and medical manpower and equipment resources.

In these instances, assistance is provided by US state government and NGOs. All states have a department or division of emergency management that is responsible for assisting local governments and individuals to prepare for, respond to, recover from and mitigate against all hazards and disasters. Since 2001, these departments are also responsible for homeland security activities at the state level.

For floods that affect more than one or two counties and/or are likely to have a significant impact on the well-being or economic status of their citizens, the state governor will declare an official public emergency. At this time, the emergency management agency will establish a state Emergency Operations Center (NC Division of Emergency Management, 2005). The centre's activities include strategically locating resources of water, meals, blankets and special equipment, such as communications gear and generators, in an affected region and providing technical expertise in disaster management. Most states will have a State Emergency Response Team manned by state agency personnel that deploys to the flood location to assist severely impacted counties to coordinate and prioritize response activity (NC Division of Emergency Management, 2005). State agriculture departments also are involved in the response to flooding and assist county agricultural agents in activities including carcass disposal and farm animal disease mitigation (NC Department of Agriculture and Consumer Services, 2005). In addition, state governments have a major role in flood disaster recovery. Much of this comes in the form of monetary assistance through grants and loans, mostly to local governments and agencies that were affected by the flood.

When resource needs are beyond the capabilities of state agencies, the state may request mutual aid from other unaffected local governments or states through intrastate cooperate agreements or interstate mutual aid agreements. Federal assistance may also be requested from a federal emergency response team. In addition, states have the authority to deploy military National Guard units during disasters. These units may be called upon for special transportation, including large off-road capable trucks and helicopters, or for power generation, communications and engineering equipment.

State health departments, in conjunction with the CDC, provide for rapid needs assessment during a flood, and disease or injury surveillance before and during the event (PHP&R, 2005). This information is essential to guide local responders to geographic areas of need and increased risk to health. Surveillance data are also important to reassure the public with accurate information, particularly when rumours of contagion or epidemics circulate. The state health department is also responsible for interacting with the mass media; developing lay person and medical provider educational materials for use before, during and after the event; and, together with state environmental protection agencies, investigating the impact of the flood on environmental and occupational health. Much of the public information that is disseminated to regions that are recovering from floods pertains to clean-up safety and personal health protection, and is generated and disseminated by the state health department in cooperation with the CDC.

Although state governments have more resources and expertise available to them than local governments, there are several potential problems that state agencies need to overcome for an effective flood relief response. These include clearing roads and other transportation routes of debris, finding routes around or over disrupted bridges, mobilizing sufficient numbers and types of vehicles and helicopter aircraft for personnel and material transportation, and rapidly assessing the needs of the population in order to appropriately triage the response. The largest obstacle is that of establishing effective communications. Communication not only requires having the proper radio and other wireless equipment, but being able to integrate, correspond and coordinate with local governments and other response elements. Frequent drills and exercises with various response elements are necessary for testing and training with communication networks. The poorly coordinated and delayed response following the 2005 New Orleans flood illustrates how these obstacles can tremendously impede an effective relief response if they are not planned for or rapidly overcome.

Federal or national responses

The highest level of flood disaster response in the US is at the level of the federal government. The federal government is involved in all levels of response, including disaster hazard identification and mitigation, individual and community disaster preparedness, acute emergency responses, and recovery. Several agencies that are involved in these activities, and their respective websites, are listed in Table 7.2. Since 2001, many of these activities have been reorganized and now come under the oversight and direction of the Department of Homeland Security (DHS). Since 2001, the level of federal funding for disaster preparedness and response has greatly increased and is budgeted by the DHS. While ostensibly directed at responses to terrorism and weapons of mass destruction, this funding has the potential to carry over into natural disaster preparedness, including flooding. The extent that these resources have been used for natural disaster preparedness and/or the rebuilding of public health infrastructure in the US varies considerably from state to state and is determined by each state or local government.

In the US, the federal government public health response to disaster is implemented only after local and state or regional responses are overwhelmed. Generally, the federal response is slower to react and local and state agencies assume the greater responsibility for the response to a flood, particularly during the first few days of the emergency phase of the disaster.

National Oceanographic and Atmospheric Agency

The responsibility for flood hazard identification, stream level and weather system monitoring and early public warning of an impending flood is assigned to the National Oceanographic and Atmospheric Agency (NOAA) and its sub-agency, the National Weather Service (NWS) (see Box 7.1). In addition to real-time monitoring and public alerts of storm and flood conditions, NOAA

Table 7.2 *Federal agencies responsible for planning for,
and responding to, flooding*

Agency	Responsibility or action	Website(s)
Department of Homeland Security (DHS)	Oversees emergency preparedness and response for all natural and human-incited disasters	www.dhs.gov
Federal Emergency Management Agency (FEMA)	Emergency preparedness training and information for communities and individuals, flood hazard mapping, risk mitigation and buyouts of property, emergency response teams, and recovery assistance	www.fema.gov www.floodsmart.gov
National Flood Insurance Program	Individual education and flood insurance	www.fema.gov/fima/nfip.shtm
Emergency Management Institute	Emergency management training	www.training.fema.gov/emiweb
Noble Training Center	Training and preparedness of hospital staff and health care professionals	www.training.fema.gov/emiweb/ntc
Mobile Emergency Operations Support	Mobile telecommunications, operational support, life support and power generation assets for on-site management	www.fema.gov/rrr/mers01.shtm
National Oceanographic and Atmospheric Administration (NOAA)	Flood disaster statistics; identify flood hazard locations; monitor river levels	www.noaa.gov
National Weather Service (NWS), a division of NOAA	Monitor weather systems; issue flood and hurricane watches and warnings; provide individual education	www.nws.noaa.gov, tadd.weather.gov
Centers for Disease Control and Prevention (CDC)	Public health planning and response, surveillance, rapid needs assessment, medical provider education and individual education	www.cdc.gov, www.bt.cdc.gov/disasters/floods
Military units	Emergency infrastructure, transportation, and field medical clinics and hospitals	

also keeps statistics on river and stream levels, flood events, flood-related mortality and its causes (NWS, 2005a). Some of the above information is used by FEMA to produce floodplain maps and to inform communities and individuals on their respective flood risk. Activities advocating direct individual action to mitigate disaster are also performed by NOAA/NWS, including the *Turn Around, Don't Drown* campaign (NWS, 2005b).

Box 7.1 *Flood early warning and dissemination in the US*

The National Weather Service (NWS) and their Storm Prediction Center (SPC) conduct real-time monitoring of stream levels across the nation, as well as large or small weather systems that are capable of producing flooding, including flash floods (NWS, 2005c, 2005d). In response to current or impending large rain events or increasing stream levels, they will issue a 'watch' or 'warning' for flash, river or coastal flooding, and for hurricanes or tropical storms. Additionally, together with the US geological survey, they will issue a tsunami warning after a recent submarine earthquake, or in response to indications from ocean monitoring buoys (NWS, 2005e).

A flood watch indicates that there is a potential risk for a flood and individuals and communities are encouraged to perform last minute preparations should it occur. A flood warning indicates that an event is currently occurring or imminent, and individuals in flood risk areas are instructed to evacuate to higher or safer ground. These warnings will also advise drivers to avoid flooded bridges or low-lying areas. Special weather statements can be found in real time on the NWS/SPC website and are broadcast live on NOAA radio and as programme interruptions in the television and radio media. Other avenues for broadcast include the Weather Channel, a 24-hour cable weather service in the US, which continuously updates its broadcasts and webpage on severe storm and flood watches and warnings, and special radio and print communications that are used by the NWS to alert state and local governments, law enforcement agencies and public safety activities. In the case of a flood warning, law enforcement officers may directly warn citizens in the path of the flood through loudspeakers or door-to-door visits. They also will pre-emptively close roadways prone to being over-washed by a flash flood. Unlike some nations, remote-controlled community speakers or sirens are not generally used in the US to disseminate flood warnings.

Federal Emergency Management Agency

The Federal Emergency Management Agency (FEMA) became part of the DHS in 2003. It has the major responsibility within the federal government for flood disaster mitigation and recovery management, and works in conjunction with other agencies on emergency responses during the event. Since coming under the DHS, FEMA has enjoyed billions of dollars in increased funding to implement its programmes (FEMA, 2004d). There is some controversy, however, on how much of this funding has been spent on reorganization, bureaucracy, and planning and training for terrorist-related disasters rather than for natural disasters.

Information is provided to communities and individuals by FEMA on how to reduce their risk from flood disasters through their 'FloodSmart' campaign (FEMA, 2005g). In addition, they provide monetary grants and low-interest loans to local communities for flood risk mitigation (FEMA, 2005h). This money is distributed through the states and can be used for the purchase of properties in regularly flooded areas and the relocation of their inhabitants, as well as for flood-proofing of structures by raising them above the historic flood level or constructing local water diversion edifices. FEMA's National Flood Insurance Program is a federally funded and managed insurance programme that offers individuals and small businesses that are located in Special Flood Hazard Areas an opportunity to buy national flood insurance (FEMA, 2004e). For most flood-risk areas, flood insurance is required by law in order to secure financing to buy, build or improve structures.

Disaster recovery is also a major function of FEMA. For any county, region or state that is declared a federal disaster area by the US president, grants and low-interest loans are made available by FEMA to individuals, small businesses and communities. These funds can be used for reconstruction or repair of homes or businesses, or for rebuilding community and public utility infrastructure. FEMA-administered monetary assistance is critical for disaster recovery and can be quite substantial. Following the inland flooding of Hurricane Floyd in 1999, the state of North Carolina alone received over US$1.9 billion in disaster recovery aid (FEMA, 2005i).

FEMA is not without controversy and the agency has been criticized in the past because of perceptions of slow response, excessive bureaucracy, waste, differential treatment and poor leadership and management (Associated Press, 2005). In addition, the agency has been censured for encouraging citizens and businesses to rebuild in flood-risk areas (Bovard, 1997). Perhaps the greatest amount of criticism that has been levelled at FEMA was in reaction to the slow and cumbersome federal response to the New Orleans flood following Hurricane Katrina (Hsu and Glasser, 2005). While it remains contentious as to the degree of blame that FEMA should shoulder from the poor public health response to this flood, it should be noted that until recent years FEMA's responsibilities have been more oriented towards fiscal mitigation and relief rather than emergency response, and that the operational response aspects of this organization have recently been drastically reorganized under the 2001 Homeland Security Act.

The Centers for Disease Control and Prevention
The Centers for Disease Control and Prevention (CDC) is one federal agency involved in responses to flooding that does not come under the umbrella of the DHS (it is within the Department of Health and Human Services). This agency largely oversees public health and clinical medical services for their

long- and short-range planning for floods and other disasters. It also assists with the emergency phase public health response to floods at the federal level. In addition, it is responsible for analysing mortality statistics from floods and, in conjunction with state health departments, for implementing and scrutinizing local, regional and state data on injury and disease in the emergency and early recovery phases. At the time of the flood, the CDC will often dispatch an epidemiology intelligence officer to the state health department to assist with rapid needs assessment and surveillance activities. The CDC has a wealth of information for individuals and medical care providers on causes of injury and disease in US floods and measures through which to reduce the risks of their occurrence. These materials are available on their website (see Table 7.2).

The role of non-governmental organizations

Selected NGOs are also involved in flood disaster responses in the US. These include the American Red Cross, the Salvation Army, local church and civic groups, amateur radio associations and the Civil Air Patrol. The largest and best organized is the American Red Cross. This organization has a well-developed programme for providing flood risk mitigation and personal preparedness information to individuals (American Red Cross, 2005). The American Red Cross is also involved in soliciting donations from the public, which it distributes to needy flood-afflicted individuals. In addition, it operates emergency shelters in conjunction with local governments and keeps basic statistics on shelter inhabitants and any diseases and injuries that they might have incurred during the flood or within the shelter. This agency also assists individuals in locating family members who may have been involved in the flood event.

Response to flooding in an era of bioterrorism and homeland security awareness

The US health-sector response to flooding has some components that are unique when compared to its responses to other natural disasters. However, to a large extent the public health, medical care, emergency services and law enforcement agencies that are called to respond are the same. Since 11 September 2001, in order to better respond to a terrorist attack, there has been a substantial increase in investment in public health and emergency service departments, as well as for improved planning and training in medical care sectors (CDC, 2005b). Any financial, equipment or personnel resources that are at the disposal of these governmental or private organizations for bioterrorism or other terrorist responses should also indirectly be available for response to natural or flooding disasters. In fiscal year 2002 over US$1 billion were distributed by the US Congress to invest in public health infrastructure (CDC, 2005b). Much of this money went to state and county health departments. Additional money was distributed to hospitals for disaster preparedness directly from the DHS (DHS, 2005b). It was speculated that this enhancement of health services infrastructure would pay off dividends in terms of an improved medical response to flooding disasters. A 2004 survey by the US Council of State and Territorial Epidemiologists showed that this investment has already enhanced state public health capabilities, but that further money and support are needed to achieve the goals outlined by the DHS (CDC, 2005b).

One example of how bioterrorism resources may be used for an enhanced public health response to flooding is found in North Carolina. This state used some of its federal funds for bioterrorism response to create seven regional Public Health Response Teams across the state (Cline, 2002). These teams are specially trained in hazard mitigation, epidemiology, surveillance, and emergency preparedness and response. While their primary mission is to plan for and respond to bioterrorism events, they are also used for other public health emergencies. During 2004 and 2005, these teams were deployed to four floods with public health implications. These teams performed rapid needs assessments using geographic information systems technology and hand-held pocket computers equipped with global positioning receivers (CDC, 2004d). These assessments were each completed during a 24- to 48-hour interval, and the results were available almost immediately due to the ability of the pocket computers to download data to a central server. In addition, during these floods the Public Health Response Teams assisted with local injury and disease surveillance.

On the other hand, the slow, poorly coordinated and inadequate response to the New Orleans flood following Hurricane Katrina has raised serious questions on whether homeland security preparedness has really advanced the US's capacity to respond to natural disasters (*The Lancet*, 2005). From the derisory public health response to this flood, it would seem that preoccupation and misdirected planning towards homeland security derailed the public health response to this natural disaster in Louisiana, particularly in New Orleans. Indeed, the mass media images of New Orleans citizens in need of basic necessities during this flood brought up severe questions across the US as to the ability of US governments to respond to any disaster. It is likely, though, that differences in regional and local use of homeland security resources for public health responses to flood disaster exist across the US. Perhaps an even more important aspect of the New Orleans flood is that it occurred in a community with serious pre-existing disparities in public health and medical care access, and that the ability of this local government to respond to the needs of its population was stressed well before the disaster of Hurricane Katrina (*The Lancet*, 2005).

Another important aspect of the governmental response to the New Orleans flood is that federal, state and local public health responses to disaster were reorganized only a few months prior to this disaster under the DHS National Response Plan (DHS, 2005c). This plan seeks to integrate all emergency services in the US using best practice and procedures from incident management disciplines. A component of the plan outlines the National Incident Management System, which integrates incident command and responses within a single framework that should provide for better coordination of federal, state and local agencies during a disaster (DHS, 2005d). At the time that the New Orleans flood occurred, the DHS National Response Plan had not been fully implemented, and state and local governments had not yet trained or exercised using the new plan. There was much confusion during the Hurricane Katrina responses as to whether the new plan should be used or whether responses outlined under previous plans still applied. This confusion contributed greatly to miscommunication and poor coordination between different response elements.

Conclusion

Response to flooding in the US occurs at many levels and involves numerous governmental and non-governmental agencies. These entities work together and coordinate their relief efforts in order to provide public health interventions and acute or chronic medical care to flood-affected persons. However, they often encounter significant barriers to their response when utility, communication and transportation infrastructure is disrupted by the flood, or when planning and training in responding elements have been deficient. In addition, past flood responses have been hampered by pre-event education campaigns that were frequently inadequate or ignored by the public and by disjointed and poorly coordinated emergency responses by both the public health and medical care sectors.

The last decade of the 20th century and the first few years of the 21st century saw several major floods in the US that provided opportunities to observe flood response and learn lessons for future responses. Many of the response sectors outlined in this chapter have attempted to address these lessons learned, some with more success than others. Perhaps most importantly there have been several important changes in US disaster and flood responses that have occurred since the terrorist events of 2001, including greater funding and resources intended to improve public health. Many of these changes were designed to improve cooperation, coordination and communication between responding agencies. The governmental public health responses to the 2005 New Orleans flood associated with Hurricane Katrina, however, has raised serious questions as to whether this investment in homeland security has increased preparedness at all, or whether it has paradoxically hampered the ability of government agencies to appropriately respond to large-scale flood and other natural disasters. It is also an open question as to how long this increase in resources for disaster preparedness will last.

One important area of flood response in the US that is currently inadequate involves the public health response to the long-term health effects of flooding, particularly those concerning mental health. As other chapters in this book suggest, the impact of flooding on mental health is considerable (Square, 1997; Ginexi et al, 2000; Verger et al, 2003; Reacher et al, 2004). There is a great need for further research in this area to examine the nature and severity of the psychological effects of flooding, and to identify effective interventions that should be employed during the emergency and recovery responses to a flood. Currently in the US, the assessment of mental health needs during a flood and the short- and long-term interventions to address these needs are insufficient and are arguably not adequately addressed by any current reform in disaster management.

There are several countries or regions of the world that currently are experiencing rapidly growing economies and a technical and industrial revolution that promises an improved standard of living for their citizens. Many of these countries have historically been plagued by floods. As these countries further develop their public utility infrastructure and public health and medical care sectors, the impacts of flooding on their population will change and will likely begin to mirror that in high-income countries. Adoption of effective public health responses to flooding currently employed in the US and study of the lessons learned from its inadequate responses may help these countries to mitigate the future effects of flooding on their populations.

8

Flood Hazards and Health: Implications for Action and Research

Roger Few, Franziska Matthies, Mike Ahern and Sari Kovats

The aim of this book has been to combine findings from studies across different disciplines in order to explore how flooding impacts upon health and how individuals, communities and agencies charged with protecting health respond to those threats. Detailed experiences from the UK, Mozambique, Viet Nam and the US in Chapters 4–7 have been brought together with reports from a wide range of countries reviewed in Chapters 2 and 3. The different approaches of the chapters reflect the different disciplinary backgrounds of the authors – among them specialists in epidemiology, medicine, public health, human geography, civil engineering and hazards research – and yet together the discussions yield many common issues and lessons. Above all, they affirm the need to take a broad, long-term approach to addressing health risks and point to the crucial role that health considerations must take in overall risk reduction.

This concluding chapter integrates the analysis from the foregoing chapters, drawing out implications for present and future response to health risks from floods. The chapter first extends the discussion of vulnerability, coping capacity and adaptation to present and future health risks from flooding. It then sets out a series of priority considerations for policy and action, now and in the future, and points to critical areas for further research.

Vulnerability, coping capacity and adaptation

Chapter 1 introduced the notion of risk as a function of hazard and vulnerability, emphasizing that it is shaped just as much by social processes as it is by natural forces. The degree to which a particular flood event will affect human health can therefore be seen to depend upon the physical nature of the flood event and the degree to which human populations and systems are vulnerable to its impacts. Vulnerability is not just a passive state since it is also determined by the responses of people and systems to health threats. Hence, coping capacity is seen as the converse of vulnerability. We also introduced the notion of adaptation as purposeful change to address recurrent or future risk. Here, we briefly review the implications of flooding for health and health care, discuss some of the determinants of differential vulnerability and coping capacity, and review the challenges of adaptation to potential changes in future flood hazards.

Health risks and response

Floods worldwide pose a range of threats to human health. In short, they can bring death, injury, disease and stress. Public and institutional concern over the health impacts of flood events is evident in the attention paid to health issues in the aftermath of disasters. Health was especially high on the agenda for relief organizations following the Indian Ocean Tsunami of 2004 – a coastal flood disaster of enormous scale that took place during the preparation of this book (see Box 8.1). Yet, the precise effects of floods on health have, to date, been poorly characterized for most health outcomes in most regions. Only a relatively small number of epidemiological studies reported in Chapter 2 are able to provide reliable evidence on disease risk during or after floods. As Chapters 4–7 and a range of other studies reveal, however, there is strong evidence of a change in risk factors during floods, of statistical associations between flood events and disease incidence, and of a perceived link between floods and ill health among people exposed to floods and those agencies responsible for public health. Together with risk of drowning and physical trauma sustained during the onset of the flood hazard, these studies especially underline the threat of disease associated with contamination of water and the creation of mosquito-breeding sites, and the mental health risks related to the emotional and psychological stress caused by flood events.

Vulnerability to disease and other health impacts is offset by coping measures undertaken both by the populations at risk and by health systems and other health-related services. Chapter 3 and each of the case studies in Chapters 4–7 discuss a range of measures that are taken at different scales at different phases in the hazard cycle across the fields of health promotion, disease control, health system disaster procedures, water supply protection and sanitation provision. The potential gains in health protection from community-based initiatives are commonly emphasized, together with the efforts of state and non-governmental agencies. These stand in addition to a wide range of more general flood management measures (both structural and non-structural), such as flood control engineering and regulations on land use.

Nevertheless, serious shortfalls in coping capacity exist in all contexts. The studies, reports and recommendations that have informed this book suggest that there are major limitations to the application of existing response

Box 8.1 *Health aspects of the Indian Ocean Tsunami, 2004*

As this book was in preparation, one of the world's worst natural disasters of recent times was unleashed on coastal communities around the Indian Ocean. At least 227,000 people lost their lives in the tsunami of 26 December 2004, with the greatest death tolls in Indonesia (especially Aceh Province), Sri Lanka, India and Thailand. Millions more were displaced from their homes, suffered loss of livelihoods and possessions, or were otherwise profoundly affected by the onrush of a series of powerful waves triggered by a huge undersea earthquake. The health implications of this disastrous coastal flood event have already been touched on in earlier chapters.

As well as the immediate fatalities, tens of thousands of people suffered injuries and complications from near-drowning (VanRooyen and Leaning, 2005; Waring and Brown, 2005). Concern over outbreaks of infectious disease was high, given the scale and intensity of the destruction and the displacement of so many households, as well as the need to meet the survivors' basic health requirements for water, sanitation, food, shelter and medical care. The capacity of health services and infrastructure in many sites was severely affected. One particularly notable aspect of this disaster was the high prominence given to the mental health repercussions. Indeed, given the level of attention paid to psychosocial support in the actions both of governments and external agencies, several commentators have stressed the need to ensure that measures follow established principles of disaster mental health response (e.g. Chatterjee, 2005; Kett et al, 2005; Silove and Zwi, 2005; WHO, 2005d).

The scale of overall international response to the tsunami disaster was unprecedented. Several hundred relief organizations became active in the region, many of them working on health-related issues, and problems over coordination of their activities rapidly emerged (VanRoyen and Leaning, 2005; WHO, 2005a). Where it was feasible, the value of local coordination of public health efforts was again demonstrated. In some sites the disaster also highlighted the value of disaster preparedness. The Centers for Disease Control and Prevention (CDC, 2005a) report that preparedness planning in Thailand enabled the government to activate mass casualty plans and rapidly deploy emergency clinical care, surveillance, health education and mental health support teams to the affected regions.

From the outset, the World Health Organization (WHO) took a major international role in supporting disease surveillance, needs assessments, mobilization of resource supplies and restoration of infrastructure through its Health Action in Crisis Network (Waring and Brown, 2005). In May 2005, the WHO held a major conference on health aspects of the tsunami, including the management of the disaster response. Once again the central role of preparedness in health risk reduction was reiterated, with special emphasis on capacities at the local level and within communities (WHO, 2005c).

mechanisms for health risks from floods – limitations broadly in terms of information, organization and resources. For health systems, at least, the needs are already well documented. In 1999, for example, the Pan American Health Organization (PAHO) held an international conference on the lessons learned from Hurricanes George and Mitch regarding emergency medical care. More than 400 experts from 48 countries compiled a comprehensive document with recommendations on topics, including disaster preparedness, needs assessment, coordination, supply management, emergency medical care and psychosocial care (PAHO, 1999). Part of the problem is that during floods, health systems have to provide ongoing care and respond to new demands at a time when the systems themselves may experience operational difficulties because of damage to health infrastructure and disruption of staffing and supplies. Chapter 7 shows how severely major floods can impact upon health systems even in a relatively resource-rich country such as the US.

What shapes vulnerability and coping capacity?

Health risks are not distributed equally. The factors that shape differential vulnerability and coping capacity in the face of floods have received little research attention to date; but we can begin to assemble a broad perspective. Vulnerability, as defined in Chapter 1, is a function both of potential exposure to flood hazard and people's underlying susceptibility to its impacts. For the presence of flood to affect health, there first has to be some form of exposure to its health-prejudicial effects – such as physical contact with water-borne pathogens. Next, there has to be development of disease in the individual, a state affected by existing health status. Final health outcome then depends further upon ability to recover from the condition, which is partly dependent upon access to treatment. The differential vulnerability of people to health impact can be seen to arise from differences at all of these stages: differences not just in environment, but in behaviour, material assets, well-being and access to health care. Those with better ability to protect their health and recover from adverse health impacts have greater coping capacity. The close interconnection between health outcomes and social aspects of vulnerability to hazards has already been emphasized by Lindsay (2003) in the field of population health.

For individuals and households, income status has a major influence on the ability to avoid and recover from health impacts. But though relative wealth plays a key role in shaping patterns of exposure and susceptibility, other assets and resources, including human and social capital, also come into the equation. Chapter 4, in particular, discusses the role that access to social support networks can play during floods. Note that in some contexts social capital may be high among certain poor or marginalized groups. Vulnerability is also differentiated by a range of wider societal factors, such as cultural norms, patterns of urbanization and policies for water provision – contextual factors that shape the likelihood of health impacts and available response options. In some countries the distinction between urban and rural settings may be important. On the one hand, populations in urban areas may benefit from easier access to health facilities and relief measures. On the other hand, there may be higher potential for environmental contamination in some urban environments and industrial zones (Harpham and Tanner, 1995; Wisner and Adams, 2002). Crucial differences in vulnerability also exist at the intra-household level and among social groups: several authors point towards higher levels of vulnerability among women, children, the elderly and people with disabilities (e.g. Enarson and Hearn-Morrow, 1998; Parkinson, 2003; Quarantelli, 2003). In some contexts, women may be more likely to become disaster victims because they are less likely to be reached by warning and evacuation procedures and may have access to fewer support systems. While recognizing such trends, however, it is also important to understand the complexity of social differentiation. Kett et al (2005), for example, point out the diversity of needs and capacities that can be masked by group labels such as 'disabled people', and Handmer (2003) warns against a tendency to stereotype social groups *a priori* as vulnerable or lacking in resilience,.

Perceptions and knowledge of health risks may play an important part, too, in shaping vulnerability, as discussed in the UK study in Chapter 4. In low-income countries, attention often focuses on the role of health and hygiene education efforts in promoting safe water use. According to Roger Young and Associates (2000), the health impact of the 1998 floods in Bangladesh was lessened by the fact that, since the previous great flood of 1988, rural people in Bangladesh had become used to drinking tube-well water and gained a generally higher awareness about the need for clean drinking water. Lack of awareness, conversely, can heighten health risks. However, as noted in Chapter 6, there is a need to be careful in making routine assumptions about the link between knowledge and behaviour. Lack of effective coping mechanisms may be a more complex matter than simply failure to recognize health risks. In the Bangladesh cyclone of 1991, Hoque et al (1993) found that many people understood the risks from contaminated water but were unable to treat their sources. Many were unable to boil water because they were displaced from their homes and possessions or could not afford fuel. They had the knowledge but not the resources.

Risk-taking behaviour is another important component of vulnerability at both community and individual levels. In a study in India, Stephens et al (1994) reveal that people living in marginal, flood-prone inner city locations made a conscious trade-off between the benefits of access to sources of income and exposure to health risks. Such a 'hazards culture' oriented towards living with floods is replicated in many parts of the world. It may contain within it aspects that heighten susceptibility to flood impact; but it also usually entails a series of customary coping mechanisms born out of experience and preparedness. In Viet Nam, the concept of living with floods has now become formalized into government policy on local capacity-building and flood preparedness (see Chapter 6).

Differential vulnerability and coping capacity can also be described at a wider scale, between countries and regions. As Chapters 2 and 3 made clear, at a crude level there is a major distinction between the health burden of floods in richer and poorer countries. It is a disparity linked partly to the geography of hazard, but, crucially, also to capacities within society to protect populations from flood hazard, to reduce and respond to the health risks of floods, and to provide baseline health care. Populations in many countries of Latin America, Africa and Asia tend to be more vulnerable not only because of individual poverty, but also because of the collective poverty manifested, for example, in low levels of investment in piped water provision and differences in the accessibility, quality and capacity of health services.

However, this gross North–South distinction hides important differences between regions and countries, both in levels of general development and health service provision, and specifically in their response to environmental hazards. A recent report on hurricane preparedness in Cuba suggests that, despite relatively low per-capita income, the country has been highly successful in risk reduction because of its investment in health care, rural infrastructure and both national-level and local-level disaster planning (Thompson and Gavira, 2004). Rather than gross patterns emerging to contrast high-income and low-income regions, country-specific variations in governance and culture may be just as prominent in shaping vulnerability and coping capacity within society.

Attention to the social determinants of vulnerability highlights that risks from flood disasters are part of the very fabric of society. Floods cannot, therefore, be addressed in isolation – as a technical problem requiring a discrete solution. In planning health risk reduction, it is important to recognize that the potential for flood hazard to cause an emergency is inherent in pre-existing conditions, rather than to view the emergency as an exogenous aberration from a 'normal' non-emergency state (White et al, 2004). In this sense, as argued in Chapter 1, the hazard cycle may be better viewed as a spiral – one that can progress positively upwards if learning from the hazard experience leads to adaptation within society, or downwards if the post-hazard phase exacerbates previous vulnerabilities still further (Wisner et al, 2004).

Future challenges

Flood hazard is an inherently episodic and variable phenomenon. There will always be year-to-year changes in the frequency and magnitude of flood events. But we can also point to forces that can bring long-term changes in flood risk, sometimes referred to as drivers of change. There are potential drivers of positive or negative change in flood hazard, such as changes in rainfall, storm patterns and sea levels, as well as vegetation changes, land-use changes and modifications in flood management. There are also potential drivers of positive and negative changes in vulnerability, including population growth, spatial shifts in human settlement and progress towards poverty reduction. The future cannot be predicted with certainty; but, on balance, there is a likelihood that the combined effect of climate change, changes in land cover and increasing human populations along coasts and in floodplains will result in a global increase in flood risk (see Chapter 1). The challenge to health further emphasizes the importance of strengthening coping capacity – a process commonly referred to as adaptation in the context of climate change.

As Chapter 1 explains, climate change, in particular, is likely to intensify future flood problems in many areas in the coming decades (McCarthy et al, 2001; Milly et al, 2002; Nicholls, 2004). In some locations under some scenarios of climate change, there may be significant changes in flooding by 2050. Sea level rise and changes in storm patterns could affect many coastal settlements throughout the world, including many of the world's megacities with populations of over 8 million (Klein et al, 2003). Increases in storm precipitation and seasonal rainfall peaks will affect many river basins, particularly, but not necessarily exclusively, in existing humid regions. Because of the many uncertainties involved, it is not possible to say precisely where, when and by how much flood hazard will change. However, we contend that it is likely such changes would entail not only an increase in risk in existing flood-prone locations, but also cause some coastal and river basin areas to become newly prone to severe flooding.

In the absence of effective adaptation measures, increased flood hazard as a result of climate change would increase the health impact of flooding. The additional hazard factor implied by climate change may place extra and potentially unanticipated demands on health care provision and other health protection services. This may be especially so in circumstances where other drivers, such as environmental degradation and the impact of HIV/AIDS in low-income African settlements, already threaten to overwhelm present adaptive capacities (Parker and Thompson, 2000). The problems may be made more complex by other climate-related changes, such as rising temperatures that could alter underlying disease ecology and the spatial distribution of pathogens (Patz et al, 2003).

Adaptation to the health implications of climate change, together with other drivers of flood risk, can encompass modifications in behaviour, practices, organization and resources at various scales (Scheraga et al, 2003). To be effective, action to address future risk may need to be taken in advance of climate impacts as anticipatory adaptation (Smit et al, 2001). Anticipatory adaptation is by no means an easy process. It requires careful assessment of long-term impacts and response options, it has inherent costs and it must be balanced against other priorities. It is also hampered by the predictive imprecision associated with climate change and the parameters of future flood risk. Yet, although uncertainty remains, a precautionary approach would posit that, given the weight of existing knowledge, absolute proof of the effects of the climate change threat should not necessarily be required before adaptive action is taken (Corvalan et al, 2003; Sperling and Szekely, 2005). Moreover, as argued in the next section, many adaptive actions within health and related sectors are likely to have multiple and tangible benefits for people living now. Efforts to build coping capacity against the health impacts of future flood risk will, in many cases, provide immediate health benefits for populations experiencing floods today.

Towards risk reduction

As reflected in the United Nations International Strategy for Disaster Reduction, modern principles of hazard management call for a move away from a solely reactive approach to floods. Risk reduction implies a broad, integrated approach to reducing present and future risks, with implications for action at all phases in the hazard cycle. At the 2005 World Conference on Disaster Reduction in Kobe, Japan, governments signed up to a framework of action that emphasizes 'the more effective integration of disaster risk considerations into sustainable development policies, planning and programming at all levels, with a special emphasis on disaster prevention, mitigation, preparedness and vulnerability reduction' (ISDR, 2005, p3). The document also supports the fundamental inter-linkage between adaptation to climate change and disaster risk reduction efforts.

The emphasis on risk reduction is reflected in all of the contributions to this book. Here we distil some concluding themes surrounding policy and intervention to reduce health risk from present and future floods. They relate to efforts to prevent health impacts and to improving the capacity of systems to provide care and essential services during and after flood events.

Acting in advance

Action in advance of flood events is, in many senses, the key to effective health risk reduction, now and in the future. Yet, a reliance on reactive response to flood emergencies remains for many populations and the health-sector institutions that serve them. Given the increased risk posed by climate change, a further shift of emphasis is required, particularly towards flood preparedness. This is increasingly advocated for flood risk reduction in general (such as improvement in early warning systems and building restrictions on floodplains), which will itself reduce overall health risk 'upstream' by reducing exposure and social vulnerability. But it is also crucial in terms of 'downstream' health protection.

Flood hazard issues need to become mainstreamed into general health system planning and development, especially in flood-prone areas. There needs to be more advance assessment of risk and planning of measures that will be taken both before and after the onset of floods. For health care agencies, such measures can include flood-proofing works at medical facilities as well as advance preparation of hospital disaster plans and national emergency medical systems with designated specialist teams. Chapter 7 discusses the role of disaster plans in the US; but emergency systems for disasters established outside resource-rich settings, as in Uzbekistan (WHO, 2004) and Thailand (CDC, 2005a) show that such initiatives can be feasible in a range of contexts. The same goes for health education. Not only is it important to enhance preparedness of individuals and communities prior to flood and storm seasons, but advance preparation of resources and delivery systems will also facilitate health and hygiene education *during* flood events. Information for the public on health and safety risks related to floods and on means of protection against those risks needs to be carefully planned and targeted to its audience in order to maximize its effect.

Where society, in general, is already undertaking flood risk reduction efforts, it is crucial that health systems are brought into the process alongside other sectors and institutions. Effective functioning of health systems in floods depends upon the activities of other sectors such as transport, communication, electricity and other utilities. Chapter 6 describes how health agency representatives are brought together with a range of officials from other sectors to form local flood protection committees in Viet Nam. In a recent European workshop on extreme climate events and health, the importance of including health agencies in flood preparedness was emphasized, together with a call for the health sector to take a proactive role (WHO, 2004). Indeed, given the importance, reach and political 'tangibility' of health impacts from floods, there is a case for arguing that the health sector can and should take the lead in galvanizing disaster preparedness planning, impact assessment and awareness-raising within society (Poncelet and de Ville de Goyet, 1996; Lindsay, 2003).

Building local capacity

Individuals, households and communities stand at the front line of both health risk and health risk reduction: it is they who ultimately face the health impacts of floods; but it is also at this level that key preventive health efforts take root. Several chapters in this book stress the importance of fostering coping capacity at the grassroots level. Chapters 4 and 6 consider the role that community support networks, volunteer organizations and local flood action groups can play in alleviating health impacts in the UK and Viet Nam. Reporting from Mozambique, Chapter 5 re-emphasizes that local people and resources often provide the bulk of relief effort, at least in the immediate post-onset phase of flood events.

Capacity-building at the community level is a key strategic goal in the international agenda on disaster reduction (ISDR, 2005), and its critical importance is recognized by many agencies engaged in both humanitarian relief and development programmes. As Tearfund (2004, p18) stresses, 'governments, aid agencies and local authorities should work alongside poor communities in vulnerable countries to identify and reduce the risks they face'. The potential for work at this level includes not only community involvement in decision-making on flood-risk reduction projects, but enabling communities to develop their own preparedness measures and emergency response plans. A number of such initiatives, both community based and in partnership with external agencies, are described in Chapter 3. They include activities such as volunteer training in medical aid for emergencies, developing local warning and evacuation systems and flood-proofing of water sources and latrines. As in many other fields, community participation in flood preparedness will often present difficult challenges, among them issues of prioritization, motivation, representation and co-option (Cooke and Kothari, 2001; Pugh and Potter,

2003). But, where effective, the gains in health protection from such efforts may prove crucial, particularly in the light of any future intensification in flood hazard (Few, 2003). As discussed below, further insights from examples of successful local capacity-building to tackle health risk from floods and storms would be highly valuable.

Coordinating responses

In all forms of health-related response to floods, effective action relies not just on the technical means to protect health, but crucially also on the flow of information and interaction between different actors and sectors. There needs to be greater dialogue and coordination between institutions and across scales: between policy-makers, agencies and communities in flood preparedness and emergency response. The importance of communication and coordination between institutions is highlighted especially in the discussion of agencies' response to floods in the US in Chapter 7. Clinton et al (1995) emphasize a need for continuous liaison between different levels of health care and response managers to ensure maintenance of effective health services.

A major problem can arise if external agencies become engaged in health care relief during flood disasters without ensuring that they communicate and coordinate effectively with domestic agencies. The form and quality of health assistance is important in flood disaster situations: if inappropriate external skills and resources do not meet the needs on the ground, they may only add to the problems (Noji and Toole, 1997). Immediate life-saving needs, for example, tend to be covered by local populations and their health professionals; therefore, the skills of incoming medical personnel should be closely matched to specific shortages within the country. The problem of ill-conceived assistance has also been highlighted in relation to donations of inappropriate drugs that are not requested by the recipient country, are unable to be used in the local context or are simply out of date. Christie and Hanlon (2001) argue that this applied to as much as 50 per cent of the drugs donated to Mozambique in 2000. Chapter 5 provides other examples of failures in coordination during the same flood disaster.

Assessing risks and needs

For health systems, the range of potential health impacts associated with floods calls for a holistic approach to assessing health needs. Together with new health demands arising from floods, health systems also have to take stock of the needs of existing patients. Prioritization of services is likely to be necessary during emergencies, and some flexibility must be retained in order to meet event-specific needs; but careful planning can ensure that important gaps in health care are avoided.

In particular, a more balanced and informed approach may be needed to assess and respond to mental health needs. As Chapter 4 and several other contributions to this book underline, until recently, the implications of floods for mental health have been largely sidelined, with resources tending to be targeted towards treatment of physical injury and prevention of infectious diseases. In part, this reflects a lack of information. Guha-Sapir et al (2005) emphasize that a better understanding of the need for and effectiveness of psychosocial interventions after disasters is required in order to assess their importance vis-à-vis other health care priorities. Commenting on mental health issues arising from the 2004 Indian Ocean Tsunami, VanRooyen and Leaning (2005, p437) note: 'psychological stress in the aftermath of a disaster and its long-term effects are only beginning to be understood'. As Chapter 6 suggests, cultural notions of resilience may possibly serve to mask the scale of psychological impacts, especially in communities frequently exposed to floods. In poor countries, in particular, inattention to mental health impacts also strongly reflects low levels of mental health care provision, in general (WHO, 2001).

In many settings, risks of infectious disease will continue to be the primary concern following floods. Again, however, the choice of response to those risks needs to be based as much as possible on informed and holistic assessment of the level of threat and the suitability of response options. McCluskey (2001) draws particular attention to judgements on water quality. Normally safe water sources that become flooded may still remain less contaminated than alternative non-flooded, but unprotected, water sources – as shown by a comparative study of water quality in flooded tube wells and other surface sources in Bangladesh. This needs to be borne in mind when decisions are taken on closing down water systems for disinfection during the emergency phase of floods.

Disseminating positive lessons

If management of health risks from floods is to improve around the globe, mechanisms for learning from past experiences need to be in place. Such lessons will be especially important for areas that may become newly exposed to flood risk as a result of climate change effects. Adaptation may arise automatically; but it may also benefit from deliberate exchange of knowledge between countries and communities on effective coping mechanisms and organization of flood preparedness at all scales.

Some studies and reports draw practical lessons from current responses to health risks from hazards and advocate replicable principles for action elsewhere. Most of the recommendations are set within more general analyses of hazard response, rather than focusing specifically on health. However, notable exceptions include a series of publications produced by PAHO on hurricane preparedness (PAHO, 1999), the protection of health facilities from natural disasters (PAHO, 2003) and contingency planning for environmental health during floods (Caribbean Environmental Health Institute, 2003).

More effort is needed to identify effective actions and strategies at different scales, and to communicate them to other contexts and regions. Thompson and Gavira (2004) argue that there may be generic aspects of disaster preparedness and mitigation that are broadly transferable, as in the artificial earthen mounds noted in Chapter 5, which are built as refuges on floodplains in some regions, or the broad principles of disaster planning for health facilities. In this sense, there is scope for international exchange of ideas, even across global regions. Lessons, however, can seldom be applied 'off the peg': generic lessons always have to be tailored to local circumstances and made appropriate to the population or system being served.

Risk reduction in the broader context of public health

Reducing risks to health from floods is not a stand-alone task. It can benefit from and contribute to broader health gains in society. For low-income countries, in particular, there is a strong argument that adaptation to future health risks from climatic hazards will be facilitated most effectively by overall strengthening of people's capacity for health protection and strengthening of the health systems and other services that are available to them (WHO, 1999b). In the broadest sense, risk reduction and adaptation are intimately linked with the development agenda (White et al, 2004; Sperling and Szekely, 2005): tackling poverty in all its forms will play a tremendous role in reducing the specific health risks from flooding. Many local-level interviewees in the Viet Nam study reported in Chapter 6 saw the key to health protection as strengthening people's livelihood assets, including income and education. In the health sector itself, general improvements in medical facilities, disease control, waste management and water supplies would also go a long way to reducing people's vulnerability to the specific risks posed by floods. They will do so by reducing chronic health hazards in the environment, improving the general health status of populations (thereby reducing susceptibility to ill health) and improving the coping capacity of systems during emergencies. The critical importance of safe water and sanitation provision for protecting public health has been re-emphasized many times (Bartram et al, 2005).

There is also a reverse reasoning. Action related to floods can, and arguably should, bring wider health benefits. Incidental benefits may stem from the targeting of extra resources during floods towards activities such as disease surveillance and control. But wider health benefits can also be an explicit goal built into project design, especially in preparedness and recovery-phase efforts geared to long-term risk reduction and sustainable development. Flood preparedness projects fostered by the aid agency Action Against Hunger in northern Cambodia, for example, have included the establishment of designated flood evacuation sites with improved water and sanitation infrastructure (British Red Cross, 2001a). The idea is that these facilities will also provide year-round benefits for the host communities. Maber (1989), reporting on sanitation recovery work following severe floods in coastal Peru, describes how community participation in one project led to a parallel activity of strengthening health promotion, in general. The floods had highlighted problems of hygiene awareness and knowledge about treatment of common diseases, and the new health promotion efforts included the establishment of a community medical centre and health education and training programmes. Training in general health promotion was also a feature of recovery work funded by aid agencies in Orissa, India, after the super-cyclone of 1999 (Palakudiyil and Todd, 2003).

In the climate change literature, the potential to derive wider gains from tackling hazard risk is commonly emphasized as a counter to short-term political constraints on adaptive capacity. Scheraga et al (2003, p245) stress that 'adaptive responses may have multiple benefits: reducing risks from climate change while, at the same time, addressing other risks to public health'. If the climate threat were to galvanize the strengthening of health systems and related services, it could certainly be seen as a 'win–win' approach – one that will provide benefits regardless of the outcome of climate change.

At present, it is not always easy to attract funding for sustainable risk reduction. Reporting from the Philippines, Luna (2001) demonstrates that it is often difficult for organizations to obtain funds for capacity-building and preparedness compared to emergency relief – the need is less visible and the impact of the work is less easy to measure. For both governmental agencies and non-governmental organizations (NGOs), it may be perceived that the financial burden of flood mitigation and preparedness is too high, particularly in countries where resources for the health sector are already under severe strain. However, according to PAHO (2000, 2003), investments in vulnerability reduction should be viewed as cost effective in the long term since they can prevent huge costs and losses to health systems in the event of a natural disaster. A key step towards risk reduction is therefore to influence the perception that risk reduction is not only effective, but also economically efficient, especially if wider health benefits and long-term risks can be brought into the equation.

Research needs

Research activity, to date, on flooding and health remains rather limited. Many of the chapters in this book highlight the need for an improved knowledge base as a platform from which to strengthen risk reduction. Research needs are discussed here in terms of health impacts and responses to health risks. However, it should be noted that there is also a need for integrated research that links findings on impact and response: the interactions between the two aspects makes it difficult to draw conclusions in isolation. There is a need, too, for integrated cross-scale research conducted at regional, national and local levels in order to capture variation in pattern and process at different spatial scales.

Health impacts research

The existing body of epidemiological research on the health impacts of floods suffers from gaps in coverage and also in quality. A better understanding is required of how disease risk alters during floods, and there is a need for more good-quality epidemiological data before vulnerability indices can be used operationally to minimize the effects of flooding on target groups.

The problem of data quality on the health impacts associated with flooding was reiterated at an expert meeting hosted by the WHO on extreme weather and health (WHO, 2004). Many of the studies that are reviewed in Chapter 2 have methodological shortcomings, including a lack of baseline (pre-flood) health data and an attempt to collect data retrospectively. Such retrospective collection is very likely to lead to recall bias in the reporting of symptoms, and in some cases health data was collected more than a year after the flood event. A further limitation in these studies was the lack of a control group (non-flooded group with whom to compare data for those who were flooded). For some health outcomes (e.g. leptospirosis and mental health disorders) a clinical diagnosis is especially important, and several studies reporting on these outcomes relied on self-reporting by the interviewee rather than on clinical diagnosis. We recognize that the relative unpredictability of floods presents methodological challenges for epidemiologists. Nevertheless, any epidemiological investigation of the health impacts of flooding should endeavour to use:

- a control (non-flooded) group for comparison with the flooded population;
- longitudinal data or routine data in order to gain information on pre-flood levels of disease at individual or population levels;
- objective measures (e.g. clinical diagnosis) of disease outcome; and
- routine surveillance information.

We recognize, too, that there are ethical, as well as methodological, issues that impinge upon research on flood impacts, especially in the immediate post-onset phase of flood disasters. Data collection during or immediately after a severe flood raises obvious issues concerning respect for those affected by the event and prioritization of resources and people's time during a period when emergency assistance is at a premium. These considerations emphasize the need for a carefully planned approach to research and perhaps for greater innovation in research design and data collection methods. Detailed discussion of ethical principles for research following disasters can be found in Collogan et al (2004).

Current state of knowledge on the health outcomes connected with flooding suggests several priority areas for research. We currently have little information on the indirect mortality attributable to flooding – deaths in addition to the immediate fatalities from drowning and injuries sustained during flood onset. Knowledge is insufficient on the impact of flooding on diarrhoeal disease and the main routes of transmission. Insufficient research attention to the impacts of flooding on long-term mental health in both high-income and low-income countries has already been highlighted, and further details on this are set out in Chapter 4. We also need a much stronger information base on the impacts on health from the disruption of health services and other life-supporting systems, especially in low-income countries.

The potential for climate change to intensify or alter flood patterns only serves to heighten the research need. We need better knowledge of the nature of future risk from floods through advances in modelling and prediction that will support the development and fine-tuning of adaptation strategies. These have to take into account complexities relating to the multi-causality of ill health. In this respect, important insights may be gained from analysis of health risk in areas currently experiencing major shifts in flooding incidence as a result of environmental change, such as land subsidence or deforestation.

Research on responses to health risks

Perhaps more so even than for health impacts, there are remarkably few studies that analyse responses to the health risks of flooding. What the often tangential literature sources discussed in Chapter 3 do show, however, is that there are many issues and considerations involved in reducing health risks that we suggest need specific attention from research and evaluation.

It is difficult, at present, to make practical statements about the utility and feasibility of different measures to tackle health risk simply because very few independent studies exist that assess their effectiveness in protecting human health. Although the task is methodologically challenging, in a technical sense there is a need to evaluate existing health protection, education, warning, monitoring, health care, water and sanitation, and system preparedness measures used in flood-prone locations (Greenough et al, 2001; Malilay, 1997; WHO, 2002). This means assessing not only their potential to interrupt the pathways towards ill health, but also assessing how feasible, appropriate and accessible they may be in different social contexts. Evaluation of effectiveness can apply in all of the spheres of response that we have considered in the book. It is also important to analyse responses to 'non-emergency' floods, as well as to extreme events. Very few studies, at present, examine how people cope with the health implications posed by predictable seasonal flooding.

In parallel, there is ample opportunity for social science approaches to strengthen our understanding of the processes of response by people and institutions to the health impacts of flooding (Matthies et al, 2003). This means analysing perceptions of health risk and coping strategies of affected populations and organizations, and the economic, social, cultural and political constraints and opportunities that shape capacity to adapt (McCluskey, 2001). Important insights can be gained from an analysis of human behaviour in response to hazard warnings and health education. A system for protecting the public from flood hazard is only effective if people take note of information and act appropriately. Understanding the social and cultural influences on response behaviour in times of emergency must therefore be a crucial consideration in the overall design and targeting of health education and public safety messages. Qualitative studies that specifically assess the knowledge, attitude and practice (KAP) of individuals or groups are designed to identify correlations, as well as discrepancies between people's knowledge and behaviour. KAP studies have already been carried out on responses to disaster (e.g. Pratinidhi and Gokhale, 1998) and could be a useful tool for analysing underlying factors that shape health behaviour in floods.

Analysis should target not just how individuals' resources and assets affect capacities and decisions, but should also examine the role of broader aspects of society that may define the parameters within which decisions and actions can be made. The latter might include, for example, the norms of organization and policy within health systems, processes of risk communication to vulnerable populations, or cultural norms on gender roles within society. As Grambsch and Menne (2003, p231) point out in relation to climate change risks, there is also a need to better understand 'the barriers and opportunities for enhancing adaptive capacity in order to protect human health'.

At a policy level, key themes of research interest include the role of community-based flood-risk management approaches in relation to health in different settings, and the prospects for integrating health-risk reduction more fully within general disaster planning. The climate change threat may heighten the need to develop new mechanisms for auditing preparedness and emergency response in health systems, and to re-examine the applicability of the precautionary principle to health policy development.

Finally, researchers, too, can seek to be proactively involved in the reduction of health risk from floods. As Chapter 7 notes, they can do so at the micro-scale for specific sites of flood risk – for example, in aiding local disease surveillance following floods. They can promote wide dissemination of research findings, and help to ensure that positive lessons on effective response to floods are deployed in order to help build the coping capacity of individuals, communities and institutions engaged in health protection and health care. They can also play a role at the macro-scale in engaging with national decision-makers and international donors on the implications of flooding for health. Armed with this improved knowledge base, it may be hoped that society will become better able to anticipate and respond to the health threats posed by any intensification of future flood hazards in the decades to come.

References

Aavitsland, P., Iversen, B., Krogh, T., Fonahn, W. and Lystad, A. (1996) 'Infections during the 1995 flood in Ostlandet: Prevention and incidence', *Tidsskrift for den Norske Lægeforening*, vol 116, pp2038–2043

Abrahams, M., Price, J., Whitlock, F. and Williams, G. (1976) 'The Brisbane floods, January 1974: Their impact on health', *Medical Journal of Australia*, vol 2, pp936–939

Action Aid (2002) *Emergencies Impact Review*, Action Aid, UK

Adam Fforde and Associates Pty Ltd (2003) *Report on Residential Clusters Research in An Giang, Dong Thap and Long An Provinces in the Mekong Delta, Vietnam*, Report for CARE International, Vietnam

Adger, N., Huq, S., Brown, K., Conway, D. and Hulme, M. (2003) 'Adaptation to climate change in the developing world', *Progress in Development Studies*, vol 3, pp179–195

Aghababian, R., Lewis, C., Gans, L. and Curley, F. (1994) 'Disasters within hospitals', *Annals of Emergency Medicine*, vol 23, pp771–777

Ahern, M., Kovats, R., Wilkinson, P., Few, R. and Matthies, F. (2005) 'Global health impacts of floods: Epidemiologic evidence', *Epidemiologic Reviews*, vol 27, pp36–46

Ahmed, M., Urasawa, S., Taniguchi, K., Urasawa, T., Kobayashi, N., Wakasugi, F., Islam, A. and Sahikh, H. (1991) 'Analysis of human rotavirus strains prevailing in Bangladesh in relation to nationwide floods brought by the 1988 monsoon', *Journal of Critical Microbiology*, vol 29, pp2273–2279

Ahmed, S., Husain, A., Sattar, M. and Chowdhury, A. (1999) 'A quick assessment of flood losses and post-flood rehabilitation needs in BRAC's programme areas', in Ahmed, S. and Ahmed, H. (eds) *Experiences of Deluge: Flood 1998*, Research Monograph Series, *15*, Bangladesh Rural Advancement Commission (BRAC), Dhaka, pp1–29

Alam, M., Rahman, S., Hossain, A. and Few, R. (2005) *Health Care Provision in the 2004 Floods in Bangladesh*, Bangladesh Centre for Advanced Studies, Dhaka

Allen, R. and Rosse, W. (1998) *Children's Response to Exposure to Traumatic Events*, Quick Response Report No 103, Hazards Center, Boulder, Colorado

American Red Cross (2005) *Disaster Services*, American Red Cross website, www.redcross.org/services/disaster/0,1082,0_319_,00.html

Anderson, M. and Woodrow, P. (1998) *Rising from the Ashes: Development Strategies in Times of Disaster*, Intermediate Technology Publications, London

Arnell, N. (2004) 'Climate change and global water resources: SRES emissions and socio-economic scenarios', *Global Environmental Change*, vol 14, pp31–52

Ashford, D., Kaiser, R., Spiegel, R., Perkins, B., Weyant, R., Bragg, S. and Plikaytis, B. (2000) 'Asymptomatic infection and risk factors for leptospirosis in Nicaragua', *American Journal of Tropical Medicine and Hygiene*, vol 63, pp249–254

Associated Press (2005) 'Perry offers no apologies for criticism of FEMA', *Houston Chronicle* website, http://www.chron.com/cs/CDA/ssistory.mpl/metropolitan/3433884

Asthana, S. (1994) 'Primary health care and selective PHC: Community participation in health and development', in Phillips, D. and Verhasselt, Y. (eds) *Health and Development*, Routledge, London, pp182–196

Atchison, C., Wintermeyer, L., Kelly, J., Currier, R. and Vogel, C. (1993) 'Public health consequences of a flood disaster – Iowa, 1993', *Morbidity and Mortality Weekly Report*, vol 42, pp653–656

Auger, C., Latour, S., Trudel, M. and Fortin, M. (2000) 'Post-traumatic stress disorder. After the flood in Saguenay', *Canadian Family Physician*, vol 46, pp2420–2427

Axelrod, C., Killam, P., Gaston, M. and Stinson, N. (1994) 'Primary health care and the Midwest flood disaster', *Public Health Reports*, vol 109, pp601–605

Balluz, L., Moll, D., Diaz Martinez, M., Merida Colindres, J and Malilay, J. (2001) 'Environmental pesticide exposure in Honduras following hurricane Mitch', *Bulletin of the World Health Organization*, vol 79, pp288–295

Bankoff, G. (2001) 'Rendering the world unsafe: 'Vulnerability' as western discourse', *Disasters*, vol 25, pp19–35

Bankoff, G., Frerks, G. and Hilhorst, D. (eds) (2004) *Mapping Vulnerability: Disasters, Development and People*, Earthscan, London

Barcellos, C. and Sabroza, P. (2000) 'Socio-environmental determinants of the leptospirosis outbreak of 1996 in western Rio de Janeiro: A geographical approach', *International Journal of Environmental Health Research*, vol 10, pp301–313

Barcellos, C. and Sabroza, P. (2001) 'The place behind the case: Leptospirosis risks and associated environmental conditions in a flood-related outbreak in Rio de Janeiro', *Cad Saude Publica*, vol 17 Supplement, pp59–67

Bartram, J., Lewis, K., Lenton, R. and Wright, A. (2005) 'Focusing on improved water and sanitation for health', *The Lancet*, vol 365, pp810–812

Baxter, P., Moller, I., Spencer, T., Spence, R and Tapsell, S. (2001) 'Flooding and climate change' in Expert Group on Climate Change and Health in the UK (ed) *Health Effects of Climate Change in the UK*, Department of Health, UK

Bayard, V., Ortega, E., Garcia, A., Caceres, L., Castillo, Z., Quiroz, E. et al (2000) 'Hantavirus pulmonary syndrome – Panama, 1999–2000', *Morbidity and Mortality Weekly Report*, vol 49, pp205–207

Becht, M., van Tilburg, M., Vingerhoets, A., Nyklicek, I., de Vries, J., Kirschbaum, C., Antoni, M. and van Heck, G. (1998) 'Watersnood Een verkennend onderzoek naar de gevolgen voor het welbevinden en de gezondheid van volwassenen en kinderen/ Flood: A pilot study on the consequences for well-being and health of adults and children' *Tijdschrift voor Psychiatrie*, vol 40, pp277–289

Beck, A. (1976) *Cognitive Therapy and the Emotional Disorders*, International Universities Press, New York

Beck, A., Emergy, G. and Greenberg, R. L. (1985) *Anxiety Disorders and Phobias*, Basic Books, New York

Becker, K., Ohl, C. and McCormick, N. (1999) 'Morbidity and mortality associated with Hurricane Floyd – North Carolina, September–October 1999', *Morbidity and Mortality Weekly Report*, vol 49, pp369–372

Benedict, S. (2003) 'Health works after the flood: Working with community partners to address public health needs following a natural disaster', Abstract 22903, 129th Annual Meeting of the American Public Health Association, Atlanta, GA, 21–25 October 2001

Bennet, G. (1970) 'Bristol floods 1968: Controlled survey of effects on health of local community disaster', *British Medical Journal*, vol 3, pp454–458

Bennish, M. and Wojtyniak, B. (1991) 'Mortality due to shigellosis; community and hospital data', *Reviews of Infectious Diseases*, vol 13(Supplement 4), ppS245–251

Bernstein, J. (1992) 'Managing hazard-prone lands in cities of the developing world', *World Bank Discussion Papers*, vol 168, pp153–174

Berrgren, R. (2005) 'Hurricane Katrina: Unexpected necessities – inside Charity Hospital', *New England Journal of Medicine*, vol 353, pp1550–1553

Beser, E., Kokal, I., Telatar, M., Okten, A. and Beser, A. (1991) 'Preventive measures after the Turkish flood disaster', *World Health Forum*, vol 12, pp445–456

Bharti, A., Nally, J., Ricaldi, J., Matthias, M., Diaz, M., Lovett, M., Levett, P., Gilman, R., Willig, M., Gotuzzo, E., Vinetz, J and Peru–United States Leptospirosis Consortium (2003) 'Leptospirosis: A zoonotic disease of global importance', *The Lancet Infectious Diseases*, vol 3, pp757–771

Biswas, R., Mazumdar, A. and Bagchi, S. (1999a) 'A study of intersectoral co-ordination in disaster management in flood prone districts of West Bengal', *Indian Journal of Public Health*, vol 43, pp106–111

Biswas, R., Pal, D and Mukhopadhyay, S. (1999b) 'A community based study on health impact of flood in a vulnerable district of West Bengal', *Indian Journal of Public Health*, vol 43, pp89–90

Bland, S., O'Leary, E., Farinaro, E and Trevisan, M. (1996) 'Long-term psychological effects of natural disasters', *Psychosomatic Medicine*, vol 58, pp18–24

Bokszczanin, A. (2000) 'Psychologiczne konsekwencje powodzi u dzieci i mlodziezy /Psychological consequences of floods in children and youth', *Psychologia Wychowawcza*, vol 43, pp172–181

Bokszczanin, A. (2002) 'Long-term negative psychological effects of a flood on adolescents', *Polish Psychological Bulletin*, vol 33, pp55–61

Bolton, P. (1983) *The Regulation of the Zambesi in Mozambique: A Study of the Origins and Impact of the Cabora Bassa Project*, PhD thesis, Science Studies Unit, University of Edinburgh, Scotland

Booker, S. (2000) 'Evaluating Floyd's effect on health in eastern North Carolina', *Environmental Health Perspectives*, vol 108, ppA67

Bovard, J. (1997) 'The FEMA snow job', CATO Institute website, www.cato.org/dailys/2-19-97.html

Bradt, D., Abraham, K and Franks, R. (2003) 'A strategic plan for disaster medicine in Australasia', *Emergency Medicine*, vol 15, pp271–282

Bravo, M., Rubio-Stipec, M., Canino, G., Woodbury, M. and Ribera, J. (1990) 'The psychological sequelae of disaster stress prospectively and retrospectively evaluated', *American Journal of Community Psychology*, vol 18, pp661–680

Breo, D. (1993) 'Flood, sweat and tears: Trying to build 'emotional levees', *Journal of the American Medical Association*, vol 270, pp2860–2862

Briceño, S. (2001) *Gender Mainstreaming in Disaster Reduction: Statement for the UN, Commission for the Status of Women*, Panel Discussion on Environmental Management and Mitigation of Natural Disasters: A Gender Perspective, 46th Session of the Commission for the Status of Women, 4–15 March 2002, New York

British Red Cross (2001a) *Preparation for Flood-Related Disasters: Case Study No 14, NGO Initiatives in Risk Reduction*, British Red Cross Society, UK

British Red Cross (2001b) *Older People in Disasters: Case Study No 11, NGO Initiatives in Risk Reduction*, British Red Cross Society, UK

British Red Cross (2001c) *Disaster Mitigation at Regional Level: Case Study No 10, NGO Initiatives in Risk Reduction*, British Red Cross Society, UK

Bromet, E., Dunn, L., Connell, M., Dew, M. and Schulberg, H. (1986) 'Long-term reliability of diagnosing lifetime major depression in a community sample', *Archives of General Psychiatry*, vol 43, pp435–440

Bronstert, A. (2003) 'Floods and climate change: Interactions and impacts', *Risk Analysis*, vol 23, pp545–557

Brown, V., Jacquier, G., Bachy, C., Bitar, D. and Legros, D. (2002) 'Prise en charge d'une épidémie de choléra dans un camp de réfugiés', *Bulletin de la Société de la Pathologie Exotique*, vol 95, pp351–354

Buckland, J. and Rahman, M. (1999) 'Community-based disaster management during the 1997 Red River Flood in Canada', *Disasters*, vol 23, pp174–191

Buckle, P., Marsh, G and Smale, S. (2000) 'New approaches to assessing vulnerability and resilience', *Australian Journal of Emergency Management*, winter, pp8–14

Cairncross, S. and Feachem, R. (1993) *Environmental Health Engineering in the Tropics: An Introductory Text*, 2nd edition, J. Wiley, Chichester

Cairncross, S., O'Neill, D., McCoy, A. and Sethi, D. (2003) *Health, Environment and the Burden of Disease: A Guidance Note*, Department for International Development, London

Caldera, T., Palma, L., Penayo, U. and Kullgren, G. (2001) 'Psychological impact of the Hurricane Mitch in Nicaragua in a one-year perspective', *Social Psychiatry and Psychiatric Epidemiology*, vol 36, pp108–114

Canino, G., Bravo, M., Rubio-Stipec, M. and Woodbury, M. (1990) 'The impact of disaster on mental health: Prospective and retrospective analyses', *International Journal of Mental Health*, vol 19, pp51–69

Cannon, T. (2000) 'Vulnerability analysis and disasters', in Parker, D. (ed) *Floods*, Routledge, London, pp45–55

Cannon, T. (2002) 'Gender and climate hazards in Bangladesh', *Gender and Development*, vol 10, pp45–50

Caribbean Environmental Health Institute (2003) *Manual for Environmental Health Contingency Planning for Floods in the Caribbean*, CEHI, Pan American Health Organization, Caribbean Office, Barbados

Caspary, H. (2004) *The August 2002 Flood in Central and Eastern Europe and Results from the EU: 'STARDEX' Project*, STARDEX, Information Sheet 2, Fachhochschule Stuttgart, Hochschule für Technik, Germany

CDC (Centers for Disease Control and Prevention) (1989) *The Public Health Consequences of Disasters 1989*, CDC, Department of Human Health and Services, Atlanta

CDC (1993a) 'Morbidity surveillance following the midwest flood: Missouri, 1993', *Journal of the American Medical Association*, vol 270, p2164

CDC (1993b) 'Public health consequences of a flood disaster, Iowa, 1993', *Morbidity and Mortality Weekly Report*, vol 42, pp653–656

CDC (1993c) 'Flood-related mortality, Missouri, 1993', *Morbidity and Mortality Weekly Report*, vol 42, pp 941–943

CDC (1993d) 'From the Centers for Disease Control and Prevention: Morbidity surveillance following the midwest flood, Missouri, 1993', *Journal of the American Medical Association*, vol 270, p2164

CDC (1994) 'Flood-related mortality, Georgia, 4–14 July 1994', *Morbidity and Mortality Weekly Report*, vol 43, pp526–530

CDC (1996) 'Surveillance for injuries and illnesses and rapid health-needs assessment following Hurricanes Marilyn and Opal, September–October 1995', *Morbidity and Mortality Weekly Report*, vol 45, pp81–85

CDC (2000) 'Morbidity and mortality associated with Hurricane Floyd, North Carolina, September–October 1999', *Morbidity and Mortality Weekly Report*, vol 49, pp369–372

CDC (2002) 'Tropical Storm Allison rapid needs assessment, Houston, Texas, June 2001', *Morbidity and Mortality Weekly Report*, vol 51, pp365–369

CDC (2004a) 'Cholera epidemic associated with raw vegetables, Lusaka, Zambia, 2003–2004', *Morbidity and Mortality Weekly Report*, vol 53, pp783–786

CDC (2004b) *Floods: Emergency Preparedness and Response*, CDC website, www.bt.cdc.gov/disasters/floods

CDC (2004c) 'Protect yourself from mold', Emergency Preparedness and Response, CDC website, www.bt.cdc.gov/disasters/mold/protect.asp

CDC (2004d) 'Rapid community health and needs assessments after Hurricanes Isabel and Charley, North Carolina, 2003–2004', *Morbidity and Mortality Weekly Report*, vol 53, pp840–842

CDC (2005a) 'Rapid health response, assessment and surveillance after a tsunami, Thailand, 2004–2005', *Morbidity and Mortality Weekly Report*, vol 54, pp61–64

CDC (2005b) 'Terrorism and emergency preparedness in state and territorial public health departments, United States, 2004', *Morbidity and Mortality Weekly Report*, vol 54, pp459–460

Cervenka, J. (1976) 'Health aspects of Danube River floods', *Annals of the Belgian Society of Tropical Medicine*, vol 56, pp217–22

Charatan, F. (2005) 'US government declares emergency following Hurricane Katrina', *British Medical Journal*, vol 331, p531

Chatterjee, P. (2005) 'Mental health care for India's tsunami survivors', *The Lancet*, vol 365, pp833–834

Chen Jiran, Deng XuHe, Xu FuKuai, Zheng GenNan and Li YunTian (2001) 'Study on the relationship between river flooding and the prevalence of schistosomiasis', *Chinese Journal of Schistosomiasis Control*, vol 13, pp27–30

Chen MingGang (1999) 'Progress in schistosomiasis control in China', *Chinese Medical Journal (Beijing)*, vol 112, pp930–933

Chen Wei, Yang XianXiang, Huang XiBao, Zhang YingHao, Cai ShunXiang, Liu JianBin, FuYi and Li ShuHua (2000) 'Influence of flood in 1998 on schistosomiasis epidemic', *Chinese Journal of Schistosomiasis Control*, vol 12, pp202–205

Chin, J. (ed) (2000) *Control of Communicable Diseases Manual: An Official Report of the American Public Health Association*, 17th edition, American Public Health Association, Washington, DC

Chopra, M., Wilkinson, D. and Stirling, S. (1997) 'Epidemic shigella dysentery in children in northern KwaZulu-Natal', *South African Medical Journal*, vol 87, pp48–51

Christensen, J. and Christensen, O. (2003) 'Climate modelling: Severe summertime flooding in Europe', *Nature*, vol 421, pp805–806

Christie, F. and Hanlon, J. (2001) *Mozambique and the Great Flood of 2000*, The International African Institute, Oxford

Church, J., Gregory, J., Huyberchts, P., Kuhn, M., Lambeck, K., Nhuan, M., Qin, D. and Woodworth, P. (2001) 'Changes in sea level' in Houghton, J., Ding, Y., Griggs, D., Noguer, M., van der Linden, P., Dai, X., Maskell, K. and Johnson, C. (eds) *Climate Change 2001: The Scientific Basis*, Cambridge University Press, Cambridge

Clemens, P., Hietala, J., Rytter, M., Schmidt, R. and Reese, D. (1999) 'Risk of domestic violence after flood impact: Effects of social support, age and history of domestic violence', *Applied Behavioural Science Review*, vol 7, pp199–206

Cline, J. (2002) 'Preparing for bioterrorism in North Carolina', *North Carolina Medical Journal*, vol 63, pp257–264

Clinton, J., Hagebak, B., Sirmons, J. and Brennan, J. (1995) 'Lessons from the Georgia floods', *Public Health Reports*, vol 110, pp684–688

Collogan, L., Tuma, F., Dolan-Sewell, R., Borja, S. and Fleischman, A. (2004) 'Ethical issues pertaining to research in the aftermath of disaster', *Journal of Traumatic Stress*, vol 17, pp363–372

Connolly, M. (ed) (2005) *Communicable Disease Control in Emergencies: A Field Manual*, World Health Organization, Geneva

Cooke, B. and Kothari, U. (2001) *Participation: The New Tyranny?* Zed Books, London

Cordova, S., Smith, D., Broom, A., Lindsay, M., Dowse, G. and Beers, M. (2000) 'Murray Valley encephalitis in Western Australia in 2000, with evidence of southerly spread', *Communicable Diseases Intelligence*, vol 24, pp368–372

Corrêa, M. (1975) 'Human leptospirosis in Brazil', *International Journal of Zoonoses*, vol 2, pp1–9

Corvalan, C., Gopalan, H. and Llanso, P. (2003) 'Conclusions and recommendations for action', in McMichael, A., Campbell-Lendrum, D., Corvalan, C., Ebi, K., Githeko, A., Scheraga, J. and Woodward, A. (eds) *Climate Change and Human Health: Risks and Responses*, World Health Organization, Geneva, pp267–283

Corwin, A., Tien, N., Bounlu, K., Winarno, J., Putri, M., Laras, K., Larasati, R., Sukri, N., Endy, T., Sulaiman, H. and Hyams, K. (1999) 'The unique riverine ecology of hepatitis E virus transmission in South-East Asia', *Transactions of the Royal Society of Tropical Medicine and Hygiene*, vol 93, pp255–260

Cosgrave, J., Selvester, K., Fidalgo, L., Hallam, A and Taimo, N. (2001) *Independent Evaluation of Expenditure of DEC Mozambique Flood Appeal Funds*, Disasters Emergency Committee, London

Craig, M., Kleinschmidt, I., Le Sueur, D. and Sharpe, M. (2004) 'Exploring 30 years of malaria data in KwaZulu-Natal, South Africa; Part II. The influence of non-climatic factors', *Tropical Medicine and International Health*, vol 9, pp1258–1266

CRED (Centre for Research on the Epidemiology of Disasters) (2005) 'EM–DAT criteria and definition', EM–DAT Emergency Disasters Database, CRED website, www.em-dat.net/criteria.htm

Curtis, L., Ross, M., Scheff, P., Persky, V., Wadden, R., Ramakrishnan, V. and Hryhorczuk, D. (1997) 'Dust-mite-allergen concentrations in asthmatics' bedrooms in the Quad Cities, Illinois, USA, and the Mississippi River floods of 1993', *Allergy*, vol 52, pp642–649

Cutter, S. (1996) 'Vulnerability to environmental hazards', *Progress in Human Geography*, vol 20, pp529–539

Daley, W., Shireley, L. and Gilmore, R. (2001) 'A flood-related outbreak of carbon monoxide poisoning, Grand Forks, North Dakota', *Journal of Emergency Medicine*, vol 21, pp249–253

D'Amore, A. and Hardin, C. (2005), 'Air Force expeditionary medical support unit at the Houston floods: Use of a military model in civilian disaster response', *Military Medicine*, vol 170, pp103–108

Dang Quang Tinh (2003) 'Flood kindergarten: Community need to community solution', in World Disaster Reduction Campaign, *Living with Risk: Turning the Tide on Disasters Towards Sustainable Development Information Kit,* United Nations International Strategy for Disaster Reduction, New York

Dang Van Chinh (2003) *Report on Health Sector Damage caused by Flooding in Central Viet Nam 2003,* World Health Organization, Western Pacific Regional Office, Manila

Dao Xuan Hoc (2003) 'Flood control for the Dong Thap Muoi Delta', *Proceedings of the International Seminar on Flood Management, Hanoi,* 17–21 November 2003, pp71–84

Davis, I. and Hall, N. (1999) 'Ways to measure community vulnerability', in Ingleton, J. (ed) *Natural Disaster Management,* Tudor Rose, Leicester, pp87–89

Davis, R. and Johnson, K. (2005) 'La looks into 215 Katrina deaths', *USA Today On Line Edition* (16 October 2005) http://www.usatoday.com/news/nation/2005-10-16-la-katrina-investigation_x.htm

Deering, C. G. (2000) 'A cognitive developmental approach to understanding how children cope with disasters', *Journal of Child and Adolescent Psychiatric Nursing,* vol 13, pp7–16

Defra (UK Department for Environment, Food and Rural Affairs) (2004) *Making Space for Water: Developing a new Government Strategy for Flood and Coastal Erosion Risk Management in England,* Consultation document, Defra, London

del Ninno, C., Dorosh, P., Smith, L. and Roy, D. (2001) *The 1998 Floods in Bangladesh: Disaster Impacts, Household Coping Strategies and Response,* International Food Policy Research Institute Research Report, Washington, DC

DHS (US Department of Homeland Security) (2005a) 'Ready America', DHS website, www.ready.gov/index.html

DHS (2005b) *Department of Health and Human Services Grants: Working with DHS,* DHS website, www.dhs.gov/dhspublic/

DHS (2005c) *National Response Plan,* Emergencies and Disasters: Planning and Prevention, DHS website, www.dhs.gov/dhspublic/

DHS (2005d) *National Incident Management System,* National Incident Management System, DHS website, www.fema.gov/nims/

Dietz, V., Gunn, R., Rigau-Perez, J., Sanderson, L. and Diaz, L. (1990) 'Health assessment of the 1985 flood disaster in Puerto Rico', *Disasters,* vol 14, pp164–170

Donnell, H. and Hamm, R. (1993) 'Flood-related mortality, Missouri, 1993', *Morbidity and Mortality Weekly Report,* vol 42, pp941–942

Duclos, P., Vidonne, O., Beuf, P., Perray, P. and Stoebner, A. (1991) 'Flash flood disaster: Nîmes, France, 1988', *European Journal of Epidemiology,* vol 7, pp365–371

Duke, C., Bon, E., Reeves, J., Miller, B., Chancellor, B. and Griffin, M. (1994) 'Flood-related mortality, Georgia, 4–14 July 1994', *Morbidity and Mortality Weekly Report,* vol 43, pp526–530

Dunston, C., McAfee, D., Kaiser, R., Rakotoarison, D., Rambeloson, L., Hoang, A. and Quick, R. (2001) 'Collaboration, cholera and cyclones: A project to improve point-of-use water quality in Madagascar', *American Journal of Public Health,* vol 91, pp1574–1576

Durkin, M., Khan, N., Davidson, L., Zaman, S. and Stein, Z. (1993) 'The effects of a natural disaster on child behaviour: Evidence for posttraumatic stress', *American Journal of Public Health,* vol 83, pp1549–1553

Durrheim, D. and Govere, J. (2002) 'Malaria outbreak control in an African village by community application of "deet" mosquito repellent to ankles and feet', *Medical and Veterinary Entomology,* vol 16, pp112–115

Easton, A. (1999) 'Leptospirosis in Philippine floods', *British Medical Journal,* vol 319, p212

Edwards, M. and Schwartz, M. (2000) 'Organized medicine's response to Hurricane Floyd', *North Carolina Medical Journal,* vol 61, pp380–382

Elidemir, O., Colasurdo, G., Rossmann, S. and Fan, L. (1999) 'Isolation of *Stachybotrys* from the lung of a child with pulmonary hemosiderosis', *Pediatrics*, vol 104 (4 Part 1), pp964–966

El-Sayed, B., Arnot, D., Mukhtar, M., Baraka, O., Dafalla, A., Elnaiem, D. and Nugud, A. (2000) 'A study of the urban malaria transmission problem in Khartoum', *Acta Tropica*, vol 75, pp163–171

Enarson, E. (2001) 'What women do: Gendered disaster work in the Red River Valley Flood', *Environmental Hazards*, vol 3, pp1–18

Enarson, E. and Hearn-Morrow, B. (eds) (1998) *The Gendered Terrain of Disaster: Through Women's Eyes*, Praeger, London

Engelthaler, D., Mosley, D., Cheeck, J., Levy, C., Komatsu, K., Ettestad, P., Davis, T., Tanda, D., Miller, L., Frampton, J., Porter, R. and Bryan, R. (1999) 'Climatic and environmental patterns associated with hantavirus pulmonary syndrome, Four Corners Region, United States', *Emerging Infectious Diseases*, vol 5, pp87–94

Environment Agency (2001) *Lessons Learned: Autumn 2000 Floods*, Environment Agency, Bristol

Environment Agency (2003) *Strategy for Flood Risk Management*, Environment Agency, Bristol

Espacios Consultores (2000) *Evaluation Report for DEC Central America Hurricane Appeal 1998*, Disasters Emergency Committee, UK

Esposito, C. (2002) *Moving Heaven and Earth: Experiences of Poor Communities Recently Exposed to Disasters in Vietnam*, CARE International Vietnam and World Health Organization Western Pacific Regional Office, Vietnam

Euripidou, E. and Murray, V. (2004) 'Public health impacts of floods and chemical contamination', *Journal of Public Health*, vol 26, pp376–383

Evans, E., Ashley, R., Hall, J., Penning-Rowsell, E., Saul, A., Sayers, P., Thorne, C. and Watkinson, A. (2004) *Foresight Future Flooding Scientific Summary, Volumes I and II*, Office of Science and Technology, London

Eyre, A. (2002) 'An overview of the traumatic effects of disasters on individuals, responders and communities', Paper presented at *Picking up the Pieces IV: A Workshop for Senior Managers*, 29–30 October, Cambridge

Feachem, R., Burns, E., Cairncross, S., Cronin, A., Cross, P., Curtis, D., Khalid Khan, M., Lamb, D. and Southall, H. (1978) *Water, Health and Development: An Interdisciplinary Evaluation*, Tri-Med Books, London

FEMA (US Federal Emergency Management Agency) (2004a) 'Inland flooding from hurricanes', Hurricane Hazards, FEMA website, www.fema.gov/hazards/

FEMA (2004b) 'Disaster preparedness for people with disabilities', Library, FEMA website, www.fema.gov/library/

FEMA (2004c) *Disaster Planning Tips for Pets, Livestock and Wildlife*, Library, FEMA website, www.fema.gov/library/

FEMA (2004d) *FEMA History: About FEMA*, FEMA website, www.fema.gov/about/historys.htm

FEMA (2004e) *National Flood Insurance Program*, Mitigation Division, FEMA website, www.fema.gov/fima/nfip.shtm

FEMA (2005a) *Top Ten Natural Disasters*, Library, FEMA website, www.fema.gov/library/df_8.shtm

FEMA (2005b) 'Under secretary of homeland security kicks off national hurricane preparedness week, urges Americans to be prepared', FEMA News, FEMA website, www.fema.gov/news/newsrelease.fema?id=17476

FEMA (2005c) *Are You Ready? In Depth Guide to Citizen Preparedness*, FEMA website, www.fema.gov/areyouready/

FEMA (2005d) *Citizen Corps*, FEMA website, www.citizencorps.gov

FEMA (2005e) *Are you Ready?: Summary of Are You Ready Training Programs*, FEMA website, www.fema.gov/areyouready/

FEMA (2005f) *Noble Training Center*, Emergency Management Institute, FEMA website, http://training.fema.gov/emiweb/ntc/

FEMA (2005g) FloodSmart.gov, FEMA website, www.floodsmart.gov/floodsmart/pages/index.jsp

FEMA (2005h) *Mitigation Division*, FEMA website, www.fema.gov/fima/

FEMA (2005i) 'Approaching one year, North Carolina Floyd assistance more than $19 billion', Declared Disasters Press Releases, FEMA website, www.fema.gov/news

Ferraro, F. R. (2003) 'Psychological resilience in older adults following the 1997 flood', *Clinical Gerontologist*, vol 26, pp139–143

Few, R. (2003) 'Flooding, vulnerability and coping strategies: Local responses to a global threat', *Progress in Development Studies*, vol 3, pp43–58

Few, R., Ahern, M., Matthies, F. and Kovats, S. (2004a) *Floods, Health and Climate Change: A Strategic Review*, Tyndall Centre Working Paper 63, UK

Few, R., Harpham, T. and Atkinson, S. (2003) 'Urban primary health care in Africa: A comparative analysis of city-wide public sector projects in Lusaka and Dar es Salaam', *Health and Place*, vol 9, pp45–53

Few, R., Pham Gia Tran and Bui Thi Thuy Hong (2004b) *Living with Floods: Health Risks and Coping Strategies of the Urban Poor in Vietnam*, Research Report, University of East Anglia, Norwich, UK

Flynn, B. and Nelson, M. (1998) 'Understanding the needs of children following large-scale disasters and the role of government', *Child and Adolescent Psychiatric Clinics of North America*, vol 1, pp211–230

Fordham, M. (1998) 'Making women visible in disasters: Problematising the private domain', *Disasters*, vol 22, pp126–143

Franklin, J., Wiese, W., Meredith, J., Lalikos, J., Dolezal, J., Brigham, D., Wooden, W. and Ohl, C. (2000) 'Hurricane Floyd: Response of the Pitt County medical community', *North Carolina Medical Journal*, vol 61, pp384–389

Frei, C. (2003) *Camouflage, Bluff, or Real? Statistical Uncertainty of Trends in Catastrophic Extremes*, STARDEX, Information Sheet 1, Fachhochschule Stuttgart-Hochschule für Technik, Germany

French, J., Ing, R., Von Allmen, S. and Wood, R. (1983) 'Mortality from flash floods: A review of national weather service reports, 1969–81', *Public Health Reports*, vol 98, pp584–588

Fullilove, M. (1996) 'Psychiatric implications of displacement: Contributions from the psychology of place', *American Journal of Psychiatry*, vol 153, pp1516–1523

Fun, B., Unicomb, L., Rahim, Z., Banu, N., Podder, G., Clemens, J., Van Loon, F., Rao, M., Malek, A. and Tzipori, S. (1991) 'Rotavirus-associated diarrhoea in rural Bangladesh: Two-year study of incidence and serotype distribution', *Journal of Critical Microbiology*, vol 29, pp1359–1363

Fuortes, L. and Nettleman, M. (1994) 'Leptospirosis: A consequence of the Iowa flood', *Iowa Medicine*, vol 84, pp449–450

Gay, E. (2002) 'Hurricane Floyd and the ensuing flood in North Carolina: A personal journal', *Journal of Emergency Nursing*, vol 28, pp216–222

Gaza Directorate of Health (2000) *Cheias 2000 na Província de Gaza; Vigilância Epidemiológica durante a Emergência Xai-Xai*, Provincial Directorate of Health, Gaza, Mozambique

Gerrity, E. and Flynn, B. (1997) 'Mental health consequences of disasters', in Noji, E. (ed) *The Public Health Consequences of Disasters*, Oxford University Press, New York, pp101–121

Gillard, M. and Paton, D. (1999) 'Disaster stress following a hurricane: The role of religious differences in the Fijian Islands', *The Australasian Journal of Disaster and Trauma Studies*, vol 1999-2, www.massey.ac.nz/~trauma/

Ginexi, E., Weihs, K., Simmens, S. and Hoyt, D. (2000) 'Natural disaster and depression: A prospective investigation of reactions to the 1993 Midwest floods', *American Journal of Community Psychology*, vol 28, pp495–518

Glantz, M. (ed) (2001) *Once Burned, Twice Shy? Lessons Learned from the 1997–1998 El Nino*, UN University Press, Tokyo

Glantz, M. (2004) *Early Warning Systems: Do's and Don'ts*, Report of Workshop, 20–23 October 2003, Shanghai, China

Gleser, G., Green, B. and Winget, C. (1981) *Prolonged Psychological Effects of Disaster: A Study of Buffalo Creek*, Academic Press, New York

Goldberg, D. and Hillier, V. (1979) 'A scaled version of the General Health Questionnaire', *Psychological Medicine*, vol 9, pp139–145

Goldberg, D. and Williams, P. (1988) *A User's Guide to the General Health Questionnaire*, NFER–Nelson, Windsor

Gordon, R. (2004) 'Community response and the recovery environment following emergency', *Australian Journal of Environmental Health*, vol 4, pp19–34

Government of Mozambique (2000) *Mozambique: Post-Emergency Reconstruction Programme*, Document presented to the Donors' Conference, Rome, April 2000, available at www.teledata.mz/html/index.html

Government of Vietnam (2001) *Second National Strategy and Action Plan for Disaster Mitigation and Management in Vietnam – 2001 to 2020*, Government of Vietnam, Hanoi

Government of Vietnam (2003) *Decree No 79/2003/ND–CP of 7 July 2003 Promulgating the Regulation on the Exercise of Democracy in Communes*, Government of Vietnam, Hanoi

Grambsch, A. and Menne, B. (2003) 'Adaptation and adaptive capacity in the public health context' in McMichael, A., Campbell-Lendrum, D., Corvalan, C., Ebi, K., Githeko, A., Scheraga, J. and Woodward, A. (eds) *Climate Change and Human Health: Risks and Responses*, World Health Organization, Geneva, pp220–236

Green, C. (1988) *The Relationships Between the Magnitude of Flooding, Stress and Health*, Flood Hazard Research Centre, Middlesex University, Enfield, UK

Green, C., Emery, P., Penning-Rowsell, E. and Parker, D. (1985) *The Health Effects of Flooding: A Survey at Uphill, Avon*, Flood Hazard Research Centre, Middlesex Polytechnic, Enfield, UK

Green, C., Penning-Rowsell, E. and Parker, D. (1987) 'Estimating the risk from flooding and evaluating worry', in Covello, V., Lave, L., Moghissi, A. and Uppuluri, V. (eds) *Uncertainty in Risk Assessment, Risk Management and Decision Making*, Plenum, New York

Green, C., Van der Veen, A., Wierstra, E. and Penning-Rowsell, E. (1994) 'Vulnerability refined: Analysing full flood impacts', in Penning-Rowsell, E. and Fordham, M. (eds) *Floods Across Europe: Flood Forecasting, Assessment, Modelling and Management*, Middlesex University Press, London

Greenough, G. and Kirsch, T. (2005) 'Hurricane Katrina: Public health response – assessing needs', *New England Journal of Medicine*, vol 353, pp1544–1546

Greenough, G., McGeehin, M., Bernard, S., Trtanj, J., Riad, J. and Engelberg, D. (2001) 'The potential impacts of climate variability and change on health impacts of extreme weather events in the United States', *Environmental Health Perspectives*, vol 109 S2, pp191–198

Guha-Sapir, D. (1991) 'Rapid assessment of health needs in mass emergencies: Review of current concepts and methods', *World Health Statistics Quarterly*, vol 44, pp171–181

Guha-Sapir, D. (1993) 'Health effects of earthquakes and volcanoes: Epidemiological and policy issues', *Disasters*, vol 3, pp255–262

Guha-Sapir, D., Lombardi, C. and Sasse, A. (1991) *Floods and Epidemics in Urban Settlements: A Case Study of Sao Paulo, Brazil*, Project Report to EEC, Contract CI1/0103, EEC, Brussels

Guha-Sapir, D., van Panhuis, W. and Lagoutte, J. (2005) 'Aid after disasters: Evidence for psychosocial services needs strengthening', *British Medical Journal*, vol 331, p50

Haines, V., Hurlbert, J. and Beggs, J. (1996) 'Exploring the determinants of support provision: Provider characteristics, personal networks, community contexts and support following life events', *Journal of Health and Social Behavior*, vol 37, pp252–264

Haines, V., Hurlbert, J. and Beggs, J. (1999) 'The disaster framing stress process: A test of an expanded model', *International Journal of Mass Emergencies and Disasters*, vol 17, pp367–397

Hales, S., Edwards, S. and Kovats, R. (2003) 'Impacts on health of climate extremes' in McMichael, A., Campbell-Lendrum, D., Corvalan, C., Ebi, K., Githeko, A., Scheraga, J. and Woodward, A. (eds) *Climate Change and Human Health: Risks and Response*, World Health Organization, Geneva, pp79–102

Hajat, S., Ebi, K., Kovats, S., Menne, B., Edwards, S. and Haines, A. (2003) 'The human health consequences of flooding in Europe and the implications for public health: A review of the evidence', *Applied Environmental Science and Public Health*, vol 1, pp13–21

Han, L. L., Popovici, F., Alexander, J. P., Jr, Laurentia, V., Tengelsen, L. A., Cernescu, C., Gary, H. E., Jr, Ion-Nedelcu, N., Campbell, G. L. and Tsai, T. F. (1999) 'Risk factors for West Nile virus infection and meningoencephalitis, Romania, 1996', *Journal of Infectious Diseases*, vol 179, pp230–233

Handmer, J. (2000) 'Are flood warnings futile? Risk communication in emergencies' *The Australasian Journal of Disaster and Trauma Studies*, vol 2000-2, www.massey. ac.nz/~trauma/

Handmer, J. (2003) 'We are all vulnerable', *The Australian Journal of Emergency Management*, vol 18, pp55–60

Handmer, J., Penning-Rowsell, E. and Tapsell, S. (1999) 'Flooding in a warmer world: The view from Europe', in Downing, T., Olsthoorn, A. and Tol, R. (eds) *Climate, Change and Risk*, Routledge, London

Handmer, J. and Smith, D. (1983) 'Health hazards of floods: Hospital admissions for Lismore', *Australian Geographical Studies*, vol 21, pp221–230

Harpham, T. and Tanner, M. (eds) (1995) *Urban Health in Developing Countries: Progress and Prospects*, Earthscan, London

Hau, C., Hien, T., Tien, N., Khiem, H., Sac, P., Nhung, V., Larasati, R., Laras, K., Putri, M., Doss, R., Hyams, K. and Corwin, A. (1999) 'Prevalence of enteric hepatitis A and E viruses in the Mekong River delta region of Vietnam', *American Journal of Tropical Medicine and Hygiene*, vol 60, pp277–280

He, Z. (1998) 'A suicide belt in China: The Yangtze basin', *Archives of Suicide Research*, vol 4, pp287–289

Heath, S., Kass, P., Beck, A. and Glickman, L. (2001) 'Human and pet-related risk factors for household evacuation failure during a natural disaster', *American Journal of Epidemiology*, vol 153, pp659–665

Hederra, R. (1987) 'Environmental sanitation and water supply during floods in Ecuador (1982–1983)', *Disasters*, vol 11, pp297–309

Hegstad, H. (2000) 'Predicting postdisaster adjustment after the Red River flood: An analysis of resource loss and pre-flood preventative behaviours', *Dissertation Abstracts International: Section B: The Sciences and Engineering*, vol 60, pp6365

Heller, L., Colosimo, E. and Antunes, C. (2003) 'Environmental sanitation conditions and health impact: A case-control study', *Revista da Sociedade Brasileira de Medicina Tropical*, vol 36, pp41–50

Herzer, H. and Clichevsky, N. (2001) 'El impacto ambiental de las inundaciones', in Kreimer, A., Kullock, D. and Valdes, J. (eds) *Inundaciones en el Area Metropolitana de Buenos Aires*, World Bank, Washington, DC, pp123–130

Hilhorst, D. and Bankoff, G. (2004) 'Introduction: Mapping vulnerability', in Bankoff, G., Frerks, G. and Hilhorst, D. (eds) *Mapping Vulnerability: Disasters, Development and People*, Earthscan, London, pp1–9

Hill, J. and O'Brien P. (1999) *Disaster in the Community: Emergency Planning for Sustainable Solutions to Long-Term Problems: Worker and Resident Perspectives of the North Wales Floods 1990 and 1993*, Disaster Recovery and Research Team Ltd, Caernarfon, Gwynedd

Holmes, T. H. and Rahe, P. H. (1967) 'The social readjustment rating scale', *Journal of Psychosomatic Research*, vol 11, pp213–218

Hopkins, C., Hollinger, F., Johnson, R., Dewlett, H., Newhouse, V. and Chamberlain, R. (1975) 'The epidemiology of St Louis encephalitis in Dallas, Texas, 1966', *American Journal of Epidemiology*, vol 102, pp1–15

Hoque, B., Sack, R., Siddiqi, M., Jahangir, A., Hazera, N. and Nahid, A. (1993) 'Environmental health and the 1991 Bangladesh Cyclone', *Disasters*, vol 17, pp143–152

Hossain, S. and Kolsteren, P. (2003) 'The 1998 flood in Bangladesh: Is different targeting needed during emergencies and recovery to tackle malnutrition?', *Disasters*, vol 27, pp172–184

Houghton, J., Ding, Y., Griggs, D., Nouger, M., van der Linden, P., Dai, X., Maskell, K. and Johnson, C. (eds) (2001) *Climate Change 2001: The Scientific Basis*, Cambridge University Press, Cambridge

Hsu, S. and Glasser, S. (2005) 'FEMA director singled out by response critics', *Washington Post* website, 6 September 2005, http://www.washingtonpost.com/wp-dyn/content/article/2005/09/05/AR2005090501590_pf.html

Huang YiXin, Rong GuoRong, Xu GuoYu, Wang XueDe, Yang HuiMin, Song HongTao, Zhang XiaoBo and Tu YuXiu (1998) 'Mass praziquantel chemoprophy-laxis against acute schistosomiasis japonica in a flood', *Chinese Journal of Schisto-somiasis Control*, vol 10, pp138–140

Hubalek, Z. (2000) 'European experience with the West Nile virus ecology and epidemiology: Could it be relevant for the New World?', *Viral Immunology*, vol 13, pp415–426

Hubalek, Z. and Halouzka, J. (1999) 'West Nile fever – A re-emerging mosquito-borne viral disease in Europe', *Emerging Infectious Diseases*, vol 5, pp643–650

Hubalek, Z., Halouzka, J. and Juricova, Z. (1999) 'West Nile fever in Czechland', *Emerging Infectious Diseases*, vol 5, pp594–595

Huerta, F. and Horton, R. (1978) 'Coping behaviour of elderly flood victims', *The Gerontologist*, vol 18, pp541–546

Hulme, M. (2003) 'Abrupt climate change: Can society cope?', *Philosophical Transactions: Mathematical, Physical and Engineering Sciences*, vol 361, pp2001–2021

Hunt, J. C. (2002) 'Floods in a changing climate: A review' *Philosophical Transactions: Mathematical, Physical and Engineering Sciences*, vol 360, pp1531–1543

Hunt, S. M. and McEwen, J. (1980) 'The development of a subjective health indicator', *Sociology of Health and Illness*, vol 2 (3), pp231–246

IFRC (International Federation of Red Cross and Red Crescent Societies) (2000) *Viet Nam: Floods and Storm Appeal No 23/00 Situation Report No 3*, Reliefweb website, www.reliefweb.int

IFRC (2002) *World Disasters Report 2002: Focus on Reducing Risk*, IFRC, Geneva

IFRC (2003) *World Disasters Report 2003: Focus on Ethics in Aid*, IFRC, Geneva

IFRC (2004) *World Disasters Report 2004: Focus on Community Resilience*, IFRC, Geneva

INE (Instituto Nacional de Estatística) (2004) *População Projectada Total e por Província Maputo*, INE website, www.ine.gov.mz/populacao/

Ingraham, J. and Ingraham, C. (1995) *Introduction to Microbiology*, Wadsworth Publishing Company, Belmont

INTRAC (International NGO Training and Research Centre) (2000) *Independent Evaluation of Expenditure of DEC India Cyclone Appeal Funds*, INTRAC, UK

ISDR (Inter-Agency Secretariat of the International Strategy for Disaster Reduction) (2002) *Living with Risk: A Global Review of Disaster Reduction Initiatives*, ISDR (UN/ISDR), Geneva

ISDR (2005) *Hyogo Framework for Action 2005–2015: Building the Resilience of Nations and Communities to Disasters*, ISDR, www.unisdr.org/wcdr

Jabry, A. (ed) (2002) *Children in Disasters: After the Cameras Have Gone*, Plan UK, London

Jamison D., Sandbu M. and Wang J. (2004) *Why has Infant Mortality Decreased at such Different Rates in Different Countries?*, Disease Control Priorities Project, Working Paper No 21, National Institutes of Health, Washington, DC, available at www.fic.nih.gov/dcpp/wps.html

Jarvis, B., Sorenson, W., Hintikka, E., Nikulin, M., Zhou, Y., Jiang, J., Wang, S., Hinkley, S., Etzel, R. and Dearborn, D. (1998) 'Study of toxin production by isolates of *Stachybotrys chartarum* and *Memnoniella echinata* isolated during a study of pulmonary hemosiderosis in infants', *Applied Environmental Microbiology*, vol 64, pp3620–3625

JCAHO (Joint Commission Accreditation of Healthcare Organizations) (2005) *Standards*, JCAHO website, www.jcaho.org

Jezierski, M. (1998) 'Flooding in the Red River Valley: Challenges met by the Grand Forks emergency medical services community', *Journal of Emergency Nursing*, vol 24, pp106–108

Jonkman, S. (2005) 'Global perspectives of loss of human life caused by floods', *Natural Hazards*, vol 34, pp151–175

Jonkman, S and Kelman, I. (2005) 'An analysis of the causes and circumstances of flood disaster deaths', *Disasters*, vol 29, pp75–97

Kabat, P. and van Schaik, H. (2003) *Climate Changes the Water Rules: How Water Managers Can Cope with Today's Climate Variability and Tomorrow's Climate Change*, The Dialogue on Water and Climate, www.waterandclimate.org/home.asp

Kaniasty, K. and Norris, F. (1993) 'A test of social support deterioration model in the context of natural disaster', *Journal of Personality and Social Psychology*, vol 64, pp395–408

Kappedal, B. (1997) 'A forty-eight hour day for Valley Memorial Homes in Grand Forks', *PrairieRose*, vol 66, pp8a–9a

Karande, S., Bhatt, M., Kelkar, A., Kulkarni, M., De, A. and Varaiya, A. (2003) 'An observational study to detect leptospirosis in Mumbai, India, 2000', *Archives of Disease in Childhood*, vol 88, pp1070–1075

Karande, S., Kulkarni, H., Kulkarni, M., De, A. and Varaiya, A. (2002) 'Leptospirosis in children in Mumbai slums', *Indian Journal of Pediatrics*, vol 69, pp855–858

Karim, F., Sultan, S. and Chowdhury, A. (1999) 'A visit to a flood shelter in Dhaka City', in Ahmed S. and Ahmed, H. (eds) *Experiences of Deluge: Flood 1998*, Research Monograph Series, vol 15, Bangladesh Rural Advancement Commission (BRAC), Dhaka, pp40–45

Katsumata, T., Hosea, D., Wasito, E., Kohno, S., Hara, K., Soeparto, P. and Ranuh, I. (1998) 'Cryptosporidiosis in Indonesia: A hospital-based study and a community-based survey', *American Journal of Tropical Medicine and Hygiene*, vol 59, pp628–632

Keene, E. (1998) 'Phenomenological study of the North Dakota flood experience and its impact on survivors' health', *International Journal of Trauma Nursing*, vol 4, pp79–84

Kett, M., Stubbs, S. and Yeo, R. (2005) *Disability in Conflict and Emergency Situations: Focus on Tsunami-Affected Areas*, KaR Disability Programme, Overseas Development Group, University of East Anglia, UK, available at www.disabilitykar.net

Kircher, T., Nelson, J. and French, J. (1987) 'Avoidance of death and injury through monitoring of dams and flood evacuation in Essex, Connecticut, June 1982', *Disasters*, vol 11, pp117–119

Klein, R., Nicholls, R. and Thomalla, F. (2003) 'The resilience of coastal megacities to weather-related hazards', in Kreimer, A., Arnold, M. and Carlin, A. (eds) *Building Safer Cities*, Disaster Risk Management Series No 3, The World Bank Group, Washington, DC, pp101–120

Ko, A. I., Reis, M., Dourado, C., Johnson, W., Riley, L. and Salvador Leptospirosis Study Group (1999) 'Urban epidemic of severe leptospirosis in Brazil', *The Lancet*, vol 354, pp820–825

Kokai, M., Fujii, S., Shinfuku, N. and Edwards, G. (2004) 'Natural disaster and mental health in Asia', *Psychiatry and Clinical Neurosciences*, vol 58, pp110–116

Korthuis, P., Jones, T., Lesmana, M., Clark, S., Okoseray, M., Ingkokusumo, G. and Wignall, F. (1998) 'An outbreak of *El Tor* cholera associated with a tribal funeral in Irian Jaya, Indonesia', *Southeast Asian Journal of Tropical Medicine and Public Health*, vol 29, pp550–554

Kosek, M., Bern, C. and Guerrent, R. (2003) 'The global burden of diarrhoeal disease, as estimated from studies published between 1992 and 2000', *Bulletin of the World Health Organization*, vol 81, pp197–204

Kotloff, K., Winickoff, J., Ivanoff, B., Clemens, J., Swerdlow, D., Sansonetti, P., Adak, G. and Levine, M. (1999) 'Global burden of shigella infections: Implications for vaccine development and implementation of control strategies', *Bulletin of the World Health Organization*, vol 77, pp651–666

Kovats, R., Bouma, M., Shakoor, H., Worrall, E. and Haines, A. (2003) 'El Nino and Health', *The Lancet*, vol 362, pp1481–1489

Kreimer, A., Arnold, M. and Carlin, A. (eds) (2003) *Building Safer Cities*, The World Bank Group, Washington, DC

Kremer, C., Zane, D., Underwood, J., Stanley, S., Stabeno, D., Simpson, D. and Perrotta, D. (2000) 'Storm-related mortality, Central Texas, 17–31 October 1998', *Morbidity and Mortality Weekly Report*, vol 49, pp133–135

Krug, E., Kresnow, M., Peddicord, J., Dahlberg, L., Powell, K., Crosby, A. and Annest, J. (1998) 'Suicide after natural disasters', *New England Journal of Medicine*, vol 338, pp373–378

Krug, E., Kresnow, M., Peddicord, J., Dahlberg, L., Powell, K., Crosby, A. and Annest, J. (1999) 'Retraction: Suicide after natural disasters', *New England Journal of Medicine*, vol 340, pp148–149

Kunii, O, Nakamura, S., Abdur, R. and Wakai, S. (2002) 'The impact on health and risk factors of the diarrhoea epidemics in the 1998 Bangladesh floods', *Public Health*, vol 116, pp68–74

Kupek, E., de Sousa Santos Faversani, M. and de Souza Philippi, J. (2000) 'The relationship between rainfall and human leptospirosis in Florianópolis, Brazil, 1991–1996', *Brazilian Journal of Infectious Diseases*, vol 4, pp131–134

Lambert, T., Soskolne, C., Bergum, V., Howell, J. and Dossetor, J. (2003) 'Ethical perspectives for public and environmental health: Fostering autonomy and the right to know', *Environmental Health Perspectives*, vol 111, pp133–137

Larson, L. (1996) 'The Great USA Flood of 1993', IAHS Conference Proceedings, *Destructive Water: Water-Caused Natural Disasters – Their Abatement and Control*, National Weather Center Northwest, available at www.nwrfc.noaa.gov/floods/papers/oh_2/great.htm

Laska, S. (2004) 'What if Hurricane Ivan had not missed New Orleans?', *Natural Hazards Observer*, vol 29, http://www.colorado.edu/hazards/o/nov04/

Last, J. (ed) (2001) *A Dictionary of Epidemiology*, 4th edition, Oxford University Press, Oxford

Lauerman, L., Birch, W., Webster, H., Stromberg, W. and Wright, M. (1984) 'Human arboviral encephalitis, United States, 1983', *Morbidity and Mortality Weekly Report*, vol 33, pp339–342, 347

Leach, M., Mearns, R. and Scoones, I. (1997) 'Challenges to community-based sustainable development: Dynamics, entitlements, institutions', *IDS Bulletin*, vol 28, pp4–14

Leal-Castellanos, C., García-Suárez, R., González-Figueroa, E., Fuentes-Allen, J. and Escobedo-De La Peña, J. (2003) 'Risk factors and the prevalence of leptospirosis infection in a rural community of Chiapas, Mexico', *Epidemiological Infections,* vol 131, pp1149–1156

Legros, D., McCormiick, M., Mugero, C., Skinnider, M., Bek'Obita, D. and Okware, S. (2000) 'Epidemiology of cholera outbreak in Kampala, Uganda', *East African Medical Journal*, vol 77, pp347–349

Leitheiser, A., Rippke, M., Sheehan, M., Korlath, J. and Ferguson, B. (1997) 'Public health response to the 1997 Minnesota flood: Lessons learned', *Minnesota Medicine*, vol 80, pp 25–28

Le Minh Nhat (2003) *Flood Disaster Management in Red River Delta*, Proceeding of the International Seminar on Flood Management, Hanoi, 17–21 November 2003, pp93–96

Le Van Tuan (2003) *Rapid Assessment on Flood Preparedness Related to Emergency Health Care in Angiang Province, 2002*, Proceeding of the International Seminar on Flood Management, Hanoi, 17–21 November 2003, pp97–104

Lewes Flood Aftercare Group (2001) *Final Report,* Lewes Flood Aftercare Group, Lewes

Lichterman, J. (2000) 'A "community as resource" strategy for disaster response', *Public Health Reports*, vol 115, pp262–265

Lilley, B., Lammie, P., Dickerson, J. and Eberhard, M. (1997) 'An increase in hookworm infection temporally associated with ecologic change', *Emerging Infectious Diseases*, vol 3, pp391–393

Lillibridge, S. (1997) 'Managing the environmental health aspects of disasters: Water, human excreta and shelter', in Noji, E. (ed) *The Public Health Consequences of Disasters*, Oxford University Press, New York

Li Tao, Yu BingGui and Dai YuHai (2000) 'Impact and countermeasures on acute schistosomiasis transmission by Yangtze River flood', *Chinese Journal of Schistosomiasis Control*, vol 12, pp268–272

Lin DanDan, Murakami, H., Zhang ShaoJi, Wu ZhongDao, Ning An, Murakami, T., Totsuya, T., Gu XiaoNan, Hu GuangHan, Gao ZuLu, Liu YueMing, Hu Fei and Chen TaiHui (1999) 'Pilot study of schistosomiasis control in Poyang Lake region', *Chinese Journal of Parasitology and Parasitic Diseases*, vol 17, pp167–171

Lindsay, J. (2003) 'The determinants of disaster vulnerability: Achieving sustainable mitigation through population health', *Natural Hazards*, vol 28, pp291–304

Lindsay, S., Bodker, R., Malima, R., Msangeni, H. and Kisinza, W. (2000) 'The effect of 1997–1998 El Niño on highland malaria in Tanzania', *The Lancet*, vol 355, pp989–990

Logue, J. and Hansen, H. (1980) 'A case-control study of hypertensive women in a post-disaster community: Wyoming Valley, Pennsylvania', *Journal of Human Stress*, vol 6, pp28–34

Logue, J., Melick, M. and Struening, E. (1981) 'A study of health and mental health status following a major natural disaster', *Research in Community and Mental Health*, vol 2, pp217–274

Lorraine, N. (1954) 'Canvey Island flood disaster, February, 1953', *Medical Officer*, vol 91, pp59–62

Lucas, M. (2000) 'Emergência em Moçambique', Sector da Saúde Powerpoint presentation for Ministry of Health, Maputo, July 2000

Luna, E. (2001) 'Disaster mitigation and preparedness: The case of NGOs in the Philippines', *Disasters*, vol 25, pp216–226

Lutgendorf, S., Antoni, M., Ironson, G., Fletcher, M., Penedo, F., Baum, A., Schneiderman, N. and Klimas, N. (1995) 'Physical symptoms of chronic fatigue syndrome are exacerbated by the stress of Hurricane Andrew', *Psychosomatic Medicine*, vol 57, pp310–323

Maber, S. (1989) 'Health care and sanitation in Peru: Developing appropriate technologies', *Waterlines*, vol 7, pp28–31

Mackowiak, P., Caraway, C. and Portnoy, B. (1976) 'Oyster-associated hepatitis: Lessons from the Louisiana experience', *American Journal of Epidemiology*, vol 103, pp181–191

Macro International (1998) *Moçambique; Inquérito Demográfico e de Saúde 1997 Calverton, MD, USA*, Instituto Nacional de Estatística and Macro International Inc, Mozambique

Malilay, J. (1997) 'Floods', in Noji, E. (ed) *The Public Health Consequences of Disasters*, Oxford University Press, New York, pp287–301

Maltais, D., Lachance, L., Fortin, M., Lalande, G., Robichaud, S., Fortin, C. and Simard, A. (2000) 'Psychological and physical health of the July 1996 disaster victims: A comparative study between victims and non-victims' ('L'état de santé psychologique et physique des sinistrés des inondations de Juillet 1996: étude comparative entre sinistrés et non sinistrés'), *Santé Mentale au Québec*, vol XXV, pp116–137

MARD (Ministry for Agriculture and Rural Development) (2003) *Living with Floods in the Mekong River Delta of Vietnam,* Proceeding of the International Seminar on Flood Management, 17–21 November 2003, Hanoi, MARD, Vietnam, pp85–92

Markenson, D., Dimaggio, C. and Redlener, I. (2005) 'Preparing health professions students for terrorism, disaster and public health emergencies: Core competencies', *Academic Medicine,* vol 80, pp517–526

Marotto, P., Marotto, M., Santos, D., Souza, T. and Seguro, A. (1997) 'Outcome of leptospirosis in children', *American Journal of Tropical Medicine and Hygiene,* vol 56, 307–310

Maskrey, A. (1999) 'Reducing global disasters', in Ingleton, J. (ed) *Natural Disaster Management,* Tudor Rose, Leicester, pp84–86

Mathur, K., Harpalani, G., Kalra, N., Murthy, G. and Narasimham, M. (1992) 'Epidemic of malaria in Barmer district (Thar desert) of Rajasthan during 1990', *Indian Journal of Malariology,* vol 29, pp1–10

Matthies, F., Few, R and Kovats, S. (2003) 'Social science and adaptation to climate change', *IHDP Update,* vol 03, p15

Mattner, M. (2004) 'Power to the people? Local governance and politics in Vietnam', *Environment and Urbanization,* vol 16, pp121–127

McCarthy, M., He, J., Hyams, K., El-Tigani, A., Khalid, I. and Carl, M. (1994) 'Acute hepatitis E infection during the 1988 floods in Khartoum, Sudan', *Transactions of the Royal Society of Tropical Medicine and Hygiene,* vol 88, p177

McCarthy, M., Haberberger, R., Salib, A., Soliman, B., El-Tigani, A., Khalid, I. and Watts, D. (1996) 'Evaluation of arthropod-borne viruses and other infectious disease pathogens as the causes of febrile illnesses in the Khartoum Province of Sudan', *Journal of Medical Virology,* vol 48, pp141–146

McCarthy, J., Canziani, O, Leary, N., Dokken, D. and White, K. (eds) (2001) *Climate Change 2001: Impacts, Adaptation and Vulnerability,* Cambridge University Press, Cambridge

McCarthy, S. (2004) *Definitions and Experience of Flooding: Residents' and Officials' Perspectives,* PhD thesis, University of Surrey, UK

McCluskey, J. (2001) 'Water supply, health and vulnerability in floods', *Waterlines,* vol 19, pp14–17

McMichael, A., Campbell-Lendrum, D., Kovats, R., Edwards, S., Wilkinson, P., Edmonds, N., Nicholls, N., Hales, S., Tanser, F., Le Sueur, D., Schlesinger, M. and Andronova, N. (2004) 'Climate change', in Ezzati, M., Lopez, A., Rodgers, A. and Murray, C. (eds) *Comparative Quantification of Health Risks: Global and Regional Burden of Disease Due to Selected Major Risk Factors,* World Health Organization, Geneva, pp1543–1650

McMichael, A., Githeko, A., Akhtar, R., Carcavallo, R., Gubler, D., Haines, A., Kovats, R., Martens, P., Patz, J. and Sasaki, A. (2001) 'Human health', in McCarthy, J., Canziani, O., Leary, N., Dokken, D. and White, K. (eds) *Climate Change 2001: Impacts, Adaptation and Vulnerability,* Cambridge University Press, Cambridge

McMillen, C., North, C., Mosley, M. and Smith, E. (2002) 'Untangling the psychiatric comorbidity of posttraumatic stress disorder in a sample of flood survivors', *Comprehensive Psychiatry,* vol 43, pp478–485

Melick, M. (1978) 'Self-reported effects of a natural disaster on the health and well-being of working class males', *Crisis Intervention,* vol 9, pp12–31

Mclick, M. and Logue, J. (1985) 'The effect of disaster on the health and well-being of older women', *International Journal of Aging and Human Development,* vol 21, pp27–38

Menne, B. (1999) *Floods and Public Health Consequences, Prevention and Control Measures, 1st Draft,* UN–ECE Task Force Meeting on Flood Prevention and Protection, 15–17 April, Berlin, WHO–European Center for Environment and Health, Rome

Milly, P., Wetherald, R., Dunne, K. and Delworth, T. (2002) 'Increasing risk of great floods in a changing climate', *Nature,* vol 415, pp514–517

Milsten, A. (2000) 'Hospital responses to acute-onset disasters: A review', *Prehospital and Disaster Medicine,* vol 15, pp32–45

Mirza, M. (2002) 'Global warming and changes in the probability of occurrence of floods in Bangladesh and implications', *Global Environmental Change,* vol 12, pp127–138

Ministry of Natural Resources and Environment (2003) *Viet Nam Initial National Communication under the United Nations Framework Convention on Climate Change,* Socialist Republic of Viet Nam, Hanoi

MMWR *(Morbidity and Mortality Weekly Report)*(1989) 'Health assessment of the population affected by flood conditions – Khartoum, Sudan', *Morbidity and Mortality Weekly Report,* vol 37, pp785–788

Moinzadeh, M. (1999) 'Trauma symptoms and retraumatization in adult survivors of child abuse following a natural disaster', *Dissertation Abstracts International: Section B: The Sciences and Engineering,* vol 59, p4476

Mondal, N., Biswas, R. and Manna, A. (2001) 'Risk factors of diarrhoea among flood victims: A controlled epidemiological study', *Indian Journal of Public Health,* vol 45, pp122–127

Moreira Cedeno, J. (1986) 'El Niño related health hazards: Rainfall and flooding in the Guayas river basin and its effects on the incidence of malaria 1982–1985', *Disasters,* vol 10, pp107–111

Morillon, M., Pina, J., Husser, J., Baudet, J., Bertherat, E. and Martet, G. (1998) 'Djibouti: The story of a cholera epidemic, 1993–1994', *Bulletin de la Societe de Pathologie Exotique,* vol 91, pp407–411

Morrow, B. (1999) 'Identifying and mapping community vulnerability', *Disasters,* vol 23, pp1–18

Morsay, T., Arafa, M., Younis, T. and Mahmoud, I. (1996) 'Studies on *Paederus alfierii Koch* (Coleoptera: Sataphylinidae) with special reference to the medical importance', *Journal of the Egyptian Society of Parasitology,* vol 26, pp337–351

Morshed, M., Konishi, H., Terada, Y., Arimitsu, Y. and Nakazawa, T. (1994) 'Seroprevalence of leptospirosis in a rural flood prone district of Bangladesh', *Epidemiological Infections,* vol 112, pp527–531

MSF (Médecins Sans Frontières) (2004) 'Mental health work alongside health care at the Haiti floods', MSF, available at www.msf.org

Mudelsee, M., Börngen, M., Tetzlaff, G. and Grünewald, U. (2003) 'No upward trends in the occurrence of extreme floods in central Europe', *Nature,* vol 425, pp166–169

Muñoz, F., Jarquin, C., González, A., Amador, J., de los Reyes, J and Jimenez, R. et al (1995) 'Outbreak of acute febrile illness and pulmonary haemorrhage – Nicaragua, 1995', *Morbidity and Mortality Weekly Report,* vol 44, pp841–843

Naidoo, A. and Patric, K. (2002) 'Cholera: A continuous epidemic in Africa', *Journal of the Royal Society for the Promotion of Health,* vol 122, pp89–94

Nandi, J. and Sharma, S. (2000) 'Efficacy of chloroquine in febrile *Plasmodium falciparum* infected children in Mewat region of Haryana', *Journal of Communicable Diseases,* vol 32, pp137–143

Nates, J. (2004) 'Combined external and internal hospital disaster: Impact and response in a Houston trauma center intensive care unit', *Critical Care Medicine,* vol 32, pp 686–690

Nathoo, K. (1997) 'Shigella dysenteriae type 1 in Zimbabwe', *Africa Health*, vol 19, pp9–10

NC (North Carolina) Department of Agriculture and Consumer Services (2005) *Preparing your Farm for Weather Disasters*, North Carolina Department of Agriculture and Consumer Services website, http://www.ncagr.com/paffairs/farmers2.htm

NC (North Carolina) Division of Emergency Management (2005) *State of North Carolina Department of Crime Control and Public Safety, Division of Emergency Management*, http://www.dem.dcc.state.nc.us/index.htm

NCPTSD (National Center for Post-Traumatic Stress Disorder) (2001) *Survivors of Human-Caused and Natural Disasters*, Fact Sheet for the NCPTSD, Department of Veterans Affairs, US

NDM (Natural Disaster Mitigation)–Partnership (2003) 'Disaster preparedness plans of VNRC', *NDM–Partnership Newsletter*, 3 June, pp2–4

Neefjes, K. (2002) *Lessons from the Floods: Voices of the People, Local Authorities and Disaster Management Agencies from the Mekong Delta in Viet Nam,* Discussion paper, Viet Nam Red Cross and the International Federation of Red Cross and Red Crescent Societies, Viet Nam

Neuberg, M., Jakubowska-Szwed, B. and Neuberg, J. (2001) 'Reproductive behaviour after the flood disaster in Klodzko region – July 1997', *Ginekologia Polska,* vol 72, pp1037–1041

Neuberg, M., Pawlosek, W., Jakubowska-Szwed, B., Waciega, A. and Turkiewicz, M. (1999) 'Repeated amenorrhea in an adolescent girl in the course of flood disaster in Klodzko Region, July 1997', *Ginekologia Polska*, vol 70, pp378–382

Nicholls, R. (2002) 'Analysis of global impacts of sea-level rise: A case study of flooding', *Physics and Chemistry of the Earth*, vol 27, pp1455–1466

Nicholls, R. (2004) 'Coastal flooding and wetland loss in the 21st century: Changes under the SRES climate and socio-economic scenarios', *Global Environmental Change*, vol 14, pp69–86

Nicholls, R., Hoozemans, F. and Marchand, M. (1999) 'Increasing flood risk and wetland losses due to global sea-level rise: Regional and global analyses', *Global Environmental Change*, vol 9, ppS69–S88

Nicholls, R., Mimura, N. and Topping, J. (1995) 'Climate change in South and South-East Asia: Some implications for coastal areas', *Journal of Global Environmental Engineering*, vol 1, pp137–154

Nishat, A., Reazuddin, M., Amin, R and Khan, A. (eds) (2000) *The 1998 Flood: Impact on the Environment of Dhaka City,* Department of Environment and IUCN Bangladesh, Dhaka

NOAA (National Oceanographic and Atmospheric Agency) (2005a) 'Billion dollar US weather disasters', *Weather Extremes*, US NOAA website, www.ncdc.noaa.gov/oa/reports/billionz.html

NOAA (2005b) *Flood Safety*, National Weather Service, US NOAA Administration website, www.floodsafety.noaa.gov/

Noji, E. (1991) 'Natural disasters', *Critical Care Clinics*, vol 7, pp271–292

Noji, E. (1997) 'The nature of disaster: General characteristics and public health effects', in Noji, E. (ed) *The Public Health Consequences of Disasters*, Oxford University Press, New York, pp3–20

Noji, E. (2005) 'Public health issues in disasters', *Critical Care Medicine*, vol 33, ppS29–S33

Noji, E. and Toole, M. (1997) 'The historical development of public health responses to disaster', *Disasters*, vol 21, pp366–376

Nolen, S. (2005) 'Katrina's other victims: Animals plight prompts outcry for change', *JAVMA News* website, 15 October 2005, www.avma.org/onlnews/javma/oct05/051015a.asp

Norris, F., Byrne, C., Diaz, E. and Kaniasty, K. (2001a) *The Range, Magnitude and Duration of Effects of Natural and Human-Caused Disasters: A Review of the Empirical Literature,* National Center for Post-Traumatic Stress Disorder, Department of Veterans Affairs, US

Norris, F., Byrne, C. and Kaniasty, K. (2001b) *Psychosocial Resources in the Aftermath of Natural and Human-Caused Disasters: A Review of the Empirical Literature, with Implications for Intervention,* National Center for Post-Traumatic Stress Disorder, Department of Veterans Affairs, US

Norris, F., Kaniasty, K., Conrad, M., Inman, G. and Murphy, A. (2002) 'Placing age differences in cultural context: A comparison of the effects of age on PTSD after disasters in the United States, Mexico and Poland', *Journal of Clinical Geropsychology,* vol 8, pp153–173

NSW (New South Wales) Health (2000) *Disaster Mental Health Response Handbook,* NSW Health, North Sydney, Australia

NWS (National Weather Service) (2005a) *Natural Hazard Statistics: Weather Fatalities,* NWS weather fatality, injury and damage statistics, US NWS website, www.nws.noaa.gov/om/hazstats.shtml

NWS (2005b) *Operation Turn Around, Don't Drown,* Hydrologic Services, US NWS, tadd.weather.gov/

NWS (2005c) *Advanced Hydrologic Prediction Service,* Hydrologic Information Center, US NWS website, www.nws.noaa.gov/oh/hic/

NWS (2005d) *National Weather Service's Warnings and Forcasts,* US NWS website, www.nws.noaa.gov

NWS (2005e) *Pacific Tsunami Warning Center,* Pacific Tsunami Warning Center, NWS, US NWS website, www.prhnoaagov/ptwc/

NWS Southern Region HDQS (2003) *Tropical Cyclones and Flooding,* Southern Region Headquarters, US NWS website, www.srh.weather.gov/floods/

Ogden, C., Gibbs-Scharf, L., Kohn, M. and Malilay, J. (2001) 'Emergency health surveillance after severe flooding in Louisiana, 1995', *Prehospital and Disaster Medicine,* vol 16, pp138–144

Ohl, C. and Tapsell, S. (2000) 'Flooding and human health: The dangers posed are not always obvious', *British Medical Journal,* vol 321, pp1167–1168

Ollendick, D. and Hoffmann, M. (1982) 'Assessment of psychological reactions in disaster victims', *Journal of Community Psychology,* vol 10, pp157–167

Orellana, C. (2002) 'Germany counts cost of flood damage to health-care services', *The Lancet,* vol 360, p698

Osorio, C. (2003) 'Lack of freshwater: A primary concern at times of disasters', in World Disaster Reduction Campaign (ed) *Living with Risk: Turning the Tide on Disasters Towards Sustainable Development: Information Kit,* United Nations International Strategy for Disaster Reduction, New York

Oxfam (2005) *The Tsunami's Impacts on Women,* Oxfam Briefing Note, March 2005

PAHO (Pan American Health Organization) (1998a) *El Niño and Its Impact on Health,* Report presented to 122nd Executive Assembly of Pan American Health Organization, May 1998, Document CE122/10, Washington, DC

PAHO (1998b) *Natural Disaster Mitigation in Drinking Water and Sewerage Systems: Guidelines for Vulnerability Analysis,* Pan American Health Organization, Washington, DC

PAHO (1999) *Meeting on Evaluation and of Preparedness and Response to Hurricanes George and Mitch, 16–19 February 1999, Santo Domingo, Dominican Republic, Conclusions and Recommendations,* Pan American Health Organization, Washington, DC

PAHO (2000) *Principles of Diaster Mitigation in Health Facilities,* Pan American Health Organization, Washington, DC

PAHO (2001) 'Editorial: Protecting the health services network', *Disaster Preparedness and Mitigation in the Americas,* vol 84, pp1, 7

PAHO (2003) *Protecting New Health Facilities from Natural Disaster: Guidelines for the Promotion of Disaster Mitigation,* Pan American Health Organization, Washington, DC

Palakudiyil, T. and Todd, M. (2003) *Facing up to the Storm: How Local Communities Can Cope with disaster – Lessons from Orissa and Gujarat,* Christian Aid, London

Palmer, T. and Rälsänen, J. (2002) 'Quantifying the risk of seasonal precipitation events in a changing climate', *Nature,* vol 415, pp512–514

Park, S. K., Lee, S. H., Rhee, Y. K., Kang, S. K., Kim, K. J., Kim, M. C., Kim, K. W. and Chang, W. H. (1989) 'Leptospirosis in Chonbuk Province of Korea in 1987: A study of 93 patients', *American Journal of Tropical Medicine and Hygiene,* vol 41, pp345–351

Parker, D. (1999) 'Criteria for evaluating the condition of a Tropical Cyclone Warning System', *Disaster,* vol 23, pp193–216

Parker, D. (2000) 'Introduction to floods and flood management', in Parker, D. (ed) *Floods,* Vol 1, Routledge, London, pp3–39

Parker, D., Green, C. and Thompson, P. (1987) *Urban Flood Protection Benefits: A Project Appraisal Guide,* Aldershot, Gower, UK

Parker, D., Green, C. and Penning-Rowsell, E. (1983) *Swalecliffe Coast Protection Proposals – Evaluation of Potential Benefits,* Flood Hazard Research Centre, Middlesex Polytechnic, Enfield, UK

Parker, D. and Thompson, P. (2000) 'Floods in Africa: Vulnerability, impacts and mitigation', in Parker, D. (ed) *Floods,* vol 1, Routledge, London, pp188–203

Parkinson, J. (2002) 'Urban drainage in developing countries – challenges and opportunities', *Waterlines,* vol 20, pp2–5

Parkinson, J. (2003) 'Drainage and stormwater management for low-income urban communities', *Environment and Urbanization,* vol 15, pp115–126

Patterson, R., Fink, J., Miles, W., Basich, J., Schleuter, D., Tinkelman, D. and Roberts, M. (1981) 'Hypersensitivity lung disease presumptively due to *Cephalosporium* in homes contaminated by sewage flooding or by humidifier water', *Journal of Allergy and Clinical Immunology,* vol 68, pp128–132

Patel, V. (2003) *Where There Is no Psychiatrist: A Mental Health Care Manual,* Gaskell, London

Patz, J., Githeko, A., McCarty, J., Hussain, S., Confalonieri, U. and de Wet, N. (2003) 'Climate change and infectious diseases' in McMichael, A., Campbell-Lendrum, D., Corvalan, C., Ebi, K., Githeko, A., Scheraga, J. and Woodward, A. (eds) *Climate Change and Human Health: Risks and Responses,* World Health Organization, Geneva, pp103–132

Pelling, M. (2003) *The Vulnerability of Cities: Natural Disasters and Social Resilience* Earthscan, London

Perez, E. and Thompson, P. (1995) 'Natural hazards: Causes and effects – Lesson 5. Tropical cyclones (hurricanes, typhoons, baguios, cordonazos, tainos)', *Prehospital and Disaster Medicine,* vol 10, pp202–215; quiz pp216–217

Peters, M. (1996) 'Hospitals respond to water loss during the Midwest floods of 1993: Preparedness and improvisation', *Journal of Emergency Medicine*, vol 14, pp345–350

Pham Thi Lan (2000) *Need Assessment in Response to Flood Disaster in Mekong River Delta,* Save the Children in Vietnam, Hanoi

Phifer, J. (1990) 'Psychological distress and somatic symptoms after natural disaster: Differential vulnerability among older adults', *Psychology and Aging*, vol 5, pp412–420

Phifer, J., Kaniasty, K. and Norris, F. (1988) 'The impact of natural disaster on the health of older adults: A multi-wave prospective study', *Journal of Health and Social Behaviour*, vol 29, pp65–78

Philippi, Jr, A., Salles, C. and Silveira, V. (2003) 'Saneamento do meio em emergencias ambientais', in Philippi, Jr (ed) *Saneamento, saude e ambiente: fundamentos para um desenvolvimento sustenavel,* Universidade de Sao Paulo, Brazil

PHLS (Public Health Laboratory Service) (2000) *Provisional Guidelines on the Public Health Implications of Flooding*, PHLS, UK

PHP&R (Public Health Preparedness and Response) (2005) 'The Office of Public Health Preparedness and Response', North Carolina Department of Epidemiology website, http://www.epi.state.nc.us/epi/phpr

Piarroux, R. (2002) 'Management of a cholera epidemic by a humanitarian organization', *Medecine Tropicale*, vol 62, pp361–367

Pilon, P. (ed) (2004) *Guidelines for Reducing Flood Losses*, United Nations (DESA, UN/ISDR) and US NOAA, Washington, DC

Piper-Jenks, N., Horowitz, H. and Schwartz, E. (2000) 'Risk of hepatitis E infection to travellers', *Journal of Travel Medicine*, vol 7, pp194–199

Poncelet, J. and de Ville de Goyet, C. (1996) 'Disaster preparedness: Institutional capacity building in the Americas', *World Health Statistics Quarterly*, vol 49, pp195–199

Potera, C. (2003) 'Fuel damage from flooding', *Environmental Health Perspectives*, vol 111, ppA228–31

Powell, B. and Penick, E. (1983) 'Psychological distress following a natural disaster: A one-year follow-up of 98 flood victims', *Journal of Community Psychology*, vol 11, pp 269–276

Power, M. (1988) 'The 'Worst Ever' version of the General Health Questionnaire', *Journal of Clinical Psychology,* vol 44, pp215–216

Pratinidhi, A. and Gokhale, R. (1998) 'Disaster management knowledge attitude and practice of urban slum dwellers', *Indian Journal of Medical Sciences*, vol 52, pp155–158

Price, J. (1978) 'Some age-related effects of the 1974 Brisbane floods', *Australian and New Zealand Journal of Psychiatry*, vol 12, pp55–58

Pugh, J. and Potter, R. (eds) (2003) *Participatory Planning in the Caribbean,* Ashgate, Aldershot, UK

Quarantelli, E. (2003) 'Urban vulnerability to disasters in developing countries: Managing risks', in Kreimer, A., Arnold, M. and Carlin, A. (eds) *Building Safer Cities*, Disaster Risk Management Series No 3, The World Bank Group, Washington, DC, pp211–232

Quayle, C. (1995) 'Learning the hard way: Veterans of disaster tell why – and how – you should be prepared', *Health Facilities Management*, vol 8, pp18–20, 22, 246

Rahman, M. and Bennish, M. (1993) 'Health related response to natural disasters: The case of the Bangladesh cyclone of 1991' *Social Science and Medicine*, vol 36, pp903–914

Ramsey, D. (1994) 'Dealing with the flood crisis of 1993: A medical center's account', *Hospital Topics*, vol 72, pp19–22

Rashid, S. (2000) 'The urban poor in Dhaka City: Their struggles and coping strategies during the floods of 1998', *Disasters*, vol 24, pp240–253

Rashid, S. and Michaud, S. (2000) 'Female adolescents and their sexuality: Notions of honour, shame, purity and pollution during the floods', *Disasters*, vol 24, pp54–70

Reacher, M., McKenzie, K., Lane, C., Nichols, T., Kedge, I., Iverson, A., Hepple, P., Walter, T., Laxton, C. and Simpson, J. (2004) 'Health impacts of flooding in Lewes: A comparison of reported gastrointestinal and other illness and mental health in flooded and non-flooded households', *Communicable Disease and Public Health*, vol 7, pp56–63

Reed, M. (1997) 'The Grand Forks disaster', *Healthcare Hazardous Materials Management*, vol 11, pp1–6

Reisberg, B., Wurtz, R., Diaz, P., Francis, B., Zakowski, P., Fannin, S., Sesline, D., Waterman, S., Sanderson, R., McChesney, T., Boddie, R., Levy, M., Miller, G., Jr and Herrera, G. (1997) 'Outbreak of leptospirosis among white water rafters – Costa Rica, 1996', *Morbidity and Mortality Weekly Report*, vol 46, pp577–579

Richards, G. (1999) *Dealing with Disaster: Lessons from Nicaragua One Year After Hurricane Mitch*, One World Action Briefing, One World Action, London

Rigau-Perez, J., Ayala-Lopez, A., Vorndam, A. and Clark, G. (2001) 'Dengue activity in Puerto Rico during an interepidemic period (1995–1997)', *American Journal of Tropical Medicine and Hygiene*, vol 64, pp75–83

Rincon, E., Linares, M. and Greenberg, B. (2001) 'Effect of previous experience of a hurricane on preparedness for future hurricanes', *American Journal of Emergency Medicine*, vol 19, pp276–279

RPA (Risk and Policy Analysis), Flood Hazard Research Centre, EFTEC and CASPAR University of Newcastle (2004) *The Appraisal of Human-Related Intangible Impacts of Flooding*, Report to Defra/Environment Agency, R&D Technical Report FD2005/TR, Defra, London

Robson, A. J. (2002) 'Evidence for trends in UK flooding', *Philosophical Transactions of the Royal Society of London. Series A. Mathematical, Physical and Engineering Sciences*, vol 360, pp1327–1343

Roger Young and Associates (2000) *Bangladesh: 1998 Flood Appeal – An Independent Evaluation*, Disasters Emergency Committee, UK

Russac, P. (1986) 'Epidemiological surveillance: Malaria epidemic following the El Niño phenomenon', *Disasters*, vol 10, pp112–117

Russoniello, C., Skalko, T., O'Brien, K., McGhee, S., Bingham-Alexander, D. and Beatley, J. (2002) 'Childhood posttraumatic stress disorder and efforts to cope after Hurricane Floyd', *Behavioral Medicine*, vol 28, pp61–70

Saenz, R., Bissell, R. and Paniagua, F. (1995) 'Post-disaster malaria in Costa Rica', *Prehospital and Disaster Medicine*, vol 10, pp154–160

Salkovskis, P. (1996) 'The cognitive approach to anxiety: Threat beliefs, safety-seeking behavior and the special case of health anxiety and obsessions', in Salkovskis, P. (ed) *Frontiers of Cognitive Therapy,* Guilford Press, New York

Sanders, E., Rigau-Pérez, J., Smits, H., Deseda, C., Vorndam, V., Aye, T., Spiegel, R., Weyant, R. and Bragg, S. (1999) 'Increase of leptospirosis in dengue-negative patients after a hurricane in Puerto Rico in 1996', *American Journal of Tropical Medicine and Hygiene*, vol 61, pp399–404

Sarkar, U., Nascimento, S., Barbosa, R., Martins, R., Nuevo, H., Kalafanos, I., Grunstein, I. and Flannery, B. (2002) 'Population-based case-control investigation of risk factors for Leptospirosis during an urban epidemic', *American Journal of Tropical Medicine and Hygiene*, vol 66, pp605–610

Save the Children (2003) *Child Drowning in the Mekong Delta: Current Situation and Solutions*, Save the Children in Vietnam, Hanoi

Scheraga, J., Ebi, K., Furlow, J. and Moreno, A. (2003) 'From science to policy: Developing responses to climate change', in McMichael, A., Campbell-Lendrum, D., Corvalan, C., Ebi, K., Githeko, A., Scheraga, J. and Woodward, A. (eds) *Climate Change and Human Health: Risks and Responses*, World Health Organization, Geneva, pp237–266

Schmidt, C. (2000) 'Lessons from the flood: Will Floyd change livestock farming?', *Environmental Health Perspectives*, vol 108, ppA74–A77

Schmidt, W., Skala, M., Donelon, I. and Donnell, H. (1993) 'Morbidity surveillance following the Midwest flood – Missouri, 1993', *Morbidity and Mortality Weekly Report*, vol 42, pp797–798

Schultz, C., Koenig, K. and Lewis, R. (2003) 'Implications of hospital evacuation after the Northridge, California, earthquake', *New England Journal of Medicine*, vol 348, pp 1349–1355

Schwarz, J. and Zuroff, D. (1979) 'Family structure and depression in female college students: Effects of parental conflict, decision-making power and inconsistency of love', *Journal of Abnormal Psychology*, vol 88, pp398–405

Scott, W. and Dua, J. (1999) 'Development of a scale to assess posttraumatic stress disorder', *International Journal of Stress Management*, vol 6, pp149–165

Seaman, J. (1984) *Epidemiology of Natural Disasters*, Karger, Basel, Switzerland

Sedyaningsih-Mamahit, E., Larasati, R., Laras, K., Sidemen, A., Sukri, N., Sabaruddin, N., Didi, S., Saragih, J., Myint, K., Endy, T., Sulaiman, A., Campbell, J. and Corwin, A. (2002) 'First documented outbreak of hepatitis E virus transmission in Java, Indonesia', *Transactions of the Royal Society of Tropical Medicine and Hygiene*, vol 96, pp398–404

Segall, M., Tipping, G., Lucas, H., Truong Viet Dung, Nguyen Thanh Tam, Dao Xuan Vinh and Dao Lan Huong (2000) *Health Care Seeking by the Poor in Transitional Economies: The Case of Vietnam*, IDS Research Report 43, Institute of Development Studies, Brighton, UK

Sehgal, S., Sugunan, A. and Vijayachari, P. (2002) 'Outbreak of leptospirosis after the cyclone in Orissa', *The National Medical Journal of India*, vol 15, pp22–23

Shahaduzzaman (1999) 'Health during disaster: Sharing experiences with 1998 flood victims', in Ahmed, S. and Ahmed, H. (eds) *Experiences of Deluge: Flood 1998 Research Monograph Series*, vol 15, Bangladesh Rural Advancement Commission (BRAC), Dhaka, pp46–56

Sharma, R., Shiv, L., Sharma, S., Joshi, R. and Dhillon, G. (1997) 'Malaria outbreak in Mewat region Gurgaon district of Haryana State', *Journal of Communicable Diseases*, vol 29, pp307–308

Siddique, A., Baqui, A., Eusof, A. and Zaman, K. (1991) '1988 floods in Bangladesh: Pattern of illness and causes of death', *Journal of Diarrhoeal Diseases Research*, vol 9, pp310–314

Sidley, P. (2000) 'Malaria epidemic expected in Mozambique', *British Medical Journal*, vol 320, p669

Silove, D. and Zwi, A. (2005) 'Translating compassion into psychosocial aid after the tsunami', *The Lancet*, vol 365, pp269–271

Sime, J. (1997) 'Informative flood warnings: Occupant response to risk, threat and loss of place', in Handmer, J. (ed) *Flood Warning: Issues and Practice in Total System Design*, Flood Hazard Research Centre, Middlesex University, Enfield, UK

Simkin P. (2000) *Floods Mozambique – Lessons Learned from the Humanitarian Flood Relief Operations*, United Nations Development Programme, Maputo

Simões, J., de Azevedo, J. and Palmeiro, J. (1969) 'Some aspects of the Weil's disease epidemiology based on a recent epidemic after a flood in Lisbon (1967)', *Anais da Escola Nacional de Saude Publica e de Medicina Tropical*, vol 3, pp19–32

Skoufias, E. (2003) 'Economic crises and natural disasters: Coping strategies and policy implications', *World Development*, vol 31, pp1087–1102

Smit, B., Pilifodova, O., Burton, I., Challenger, B., Huq, S., Klein, R., Yohe, G., Adger, N., Downing, T., Harvey, E., Kane, S., Parry, M., Skinner, M., Smith, J., Wandel, J., Patwardhan, A. and Soussana, J. (2001) 'Adaptation to climate change in the context of sustainable development and equity', in McCarthy, J., Canziani, O., Leary, N., Dokken, D. and White, K. (eds) *Climate Change 2001: Impacts, Adaptation and Vulnerability*, Cambridge University Press, Cambridge

Smith, B. (1996) 'Coping as a predictor of outcomes following the 1993 midwest flood', *Journal of Social Behavior and Personality*, vol 11, pp225–239

Smith, D. (2000) 'Floodplain management: Problems, issues and opportunities', in Parker, D. (ed) *Floods*, Routledge, London

Smith, D., Mackenzie, J. and Broom, A. (1993) 'Preliminary report of Australian encephalitis in Western Australia and the Northern Territory, 1993', *Communicable Disease Intelligence*, vol 17, pp209–210

Sneddon, C. and Nguyen Thanh Binh (2001) 'Politics, ecology and water: The Mekong Delta and development of the Lower Mekong Basin', in Adger, W., Kelly, P. and Nguyen Huu Ninh (eds) *Living with Environmental Change: Social Vulnerability, Adaptation and Resilience in Vietnam*, Routledge, London, pp234–262

Solomon, S., Smith, E., Robins, L. and Fischbach, R. (1987) 'Social involvement as a mediator of disaster-induced stress', *Journal of Applied Social Psychology*, vol 17, pp1092–1112

Sperling, F. and Szekely, F. (2005) *Disaster Risk Management in a Changing Climate*, Discussion Paper, Vulnerability and Adaptation Resource Group (VARG), Washington, DC

Square, D. (1997) 'Hospital evacuated, mental-health issues dominated as Manitoba coped with flood of century', *Canadian Medical Association Journal*, vol 156, pp 1742–1745

Steinglass, P. and Gerrity, E. (1990) 'Natural disaster and post-traumatic stress disorder: Short-term versus long-term recovery in two disaster-affected communities', *Journal of Applied Social Psychology*, vol 20, pp1746–1765

Staes, C., Orengo, J., Malilay, J., Rullan, J. and Noji, E. (1994) 'Deaths due to flash floods in Puerto Rico, January 1992: Implications for prevention', *International Journal of Epidemiology*, vol 23, pp968–975

Stephens, C., Patnaik, R. and Lewin, S. (1994) *This Is My Beautiful Home. Risk Perceptions Towards Flooding and Environment in Low Income Urban Communities: A Case Study in Indore, India*, Research Report, London School of Hygiene and Tropical Medicine, London

Sternberg, E., Lee, G. and Huard, D. (2004) 'Counting crises: US hospital evacuations, 1971–1999', *Prehospital and Disaster Medicine*, vol 19, pp150–157

Suárez Hernández, M., Martínez Sánchez, R., Posada Fernández, P., Vidal García, I., Bravo Fleites, F. and Sánchez Sibello, A. (1999) 'Human leptospirosis outbreak in the district of Ciego de Ávila, Cuba', *Revista da Sociedade Brasileira de Medicina Tropical*, vol 32, pp13–18

Summerfield, D. (2001) 'The invention of post-traumatic stress disorder and the social usefulness of a psychiatric category', *British Medical Journal*, vol 322, pp95–98

Sun–Sentinel (2005) 'Florida Power & Light Co works on improving hurricane response plan for 2005', Archives, *Sun–Sentinel* web edition, www.sun-sentinel.com

Sur, D., Dutta, P., Nair, G. and Bhattacharya, S. (2000) 'Severe cholera outbreak following floods in a northern district of West Bengal', *Indian Journal of Medical Research*, vol 112, pp178–182

Tapsell, S. and Tunstall, S. (2000) *Follow-up Study of the Health Effects of the 1998 Easter Flooding in Banbury and Kidlington,* Final report to the Environment Agency, Flood Hazard Research Centre, Middlesex University, Enfield, UK

Tapsell, S. and Tunstall, S. (2001) *The Health and Social Effects of the June 2000 Flooding in the North East Region: Report to the Environment Agency, Thames Region,* Flood Hazard Research Centre, Middlesex University, Enfield, UK

Tapsell, S., Tunstall, S., Penning-Rowsell, E. and Handmer, J. (1999) *The Health Effects of the 1998 Easter Flooding in Banbury and Kidlington: Report to the Environment Agency, Thames Region,* Flood Hazard Research Centre, Middlesex University, Enfield, UK

Tapsell, S., Tunstall, S. and Wilson, T. (2003) *Banbury and Kidlington Four Years After the Flood: An Examination of the Long-Term Health Effects of Flooding: Report to the Environment Agency, Thames Region,* Flood Hazard Research Centre, Middlesex University, Enfield, UK

Tearfund (2004) *Before Disaster Strikes: Why Thousands Are Dying Needlessly Each Year in Preventable Disasters,* Tearfund, London

Thai Thi Ngoc Du, Pham Gia Tran, Nguyen Thi Thu Ha, Nguyen Thi Nhan and Duong Thi Ry (2002) 'Housing and infrastructure constraints faced by the urban poor in Hochiminh City and Cantho City', in World Bank (ed) *The Most Urgent Problems of the Poor: Study Report,* World Bank, Hochiminh City, pp43–51

The Center for an Accessible Society (2005) *Disaster Mitigation for Persons with Disabilities,* The Center for an Accessible Society website, www.accessiblesociety. org/topics/independentliving/disasterprep.htm

The Daily Star (2004) 'Ways to confront the flood situation', *The Daily Star,* vol 6, p2

The Lancet (2005) 'Katrina reveals fatal weaknesses in US public health', *The Lancet,* vol 366, p867

The Sphere Project (2004) *Humanitarian Charter and Minimum Standards in Disaster Response,* The Sphere Project, Geneva

The Times-Picayune (2002) 'Washing away. Special report from *The Times-Picayune*', NOLA.com Hurricane Center website, http://www.nola.com/hurricane/?/washingaway/

Thomas, T., Hsu, E., Kim, H., Colli, S., Arana, G. and Green, G. (2005) 'The incident command system in disasters: Evaluation methods for a hospital-based exercise', *Prehospital and Disaster Medicine,* vol 20, pp4–23

Thompson, M. and Gavira, I. (2004) *Weathering the Storm: Lessons in Risk Reduction from Cuba,* Oxfam America, Boston and Washington, DC

Ticehurst, S., Webster, R., Carr, V and Lewin, T. (1996) 'The psychosocial impact of an earthquake on the elderly', *International Journal of Geriatric Psychiatry,* vol 11, pp943–951

Tierney, K. (2000) *Controversy and Consensus in Disaster Mental Health Research,* Disaster Research Center Preliminary Paper 305, Disaster Research Center, University of Delaware, Newark

Tobin, G. and Ollenburger, J. (1996) 'Predicting levels of postdisaster stress in adults following the 1993 floods in the upper Midwest', *Environment and Behaviour,* vol 28, pp340–357

Tran Thanh Tung, Le Phan Hong Anh, Nguyen Tuan Hap, Tran Thi Thanh Nhan, Dinh Thi Hong Quyet, Hoang Thanh Sang, Trinh Thi Thu Thao, Doan Dang Bao

Tran, Tran Minh Tri, Vo Thi Nhat Tam, Nguyen Doan Vu Tuyen, Tran Thi Doan Trinh and Nguyen Tran Thanh Quyen (2005) *The Fact of Flooding and Living with Flood of Rural Residential Community in An Giang Province,* Research report, Department of Geography, University of Social Sciences and Humanities, National University of Ho Chi Minh City, Vietnam

Trevejo, R., Rigau-Pérez, J., Ashford, D., McClure, E., Jarquín-González, C., Amador, J., de los Reyes, J., González, A., Zaki, S., Shieh WunJu, McLean, R., Nasci, R., Weyant, R., Bolin, C., Bragg, S., Perkins, B. and Spiegel, R. (1998) 'Epidemic leptospirosis associated with pulmonary haemorrhage, Nicaragua, 1995', *Journal of Infectious Diseases,* vol 178, pp1457–1463

Tsai, T., Popovici, F., Cernescu, C., Campbell, G. and Nedelcu, N. (1998) 'West Nile encephalitis epidemic in southeastern Romania', *The Lancet,* vol 352, pp767–771

Tunstall, S., Tapsell, S., Green, C., Floyd, P. and George, C. (2006) 'The health effects of flooding in the developed world: Research results for England and Wales', *Journal of Water and Health* (in press)

Twigg, J. (2004) *Disaster Risk Reduction: Mitigation and Preparedness in Development and Emergency Programming,* Overseas Development Institute, London

UNC (University of North Carolina) Chapel Hill (2005a) *Community Preparedness and Disaster Management,* Health Policy and Administration, Carolina School of Public Health, available at www.sph.unc.edu/hpaa/academic/disaster.htm

UNC Chapel Hill (2005b) *North Carolina Center of Public Health Preparedness,* Center of Public Health Preparedness, University of North Carolina School of Public Health, available at www.sph.unc.edu/nccphp/

UNDP (United Nations Development Programme) (2002) *Mozambique National Human Development Report 2001,* UNDP, Maputo

UNDP (2004a) *Reducing Disaster Risk: A Challenge for Development,* UNDP, New York

UNDP (2004b) *Human Development Report 2004,* UNDP, New York

UNICEF (United Nations Children's Fund) (2003) *UNICEF Donates Relief Items Worth KSHS 13 Million to Flood Victims in Western Kenya,* Press Center News Note, UNICEF, available at www.unicef.org/newsline/2003/03nn33kenya.htm

UNICEF Cyclone Evaluation Team (1993) 'Health effects of the 1991 Bangladesh cyclone: Report of a UNICEF evaluation team', *Disasters,* vol 17, pp153–165

UNICEF Vietnam (2002) *Psychosocial Impact of Child Drowning Deaths in the Mekong River Province of Dong Thap: A Preliminary Assessment,* UNICEF, Hanoi

UNICEF Vietnam (2004) *Injury a Leading Killer of Children in Asia and the Pacific Region,* Press release, United Nations Children's Fund, Vietnam, 20 April 2004

Union of Concerned Scientists (2003) *Confronting Climate Change in the Gulf Coast Region,* Union of Concerned Scientists website, www.ucsusa.org, accessed 18 March 2003

Vanasco, N., Sequeira, G., Fontana, M., Fusco, S., Sequeira, M. and Enría, D. (2000) 'Description of leptospirosis outbreak in the city of Santa Fe, Argentina, March–April 1998', *Revista Panamericana de Salud Publica/Pan American Journal of Public Health,* vol 7, pp35–40

Van Dyke, C., Zilbert, N. and McKinnon, J. (1985) 'Posttraumatic stress disorder: A thirty-year delay in a World War II veteran', *American Journal of Psychiatry,* vol 142, pp1070–1073

van Middelkoop, A., Wyk, J. and Kustner, H. (1992) 'Poliomyelitis outbreak in Natal/ KwaZulu, South Africa, 1987–1988' *Transactions of the Royal Society of Tropical Medicine and Hygiene,* vol 86, pp80–82

VanRooyen, M. and Leaning, J. (2005) 'After the Tsunami: Facing the public health challenges' *New England Journal of Medicine*, vol 352, pp435–438

Verger, P., Rotily, M., Hunault, C., Brenot, J., Baruffol, E. and Bard, D. (2003) 'Assessment of exposure to a flood disaster in a mental health study', *Journal of Exposure Analysis and Environmental Epidemiology*, vol 13, pp436–442

Victoria, L. (2002) *Impact Assessment Study of the Orissa Disaster Management Project*, Asian Disaster Preparedness Centre, Klong Luang, Thailand

Vollaard, A., Ali, S., van Asten, H., Widjaja, S., Visser, L., Surjadi, C. and van Dissel, J. (2004) 'Risk factors for typhoid and paratyphoid fever in Jakarta, Indonesia', *Journal of the American Medical Association*, vol 291, pp2607–2615

Wade, T., Sandhu, S., Levy, D., Lee, S., LeChevallier, M., Katz, L. and Colford, J. (2004) 'Did a severe flood in the Midwest cause an increase in the incidence of gastrointestinal symptoms?', *American Journal of Epidemiology*, vol 159, pp398–405

Waelde, L., Koopman, C., Rierdan, J. and Spiegel, D. (2001) 'Symptoms of acute stress disorder and posttraumatic stress disorder following exposure to disastrous flooding', *Journal of Trauma and Dissociation*, vol 2, pp37–52

Waelde, L., Koopman, C. and Spiegel, D. (1998) *Dissociative and Post-Traumatic Reactions to the Northern California Flooding of 1997*, Quick Response Report No 104, Hazards Center, Boulder, Colorado

Ward, R. (1978) *Floods: A Geographical Perspective*, Macmillan, London

Waring, S. and Brown, B. (2005) 'The threat of communicable diseases following natural disasters: A public health response', *Disaster Management and Response*, April–June 2005, pp41–47

Waring, S., Reynolds, K., D'Souza, G. and Arafat, R. (2002) 'Rapid assessment of household needs in the Houston area after Tropical Storm Allison', *Disaster Management Response*, September 2002, pp3–9

Western, K. (1982) *Epidemiologic Surveillance after Natural Disaster*, Pan American Health Organization, Washington, DC

White, P., Pelling, M., Sen, K., Seddon, D., Russell, S. and Few, R. (2004) *Disaster Risk Reduction: A Development Concern – A Scoping Study on Links between Disaster Risk Reduction, Poverty and Development*, Department for International Development, London

WHO (World Health Organization) (1998) 'Cholera in 1997', *Weekly Epidemiological Record*, vol 73, pp201–208

WHO (1999a) *Rapid Health Assessment Protocols for Emergencies*, World Health Organization, Geneva

WHO (1999b) *Climate and Health*, Working Group Meeting Report, WHO/SDE/OEH/99.6, World Health Organization, Geneva

WHO (2000) 'Leptospirosis, India Report of the investigation of a post-cyclone outbreak in Orissa, November 1999', *Epidemiological Record*, vol 75, pp217–224

WHO (2001) *The World Health Report 2001 – Mental Health: New Understanding, New Hope*, World Health Organization, Geneva

WHO (2002) *Floods: Climate Change and Adaptation Strategies for Human Health*, Report on a WHO meeting 30 June–2 July 2002, London, UK, World Health Organization Regional Office for Europe, Denmark

WHO (2003a) *WHO Recommends Close Disease Surveillance in Flood Affected Areas in Sri Lanka*, Press Release, World Health Organization Media Centre, Geneva

WHO (2003b) *Mental Health in Emergencies: Mental and Social Aspects of Health of Populations Exposed to Extreme Stressors*, World Health Organization, Geneva

WHO (2004) *Extreme Weather and Climate Events and Public Health Responses*, Report on a WHO meeting, 9–10 February 2004, Bratislava, Slovakia

WHO (2005a) *Inter-agency Rapid Health Assessment, West Aceh, Indonesia, 13–19 January 2005*, World Health Organization website, www.who.int/hac/crises/international/asia_tsunami/final_report/en/print.html

WHO (2005b) *Tsunami and Health Situation Report 41, 11 March 2005*, World Health Organization, Geneva

WHO (2005c) *Proceedings from the WHO Conference on the Health Aspects of the Tsunami Disaster in Asia*, 4–6 May 2005, Phuket, Thailand, www.who.int/hac/events/tsunamiconf/proceedings/en

WHO (2005d) *Mental Health Assistance to the Populations Affected by the Tsunami in Asia*, World Health Organization, Geneva, www.who.int/mental_health/resources/tsunami/en

Wickramanayake, E. (1994) 'Flood mitigation problems in Vietnam', *Disasters,* vol 18, pp81–86

Wisner, B. and Adams, J. (eds) (2002) *Environmental Health in Emergencies and Disasters*, World Health Organization, Geneva

Wisner, B., Blaikie, P., Cannon, T. and Davis, I. (2004) *At Risk: Natural Hazards, People's Vulnerability and Disasters*, Routledge, London

Wolk, M. (2005) 'How Hurricane Katrina's costs are adding up: Insurance industry costs plus federal outlays could equal "$200 billion event"', MSNBC website, http://msnbc.msn.com/id/9329293/

Woodruff, B., Toole, M., Rodrigue, D., Brink, E., Mahgoub, E., Ahmed, M. and Babikar, A. (1990) 'Disease surveillance and control after a flood: Khartoum, Sudan, 1988' *Disasters*, vol 14, pp151–163

Woodworth, P., Gregory, J. and Nicholls, R. (2005) 'Long term sea level changes and their impacts', in Robinson, A. and Brink, K. (eds) *The Global Coastal Ocean, Volume 13: Multiscale Interdisciplinary Processes,* Harvard University Press, Cambridge, MA, pp715–753

World Bank (2000) *Technical Annex for a Proposed Credit of SDR 224 Million to the Republic of Mozambique for a Flood Recovery Project*, Report No t–7370–MOZ, 7 April 2000, World Bank, Washington, DC

Xiaohong, S. (1993) 'The role of health sectors in disaster preparedness: Floods in southeastern China, 1991', *Prehospital and Disaster Medicine*, vol 8, pp173–175

Yang MeiXia, Tan HongZhuan, Zhou YiBiao, Tang GuanMing, Li PeiAn, Yun CongYa and Xu Xi (2002) 'Quantitative study on human water contact during 1998 in an endemic region of schistosomiasis japonica', *Chinese Journal of Schistosomiasis Control*, vol 14, pp109–114

Zhang YuQi, Zhang Juan and Yang Hui (2002) 'Schistosomiasis investigation at 4 villages of Yangjiayuan during a flood in 1999', *Chinese Journal of Parasitology and Parasitic Diseases*, vol 20, pp59–60

Index